# The Paretian Tradition during the Interwar Period

The years in between the two World Wars were a crucial period for the building of economic dynamics as an autonomous field. Different competing research programmes arose at international level. Great progress was achieved by studies on the business cycle, with the first statistical applications. Outside the theory of the business cycle, a significant line of inquiry was that pursued at the end of the 1930s by Hicks and Samuelson. This period also saw the formulation of another approach to formal economic dynamics which in the 1930s represented the frontier of research from the analytical point of view. It was an approach which set the notion of equilibrium at the basis of dynamics, exactly as in the case of statics, thus leading to the definition of a dynamic equilibrium approach. The aim of this volume is to take into consideration this original research field sparked from Pareto's works and initially developed during the 1920s in the United States by two American mathematicians, G. Evans and C. Roos.

In the 1930s, the concept of dynamic equilibrium became the main research field of the Pareto school which gave its most important contributions in this field. The Paretian economists such as Amoroso, de Pietri Tonelli, Sensini, and the younger, such as Bordin, Palomba, La Volpe, Fossati and Zaccagnini, for the most part students of the former, developed this approach in many directions. The theory of dynamic equilibrium reached remarkable results from an analytical viewpoint through the wide application of the functional calculus, thus anticipating a perspective which was taken into consideration in the 1960s with the theory of optimal growth. Despite the Pareto school's relevance, it remained widely unknown, not only at international level, but also in Italy. Recently, it has been the object of renewed interest. This present work aims at reconstructing the fundamental contributions offered by the Pareto school in forming the theory of economic dynamics.

**Mario Pomini** is Associate Professor of Economics at the Department of Economics, University of Padua, Italy.

# Routledge Studies in the History of Economics

1 **Economics as Literature**
*Willie Henderson*

2 **Socialism and Marginalism in Economics 1870–1930**
*Edited by Ian Steedman*

3 **Hayek's Political Economy**
The socio-economics of order
*Steve Fleetwood*

4 **On the Origins of Classical Economics**
Distribution and value
from William Petty to
Adam Smith
*Tony Aspromourgos*

5 **The Economics of Joan Robinson**
*Edited by Maria Cristina
Marcuzzo, Luigi Pasinetti
and Alesandro Roncaglia*

6 **The Evolutionist Economics of Léon Walras**
*Albert Jolink*

7 **Keynes and the 'Classics'**
A study in language, epistemology
and mistaken identities
*Michel Verdon*

8 **The History of Game Theory, Vol. 1**
From the beginnings to 1945
*Robert W. Dimand and Mary
Ann Dimand*

9 **The Economics of W. S. Jevons**
*Sandra Peart*

10 **Gandhi's Economic Thought**
*Ajit K. Dasgupta*

11 **Equilibrium and Economic Theory**
*Edited by Giovanni Caravale*

12 **Austrian Economics in Debate**
*Edited by Willem Keizer,
Bert Tieben and Rudy van Zijp*

13 **Ancient Economic Thought**
*Edited by B. B. Price*

14 **The Political Economy of Social Credit and Guild Socialism**
*Frances Hutchinson
and Brian Burkitt*

15 **Economic Careers**
Economics and economists
in Britain 1930–1970
*Keith Tribe*

16 **Understanding 'Classical' Economics**
Studies in the long-period theory
*Heinz Kurz and Neri Salvadori*

17 **History of Environmental Economic Thought**
*E. Kula*

18 **Economic Thought in Communist and Post-Communist Europe**
*Edited by Hans-Jürgen Wagener*

19 **Studies in the History of French Political Economy**
From Bodin to Walras
*Edited by Gilbert Faccarello*

20 **The Economics of John Rae**
*Edited by O. F. Hamouda, C. Lee and D. Mair*

21 **Keynes and the Neoclassical Synthesis**
Einsteinian versus Newtonian macroeconomics
*Teodoro Dario Togati*

22 **Historical Perspectives on Macroeconomics**
Sixty years after the 'General Theory'
*Edited by Philippe Fontaine and Albert Jolink*

23 **The Founding of Institutional Economics**
The leisure class and sovereignty
*Edited by Warren J. Samuels*

24 **Evolution of Austrian Economics**
From Menger to Lachmann
*Sandye Gloria*

25 **Marx's Concept of Money**
The god of commodities
*Anitra Nelson*

26 **The Economics of James Steuart**
*Edited by Ramón Tortajada*

27 **The Development of Economics in Europe since 1945**
*Edited by A. W. Bob Coats*

28 **The Canon in the History of Economics**
Critical essays
*Edited by Michalis Psalidopoulos*

29 **Money and Growth**
Selected papers of Allyn Abbott Young
*Edited by Perry G. Mehrling and Roger J. Sandilands*

30 **The Social Economics of Jean-Baptiste Say**
Markets and virtue
*Evelyn L. Forget*

31 **The Foundations of Laissez-Faire**
The economics of Pierre de Boisguilbert
*Gilbert Faccarello*

32 **John Ruskin's Political Economy**
*Willie Henderson*

33 **Contributions to the History of Economic Thought**
Essays in honour of R. D. C. Black
*Edited by Antoin E. Murphy and Renee Prendergast*

**34 Towards an Unknown Marx**
A commentary on the manuscripts
of 1861–63
*Enrique Dussel*

**35 Economics and Interdisciplinary
Exchange**
*Edited by Guido Erreygers*

**36 Economics as the Art
of Thought**
Essays in memory of G. L. S.
Shackle
*Edited by Stephen F. Frowen and
Peter Earl*

**37 The Decline of Ricardian
Economics**
Politics and economics in post-
Ricardian theory
*Susan Pashkoff*

**38 Piero Sraffa**
His life, thought and cultural
heritage
*Alessandro Roncaglia*

**39 Equilibrium and Disequilibrium
in Economic Theory**
The Marshall–Walras divide
*Michel de Vroey*

**40 The German Historical School**
The historical and ethical
approach to economics
*Edited by Yuichi Shionoya*

**41 Reflections on the Classical
Canon in Economics**
Essays in honour of Samuel
Hollander
*Edited by Sandra Peart
and Evelyn Forget*

**42 Piero Sraffa's Political Economy**
A centenary estimate
*Edited by Terenzio Cozzi
and Roberto Marchionatti*

**43 The Contribution of Joseph
Schumpeter to Economics**
Economic development and
institutional change
*Richard Arena and Cecile Dangel*

**44 On the Development of Long-
run Neo-Classical Theory**
*Tom Kompas*

**45 F. A. Hayek as a Political
Economist**
Economic analysis and values
*Edited by Jack Birner,
Pierre Garrouste and
Thierry Aimar*

**46 Pareto, Economics and Society**
The mechanical analogy
*Michael McLure*

**47 The Cambridge Controversies
in Capital Theory**
A study in the logic of theory
development
*Jack Birner*

**48 Economics Broadly Considered**
Essays in honour of Warren J.
Samuels
*Edited by Steven G. Medema,
Jeff Biddle and John B. Davis*

**49 Physicians and Political
Economy**
Six studies of the work
of doctor-economists
*Edited by Peter Groenewegen*

50 **The Spread of Political Economy and the Professionalisation of Economists**
Economic societies in Europe, America and Japan in the nineteenth century
*Massimo Augello and Marco Guidi*

51 **Historians of Economics and Economic Thought**
The construction of disciplinary memory
*Steven G. Medema and Warren J. Samuels*

52 **Competing Economic Theories**
Essays in memory of Giovanni Caravale
*Sergio Nisticò and Domenico Tosato*

53 **Economic Thought and Policy in Less Developed Europe**
The nineteenth century
*Edited by Michalis Psalidopoulos and Maria-Eugenia Almedia Mata*

54 **Family Fictions and Family Facts**
Harriet Martineau, Adolphe Quetelet and the population question in England 1798–1859
*Brian Cooper*

55 **Eighteenth-Century Economics**
*Peter Groenewegen*

56 **The Rise of Political Economy in the Scottish Enlightenment**
*Edited by Tatsuya Sakamoto and Hideo Tanaka*

57 **Classics and Moderns in Economics, Vol. I**
Essays on nineteenth and twentieth century economic thought
*Peter Groenewegen*

58 **Classics and Moderns in Economics, Vol. II**
Essays on nineteenth and twentieth century economic thought
*Peter Groenewegen*

59 **Marshall's Evolutionary Economics**
*Tiziano Raffaelli*

60 **Money, Time and Rationality in Max Weber**
Austrian connections
*Stephen D. Parsons*

61 **Classical Macroeconomics**
Some modern variations and distortions
*James C. W. Ahiakpor*

62 **The Historical School of Economics in England and Japan**
*Tamotsu Nishizawa*

63 **Classical Economics and Modern Theory**
Studies in long-period analysis
*Heinz D. Kurz and Neri Salvadori*

64 **A Bibliography of Female Economic Thought to 1940**
*Kirsten K. Madden, Janet A. Sietz and Michele Pujol*

65 **Economics, Economists and Expectations**
From microfoundations to macroeconomics
*Warren Young, Robert Leeson and William Darity Jnr.*

66 **The Political Economy of Public Finance in Britain, 1767–1873**
*Takuo Dome*

67 **Essays in the History of Economics**
*Warren J. Samuels, Willie Henderson, Kirk D. Johnson and Marianne Johnson*

68 **History and Political Economy**
Essays in honour of P. D. Groenewegen
*Edited by Tony Aspromourgos and John Lodewijks*

69 **The Tradition of Free Trade**
*Lars Magnusson*

70 **Evolution of the Market Process**
Austrian and Swedish economics
*Edited by Michel Bellet, Sandye Gloria-Palermo and Abdallah Zouache*

71 **Consumption as an Investment**
The fear of goods from Hesiod to Adam Smith
*Cosimo Perrotta*

72 **Jean-Baptiste Say and the Classical Canon in Economics**
The British connection in French classicism
*Samuel Hollander*

73 **Knut Wicksell on Poverty**
No place is too exalted
*Knut Wicksell*

74 **Economists in Cambridge**
A study through their correspondence 1907–1946
*Edited by M. C. Marcuzzo and A. Rosselli*

75 **The Experiment in the History of Economics**
*Edited by Philippe Fontaine and Robert Leonard*

76 **At the Origins of Mathematical Economics**
The Economics of A. N. Isnard (1748–1803)
*Richard van den Berg*

77 **Money and Exchange**
Folktales and reality
*Sasan Fayazmanesh*

78 **Economic Development and Social Change**
Historical roots and modern perspectives
*George Stathakis and Gianni Vaggi*

79 **Ethical Codes and Income Distribution**
A study of John Bates Clark and Thorstein Veblen
*Guglielmo Forges Davanzati*

80 **Evaluating Adam Smith**
Creating the wealth of nations
*Willie Henderson*

81 **Civil Happiness**
Economics and human flourishing in historical perspective
*Luigino Bruni*

82 **New Voices on Adam Smith**
*Edited by Leonidas Montes
and Eric Schliesser*

83 **Making Chicago Price Theory**
Milton Friedman–George Stigler
correspondence, 1945–1957
*Edited by J. Daniel Hammond and
Claire H. Hammond*

84 **William Stanley Jevons and the
Cutting Edge of Economics**
*Bert Mosselmans*

85 **A History of Econometrics
in France**
From nature to models
*Philippe Le Gall*

86 **Money and Markets**
A doctrinal approach
*Edited by Alberto Giacomin
and Maria Cristina Marcuzzo*

87 **Considerations on the
Fundamental Principles of Pure
Political Economy**
*Vilfredo Pareto (Edited by
Roberto Marchionatti and
Fiorenzo Mornati)*

88 **The Years of High Econometrics**
A short history of the generation
that reinvented economics
*Francisco Louçã*

89 **David Hume's Political
Economy**
*Edited by Carl Wennerlind
and Margaret Schabas*

90 **Interpreting Classical
Economics**
Studies in long-period analysis
*Heinz D. Kurz and Neri Salvadori*

91 **Keynes's Vision**
Why the great depression
did not return
*John Philip Jones*

92 **Monetary Theory in Retrospect**
The selected essays of Filippo
Cesarano
*Filippo Cesarano*

93 **Keynes's Theoretical
Development**
From the tract to the general
theory
*Toshiaki Hirai*

94 **Leading Contemporary
Economists**
Economics at the cutting edge
*Edited by Steven Pressman*

95 **The Science of Wealth**
Adam Smith and the framing
of political economy
*Tony Aspromourgos*

96 **Capital, Time and Transitional
Dynamics**
*Edited by Harald Hagemann
and Roberto Scazzieri*

97 **New Essays on Pareto's
Economic Theory**
*Edited by Luigino Bruni
and Aldo Montesano*

98 **Frank Knight and the Chicago
School in American Economics**
*Ross B. Emmett*

99 **A History of Economic Theory**
Essays in honour of Takashi
Negishi
*Edited by Aiko Ikeo and
Heinz D. Kurz*

100 **Open Economics**
Economics in relation to other
disciplines
*Edited by Richard Arena, Sheila
Dow and Matthias Klaes*

101 **Rosa Luxemburg and the
Critique of Political Economy**
*Edited by Riccardo Bellofiore*

102 **Problems and Methods
of Econometrics**
The Poincaré lectures of Ragnar
Frisch 1933
*Edited by Olav Bjerkholt and
Ariane Dupont-Keiffer*

103 **Criticisms of Classical Political
Economy**
Menger, Austrian economics and
the German historical school
*Gilles Campagnolo*

104 **A History of Entrepreneurship**
*Robert F. Hébert
and Albert N. link*

105 **Keynes on Monetary Policy,
Finance and Uncertainty**
Liquidity preference theory and
the global financial crisis
*Jorg Bibow*

106 **Kalecki's Principle of
Increasing Risk and Keynesian
Economics**
*Tracy Mott*

107 **Economic Theory and
Economic Thought**
Essays in honour
of Ian Steedman
*John Vint, J Stanley Metcalfe,
Heinz D. Kurz, Neri Salvadori
and Paul Samuelson*

108 **Political Economy, Public
Policy and Monetary Economics**
Ludwig von Mises and the
Austrian tradition
*Richard M. Ebeling*

109 **Keynes and the British
Humanist Tradition**
The moral purpose of the market
*David R. Andrews*

110 **Political Economy
and Industrialism**
Banks in Saint-Simonian
economic thought
*Gilles Jacoud*

111 **Studies in Social Economics**
Leon Walras
*Translated by Jan van Daal and
Donald Walker*

112 **The Making of the Classical
Theory of Economic Growth**
*Anthony Brewer*

113 **The Origins of David Hume's
Economics**
*Willie Henderson*

114 **Production, Distribution and
Trade**
*Edited by Adriano Birolo,
Duncan Foley, Heinz D. Kurz,
Bertram Schefold and
Ian Steedman*

115 **The Essential Writings
of Thorstein Veblen**
*Edited by Charles Camic and
Geoffrey Hodgson*

116 **Adam Smith and the Economy
of the Passions**
*Jan Horst Keppler*

117 **The Analysis of Linear Economic Systems**
Father Maurice Potron's pioneering works
*Translated by Christian Bidard and Guido Erreygers*

118 **A Dynamic Approach to Economic Theory: Frisch**
*Edited by Olav Bjerkholt and Duo Qin*

119 **Henry A. Abbati: Keynes' Forgotten Precursor**
*Serena Di Gaspare*

120 **Generations of Economists**
*David Collard*

121 **Hayek, Mill and the Liberal Tradition**
*Edited by Andrew Farrant*

122 **Marshall, Marshallians and Industrial Economics**
*Edited by Tiziano Raffaelli*

123 **Austrian and German Economic Thought**
*Kiichiro Yagi*

124 **The Evolution of Economic Theory**
*Edited by Volker Caspari*

125 **Thomas Tooke and the Monetary Thought of Classical Economics**
*Matthew Smith*

126 **Political Economy and Liberalism in France**
The contributions of Frédéric Bastiat
*Robert Leroux*

127 **Stalin's Economist**
The economic contributions of Jenö Varga
*André Mommen*

128 **E.E. Slutsky as Economist and Mathematician**
Crossing the limits of knowledge
*Vincent Barnett*

129 **Keynes, Sraffa, and the Criticism of Neoclassical Theory**
Essays in honour of Heinz Kurz
*Edited by Neri Salvadori and Christian Gehrke*

130 **Crises and Cycles in Economic Dictionaries and Encyclopaedias**
*Edited by Daniele Bensomi*

131 **General Equilibrium Analysis**
A century after Walras
*Edited by Pascal Bridel*

132 **Sraffa and Modern Economics, Vol. I**
*Edited by Roberto Ciccone, Christian Gehrke and Gary Mongiovi*

133 **Sraffa and Modern Economics, Vol. II**
*Edited by Roberto Ciccone, Christian Gehrke and Gary Mongiovi*

134 **The Minor Marshallians and Alfred Marshall**
An evaluation
*Peter Groenewegen*

135 **Fighting Market Failure**
Collected essays in the
Cambridge tradition of
economics
*Maria Cristina Marcuzzo*

136 **The Economic Reader**
*Edited by Massimo M. Augello
and Marco E. L. Guido*

137 **Classical Political Economy
and Modern Theory**
Essays in honour of Heinz Kurz
*Edited by Neri Salvadori and
Christian Gehrke*

138 **The Ideas of Ronald H. Coase**
*Lawrence W. C. Lai*

139 **Anticipating the Wealth
of Nations**
*Edited by Maren Jonasson
and Petri Hyttinen, with an
Introduction by Lars Magnusson*

140 **Innovation, Knowledge
and Growth**
*Edited by Heinz D. Kurz*

141 **A History of *Homo Economicus***
The nature of the moral in
economic theory
*William Dixon and David Wilson*

142 **The Division of Labor
in Economics**
A history
*Guang-Zhen Sun*

143 **Keynes and Modern
Economics**
*Ryuzo Kuroki*

144 **Macroeconomics and the
History of Economic Thought**
Festschrift in honour of Harald
Hagemann
*Edited by Hagen M. Krämer,
Heinz D. Kurz and Hans-Michael
Trautwein*

145 **French Liberalism
in the Nineteenth Century**
An anthology
*Edited by Robert Leroux*

146 **Subjectivisim and Objectivism
in the History of Economic
Thought**
*Edited by Yukihiro Ikeda
and Kiichiro Yagi*

147 **The Rhetoric of the Right**
Language change and the spread
of the market
*David George*

148 **The Theory of Value and
Distribution in Economics**
Discussions between Pierangelo
Garegnani and Paul Samuelson
*Edited by Heinz Kurz*

149 **An Economic History of
Ireland Since Independence**
*Andy Bielenberg*

150 **Reinterpreting the Keynesian
Revolution**
*Robert Cord*

151 **Money and Banking in
Jean-Baptiste Say's Economic
Thought**
*Gilles Jacoud*

152 **Jean-Baptiste Say**
Revolutionary, entrepreneur, economist
*Evert Schoorl*

153 **Essays on Classical and Marxian Political Economy**
*Samuel Hollander*

154 **Marxist Political Economy**
Essays in retrieval: selected works of Geoff Pilling
*Geoff Pilling; Edited by Doria Pilling*

155 **Interdisciplinary Economics**
Kenneth E. Boulding's engagement in the sciences
*Edited by Wilfred Dolfsma and Stefan Kestin*

156 **Keynes and Friedman on Laissez-Faire and Planning**
'Where to draw the line?'
*Sylvie Rivot*

157 **Economic Justice and Liberty**
The social philosophy in John Stuart Mill's utilitarianism
*Huei-chun Su*

158 **German Utility Theory**
Analysis and translations
*John Chipman*

159 **A Re-Assessment of Aristotle's Economic Thought**
*Ricardo Crespo*

160 **The Varieties of Economic Rationality**
From Adam Smith to contemporary behavioural and evolutionary economics
*Michel S. Zouboulakis*

161 **Economic Development and Global Crisis**
The Latin American economy in historical perspective
*Edited by José Luís Cardoso, Maria Cristina Marcuzzo and María Eugenia Romero*

162 **The History of Ancient Chinese Economic Thought**
*Edited by Cheng Lin, Terry Peach and Wang Fang*

163 **A History of Economic Science in Japan**
The internationalization of economics in the twentieth century
*Aiko Ikeo*

164 **The Paretian Tradition during the Interwar Period**
From dynamics to growth
*Mario Pomini*

# The Paretian Tradition during the Interwar Period

From dynamics to growth

Mario Pomini

LONDON AND NEW YORK

First published 2014
by Routledge
2 Park Square, Milton Park, Abingdon, Oxon OX14 4RN

and by Routledge
711 Third Avenue, New York, NY 10017

*Routledge is an imprint of the Taylor & Francis Group, an informa business*

© 2014 Mario Pomini

The right of Mario Pomini to be identified as author of this work has been asserted by him in accordance with the Copyright, Designs and Patent Act 1988.

All rights reserved. No part of this book may be reprinted or reproduced or utilized in any form or by any electronic, mechanical, or other means, now known or hereafter invented, including photocopying and recording, or in any information storage or retrieval system, without permission in writing from the publishers.

*Trademark notice*: Product or corporate names may be trademarks or registered trademarks, and are used only for identification and explanation without intent to infringe.

*British Library Cataloguing in Publication Data*
A catalogue record for this book is available from the British Library

*Library of Congress Cataloging-in-Publication Data*
Pomini, Mario.
The Paretian tradition during the interwar period : from dynamics to growth / Mario Pomini.
pages cm
1. Economics–Italy–History–20th century. 2. Equilibrium (Economics) 3. Pareto, Vilfredo, 1848–1923. I. Title.
HB109.A2P66 2014
330.15'43092–dc23
2013044400

ISBN: 978-0-415-66140-9 (hbk)
ISBN: 978-1-315-77649-1 (ebk)

Typeset in Times New Roman
by Cenveo Publisher Services

Printed and bound in the United States of America by
Edwards Brothers Malloy on sustainably sourced paper

# Contents

| | | |
|---|---|---:|
| | Introduction | 1 |
| 1 | The Paretian school in Italy | 5 |
| 2 | Pareto's legacy in economic dynamics | 28 |
| 3 | Dynamic equilibrium in the international context | 48 |
| 4 | Dynamic equilibrium and economic mechanics in Luigi Amoroso | 64 |
| 5 | Dynamic equilibrium and expectations in Giulio La Volpe | 86 |
| 6 | Eraldo Fossati and the role of uncertainty | 106 |
| 7 | Dynamic equilibrium and the economic cycle | 125 |
| 8 | From dynamic equilibrium to the theory of optimal growth | 143 |
| | *Bibliography* | 148 |
| | *Index* | 156 |

# Introduction

The rise of the Pareto school and its sudden decline in the years following the Second World War can be considered as one of the most significant events in the history of economic thought in Italy in the first half of the twentieth century. While Walras remained an isolated innovator in France, Pareto managed to gather a large number of followers and students, at least in Italy, owing to his exceptional personality and to his wide variety of interests in many fields. This led to the forming of the Pareto school which experienced its golden age in the years between the two World Wars. It was initially formed by a group of people in direct contact with Pareto, such as Amoroso, de Pietro Tonelli and the combative Sensini; then, other younger economists joined the group, such as Bordin, Palomba, La Volpe, Fossati and Zaccagnini, for the most part students of the former. The Pareto economists were a recognizable group within the community of the Italian economists, both for the specificity of the issues faced and for their characteristic methodological approach. Essentially, their main aim was to extend their teacher's theory of general economic equilibrium to new ambits. In particular, more than other Italian economists in those years, they tended towards mathematical formalization which they took to a very high level. They were often identified as mathematical economists. This is what distinguished them from Marshall's followers: that is economists who tended more towards descriptive, institutional and scarcely formalized analysis, such as Del Vecchio. Generally speaking, despite the Pareto school's relevance, it remained widely unknown, not only at international level, but also in Italy. Recently, it has been the object of renewed interest. In particular, in an important monograph McLure (2007) reconstructed Pareto's influence in establishing the Pareto school in Italy in the field of public finance. This present work, fitting within this perspective, aims at reconstructing the fundamental contributions offered by the Pareto school in forming the economic dynamics theory.

The years between the two World Wars were a crucial period for the beginning of economic dynamics as an autonomous research field. The first generation of marginalists had completed the statics theory and now, also due to the need of more realism in theory, it was a matter of passing on to the analysis of dynamics. During those two decades, different research programmes emerged in competition with each other; some were mainly empirical and statistical

2  *Introduction*

(Tinbergen 1934, Frisch 1933), others were essentially theoretical (Hicks, 1939). The aim of this volume is to take into consideration the research trend which manifested remarkable originality and liveliness in the 1920s and 1930s, distinguishing itself for its analytical rigour and its primarily theoretical character. It was an approach which set the notion of equilibrium at the basis of dynamics, exactly as in the case of statics, thus leading to the definition of a *dynamic equilibrium approach*. This approach was sparked by Pareto's works and initially was developed during the 1920s in the United States by two American mathematicians, G. Evans and his student C. Roos, at the Rice Institute, Texas. In the 1930s, the concept of dynamic equilibrium became the privileged and characteristic research area of the Pareto school which, in fact, gave its most important contributions in this field. The theory of dynamic equilibrium reached remarkable results from an analytical viewpoint through the wide application of the functional calculus, thus anticipating a perspective which was taken into consideration in the 1960s with the theory of optimal growth. The theory of economic dynamics proposed by the Pareto school laid out an original path towards the construction of economic dynamics. However, in the years following the Second World War, for reasons which we will try to highlight, this research programme lost its vigour together with the general decline of the school. Other research programmes in the field of dynamics, and in particular that of Samuelson-Frisch, seemed more convincing and surely easier to deal with from an analytical viewpoint. In the field of dynamics there was no longer room for the wide theorizations of the Pareto school, anchored to the theory of general economic equilibrium. The theory of economic dynamics became more modestly the theory of economic growth, a less ambitious perspective from a theoretical viewpoint but richer in applications on an interpretative level.

This volume is articulated in eight chapters. The second chapter offers a general view of Pareto's dynamic theory. Pareto's main notion consists in dynamic equilibrium which may be considered from two viewpoints. A first definition resumed by Walras consists of the idea that dynamic equilibrium is constituted by equilibria which the system reaches in successive moments. This is the first-order dynamics or the successive equilibria. The second notion derives from the analogy with rational mechanics according to which dynamic equilibrium is constituted by the continuous variation of the economic quantities in function of time. This second-order dynamics is the one which was more developed within the Pareto school, with contributions of remarkable originality. However, both these formulations were unsatisfying for Pareto who soon abandoned the idea of being able to formalize economic dynamics, as he had done instead with statics, leaving the problem open. The development of these issues in the Pareto school constituted his students' field of investigation.

The third chapter considers the attempts brought forward in the second half of the 1920s at international level to dynamize general economic equilibrium. In this case, we will mention two American mathematicians, Griffith Evans and Charles Roos, and a direct student of Walras's, Henry Ludwell Moore. Evans studied in Italy under the guidance of Vito Volterra and together with his student Roos he

*Introduction* 3

tried to dynamize the economic theory applying Volterra's functional calculus and integral equations. Moore followed a different path with the aim of drawing dynamic equations of general economic equilibrium through statistical analysis. These authors were well-known in the Italian debate and constituted an important point of reference. In particular, Evans's contribution was decisive as he was the first to apply the functional calculus (Evans 1924) to a problem of economic dynamics. The third chapter has the aim to expose these author's contributions in the construction of economic dynamics.

In the fourth chapter we will take into consideration Amoroso: he was educated in Mathematics and the most important exponent of Pareto's school in Italy. Amoroso's contributions to dynamic analysis cover a very wide range of topics, from the dynamization of the offer curve, to a non-monetary theory of the economic cycle, to the study of demographic dynamics. In the 1930s he resumed his project to dynamize Pareto's theory of general equilibrium, a project which he realized gradually. This found a first complete expression in the article published in *Ecometrica, The Transformation of Value in the Productive Process,* (Amoroso 1940) and its full exposition in the substantial lessons of the academic year 1940–1941 carried out at Regio Istituto di Alta Matematica in Rome, collected in the volume *Meccanica Economica* (Amoroso 1942). The aim of the chapter is to reconstruct the evolution of Amoroso's dynamic theory from the first drafts of the 1920s to the intertemporal theory of consumption based on the consumer's habits and inertia. His dynamic concept is inserted in an energetic view of the economic processes, in conformity with its initial scientific education linked to classical physics and in particular to rational mechanics. The research of the analogies with classical mechanics constituted the fundamental approach followed by Amoroso.

The fifth chapter is dedicated to La Volpe's first but important contribution to economic dynamics. The dynamic theory of general economic equilibrium developed by La Volpe is contained in the essay published in 1936, *Studi sulla teoria dell'equilibrio dinamico generale.* Here, La Volpe demonstrated how dynamic equilibrium depends on the expectations of the economic operators. If these change, for any reason whatsoever, the path of economic development will also change. In this way La Volpe managed to anticipate the concept of temporary equilibrium formulated by Hicks three years later in *Value and Capital* (1939). His contribution constitutes perhaps the most important result reached by the Pareto tradition in the field of dynamics. La Volpe's contribution is fundamental also because he was the first to find the correct form of the condition of transversality, a necessary condition in the problems of intertemporal optimum. He may thus be considered a forerunner of the theories of the life-cycle of consumption which were expressed in the 1950s and 1960s.

In the sixth chapter we will take into consideration Fossati. Fossati proposed a dynamic theory of general economic equilibrium in the 1930s, on the basis of the contribution of the Austrian school and in particular on von Wieser's approach. For Fossati the theory of general economic equilibrium becomes dynamic when taking into account the uncertainty which characterizes the

## 4  Introduction

economic phenomena. Analytically he proposed to introduce at the level of economic agents a loss function which was not quantifiable with the application of the calculus of probabilities. On an analytical level, Fossati's contribution is less innovative than Amoroso's and La Volpe's. In the 1940s, he tried to connect the combination dynamic-uncertainty to the role of money. In this way he was the only one among Pareto's followers who grew very close to the Keynesian theory, considering it a first step towards dynamic analysis, while he was critical of the axiomatic turning point.

The seventh chapter is dedicated to the mathematical theory of the economic cycle developed by Pareto's followers. In the 1930s, Pareto economists proposed a mathematical theory of the economic cycle. The contributions came essentially from Amoroso, Vinci, Bordin and Palomba. This course also had international visibility since some contributions (Vinci 1934; Amoroso 1935) were published in *Econometrica*, the journal of the Econometric Society, just founded through the contribution of some of the most renowned Italian economists. It is interesting that in their models the Italian economists widely drew inspiration on Keynes' writings, both the *Treatise* (1930) and *General Theory* (1936). The analytical model proposed was totally similar to that of Frisch's (1933), while the economic interpretation based on the interaction among the various sectors of economy was completely different. The novelty of the theory of the economic cycle is that it represents the oscillatory trend of the economic quantities as a real phenomenon of equilibrium. An analogous approach will be found in the real theory of the economic cycle a couple of decades later.

The eighth chapter contains several final observations. The fundamental idea is that the theory of dynamic equilibrium constituted an important contribution to the forming of the dynamic theory in the 1930s. In particular, it anticipated some elements which will be resumed and developed by the theory of optimal growth which was developed in the 1960s. Several factors contributed to the decline of the idea of dynamic equilibrium in the years following the Second World War. Some were internal traits, such as the relevant analytical difficulties in dynamizing the equations of general economic equilibrium. Others were external traits, such as the excessive closeness of these authors with corporative economics or the difficulty in competing with a rival research programme such as the Keynesian's, which was starting in Italy. The attempt to formalize the construction of dynamic equilibrium was an episode which significantly characterized the history of general economic equilibrium not only in Italy but also at international level. The fact that many acknowledgements concerning the important analytical conquests of that period occurred late, shows how the evolution of the economic ideas is neither a linear nor a cumulative process.

# 1 The Paretian school in Italy

## Introduction

In Italy, at the beginning of the 1920s, an important change took place in economics. In 1923, the solitary of Cèligny, Vilfredo Pareto, passed away. The following year, Maffeo Pantaleoni passed away as well. Within a couple of months the two main protagonists, who had marked the turning point of marginalism in Italy, had died. After the publishing of Pantaleoni's *Principi di economia pura* in 1889, the scenario changed completely. Within a generation the subjective theory of value became the dominating paradigm substituting all other approaches (historicist, evolutionary, sociological). Nothing had indicated that such a rapid and radical change was going to take place. In 1891, Ugo Rabbeno published a long article in *Political Science Quarterly* reviewing the situation of the economic theory in Italy and commenting on the fact that there were many lines of thought: the historicist and sociological approaches, which insisted on the need of state intervention; the eclectic approach, which attempted to group the various viewpoints; the socialist approach, and lastly the more recent approach which drew on the Austrian school. However, none of the above seemed to definitively prevail over the others, all of them likely promising new results. Pareto was hardly mentioned, and also Pantaleoni's work was considered with scepticism, since it was the expression of a theoretical approach considered too abstract and distant from the practical economic reality. Rabbeno observed in this regard:

> The *Principi di Economia Pura* is a remarkable piece of work. As a monument of abstract logic, it bears fresh fitness to the unusual quantities of the author's genius: but it is based on a method which, frankly speaking, I consider dangerous.
>
> (Rabbeno 1891: 462)

Contrary to Rabbeno's preference for a historicist approach, a few years after the above assessment of his, the marginalist viewpoint triumphed in Italy as well.

On the occasion of the celebration of F. Wieser's 75th birthday, one of the fifteen contributions dedicated to the economic theory in the main countries was Augusto Graziani's essay, in which he well described the situation of economic

## 6 *The Paretian school in Italy*

studies in Italy during the first years of the 1920s. The curators of the event chose Graziani owing to his widely read manual on economics, *Istituzioni di economia politica* dated 1904, a piece of work which had played a determining role in the diffusion of marginalism in Italy. According to Graziani the main characteristic of the Italian economic line of thought was the establishment of a unifying tendency aimed at toning down the differences among the different approaches. In his opinion the three main approaches battling for the scene in the Italian context were: the classical tradition based on the cost of production; Marshall's approach based on partial equilibriums; and Walras's and Pareto's general economic equilibrium. He believed that the three approaches were not antithetical and mutually irreducible. Graziani was convinced that this attitude towards synthesis was stronger in Italy than elsewhere because, generally speaking, the theory of general economic equilibrium had been kept in the background in the other countries, whereas in Italy it was cultivated by many economists. The establishment of the marginalist approach was not considered by Graziani – as well as by other Italian economists – as a revolutionary rift, but rather a further step in the development of economics as a scientific discipline. This was a sign that the basis of the marginalist revolution had been well prepared by a previous cultural development. Graziani also highlighted how Pantaleoni had moved in this direction of continuity, putting into evidence the complementary role between the utility principle and that of the cost of production. In fact, Pantaleoni played a decisive role in affirming Marshall's system in Italy, which on one hand reduced the determining factors of the exchange value at the cost of production, and on the other hand at the final degree of utility. Pantaleoni evidenced how the two theories were not in conflict, but both indispensable for pricing. The turning point in the system of economic relationships was to be found in the double factor of marginal utility and cost of production.

For Graziani, Pareto's theory represented the next step necessary for the development of economics. It offered a synthetic view of the entire economic system as an ensemble of elements, subjects, goods and markets, all determining each other. However, Graziani continued to believe in the basic interpretation of the economic reasoning: despite this more general context, the economic action was still traced back to the two categories of economic reasoning: tastes and obstacles, the level of utility on one hand and the cost of production on the other. For Graziani, Pareto's theory of general economic equilibrium was not in contrast with Marshall's theory of partial equilibriums, but rather constituted its necessary completion. If Pareto's theory, compared to Marshall's, was superior for rigour and formal elegance, nonetheless the latter's was to be preferred because it was more appropriate when studying the economic phenomenon from a practical viewpoint. This was a widespread thought among the Italian economists, and it was reasserted in the following decade by one of Marshall's followers, Ricci (1939). Therefore, during the second half of the 1920s in Italy, Marshall's and Pareto's systems were the two scientific paradigms of reference within the marginalist current, at least as regards the main issues concerning economic theory, such as the theory of value. Even the economists were classified depending

*The Paretian school in Italy*   7

on whose views they supported, Marshall's or Pareto's, as regards the functioning of the economic system.

The events surrounding Marshall's line of thought, at least until Pantaleoni's death, were the object of accurate historiographic reconstructions (Gallegati 1984). Marshall's *Principles* spread immediately in Italy owing to Pantaleoni, Dalla Volta and Luigi Cossa, author of a fortunate manual on political economy. Initially, Marshall was viewed – in the Italian context – as a compromise between Ricardo and Jevons, even if the tones varied depending on the authors. Only afterwards, Marshall's *Principles* were acknowledged in all their relevance as a fundamental contribution in marking the marginalist's turning point. This initial questioning if Marshall belonged to the classical school or among the marginalists, led to the most important issue concerning the compatibility between the analysis of partial economic equilibrium and general economic equilibrium. A leading role in the diffusion of the marginalist viewpoint, and thus of Marshall's theory, was carried out by *Giornale degli Economisti*. The Journal was founded in 1875 in Padua as an organ of *Associazione per il progresso degli studi di economia* under the direction of De Viti, Mazzola and Pantaleoni. In 1890, the *Giornale* took on a highly marginalist approach from a theoretical viewpoint and a liberalist approach as regards economic policy.

For the purposes of this work, it is important to highlight that a relevant aspect concerning the introduction of marginalism in Italy consists in the fact that no school was formed around Pantaleoni, at least in the traditional sense of the term. Pantaleoni did not become a recognized leader of a group of scholars aiming at spreading and developing their teacher's work. In fact, Marshall's tradition was fuelled by individual contributions which had two main centres of influence: Rome, around Pantaleoni and Barone, to whom we can add Fanno who taught in Genoa; and the axis Turin-Milan, around Einaudi and Jannaccone (Gallegati 1984). Pantaleoni, Ricci and Fanno were particularly sensitive towards the topics concerning general economic equilibrium which they tried to mitigate through Marhall's instruments. The most rigorous example, from an analytical viewpoint, consists of two of Fanno's contributions on the offer at joint costs and substitute goods. In these works, Fanno analysed the functional relationships among the various goods, starting from Pantaleoni's contributions on the compatibility between Marshall's and Walras's systems. Fanno identified four main relationships: joint products, complementary products, rival products as regards the demand, rival products as regards the supply. He dedicated two specific monographs to the first two groups laying the foundations for an organic theory capable of leading all the cases to a single principle. Also Einaudi and Jannaccone were close followers of Marshall's method and were convinced positivists. Moreover, Marshall's works were taken into consideration also in relation to an evolutionist concept of economy founded on biological analogies. All of the Italian exponents of Marshall's tradition were united in the fact that they considered the theory of general economic equilibrium as a construction worthy of great theoretical admiration, but too abstract and basically not useful for an in-depth understanding of the economic reality. Marshall's method based on partial equilibriums – which

## 8 *The Paretian school in Italy*

privileged only the most relevant economic relationships – seemed to be the most fruitful path. However, this did not hold them back from considering general economic equilibrium as an obligatory point of reference in the field of pure theory.

## The Pareto school: the people

A very different situation from the one just mentioned is given by Pareto's case and his influence on Italian economists. Scholars studying the evolution of the economic theory in Italy have highlighted how, at the beginning of the twentieth century, a group of scholars gathered around this extraordinary personality with the aim to develop and spread their teacher's ideas, thus forming an actual school. In Schumpeter's words:

> As mentioned above, when observing his disciples, if we want to talk about a Pareto period, we have to date it around the beginning of the 1900's, when Pareto started to define his position and form his own school. Similarly to all schools, it had a nucleus, allies and supporters, as well as a sphere of external influence.

> (Schumpeter 1954: 1003)

The only people mentioned by Schumpeter in Pareto's school were Amoroso and de Pietri Tonelli, as they were the only two members renowned at international level. A couple of decades later, Giorgio Fuà mentioned the situation in similar terms:

> However, Pareto's orientation is what gave the most characteristic imprint to the Italian construction throughout half a century. I say the most characteristic also because Pareto was the only teacher in Italy followed by such a homogeneous group of continuators (such as L. Amoroso, P. Boninsegni, A. de Pietri Tonelli, G. Sensini), to the point that, as for the physiocrats, one could almost use the term sect.

> (Fuà 1980: 76)

Therefore, Fuà also mentioned how, in the first half of the twentieth century, Pareto economists formed a recognizable group which contributed, in a determining way, to delineating the aspects of economic research in Italy, at least until the years following the Second World War.

Owing to de Pietri Tonelli's reconstruction, provided in a contribution dated 1936, it is possible to distinguish two distinct phases in the evolution of the Pareto school. The first phase consists of its formation and consolidation, covering a period which lasted until the first years of the 1920s. The names to take into consideration are Pasquale Boninsegni, Guido Sensini, Luigi Amoroso, Alfonso de Pietri Tonelli, Roberto Murray and Gino Borgatta. In this first period, Pareto's followers – with the sole exception of Sensini – published short contributions

*The Paretian school in Italy* 9

clarifying and defending Pareto's theory, both in its contents and methodologies. These first works were not at all original, and for this reason Paretian first scholars were accused of being simple popularizers. The period of the school's adjustment finished around the beginning of the 1920s. In 1921, two important works were produced: *Lezioni di scienza economica razionale e sperimentale* by Alfonso de Pietri Tonelli and *Lezioni di Economia Matematica* by Luigi Amoroso. These two substantial volumes marked a turning point: although containing the usual simplified exposition of the theory of general economic equilibrium, they also presented new and original results. The two texts, created for educational purposes, were immediately imposing due to their authoritativeness. The first volume was also published in French in 1927, as it had already occurred for Pareto's *Manuale*. These volumes contributed in turning mathematical economics into an autonomous subject, and for many years Amoroso's lessons were the text of reference for this subject.

Pareto's school reached its mature phase in the 1930s. New economists added on to the original group. These were no longer just economists who had experienced direct contact with Pareto, but actually students of Pareto's first followers. For this reason we can talk about a second generation of Pareto economists. The main names are Giulio La Volpe, Eraldo Fossati, Arrigo Bordin and Giuseppe Palomba. This was the golden period of the Pareto school in which the most important theoretical results were reached. Their contributions were published in the most prestigious foreign journals. Amoroso was recognized as the most important Italian mathematical economist and, together with other Italian economists, he was involved in the creation of the *Econometric Society*, the new association of quantitative economists at international level.

After the Second World War, the Pareto school entered into its fast declining phase. Within a few years, the events which had characterized the Pareto school came to an end. Several factors contributed towards this outcome. First of all, several important theoretical results had already been achieved and were quite problematic to extend on the basis of the indications inherited from Pareto. Second, the new directions of research, such as the Keynesian macroeconomic theory, did not have much in common with the approach of general economic equilibrium. Even the axiomatic developments saw Pareto's followers take on a definitely critical position. Basically, right after the war, Pareto's followers – with a few exceptions – remained detached from the most vital and innovative currents of research at international level. Besides, their ages also started to weigh on the situation. In the 1950s, Pareto's direct students were passing away without leaving any direct heirs. The epoch of the great teachers was at an end, and a new generation of economists started to form in the United States and in England, also owing to a generous scholarship policy. Lastly, in the second half of the 1930s, Pareto economists' closeness to corporativism did not help. However, they were not the only ones. This aspect, in the new cultural context of the years following the war, contributed to overshadowing the genuine scientific conquests of mathematical economists. Within a few years, the Pareto school was completely forgotten or considered totally negligible also in Italy (Graziani 1991).

10   *The Paretian school in Italy*

We will now briefly take into consideration the main exponents of the Pareto school, with the exclusion of those whom we will consider in the following chapters. Starting from 1904, a growing group of students started to gather around Pareto, as documented by an abundant correspondence. Pareto's influence on these young students, animated by the most various interests, was enormous and it concerned not only the contents of economic theory, but also the way of approaching this discipline, very combative and polemical towards the other theoretical approaches. Pareto's first followers had the feeling of being at a decisive turning point in economics, which needed to be founded on new bases.

Pareto's first follower was Pasquale Boninsegni (1869–1939), a young graduate in Mathematics who had taken refuge in Switzerland in 1900 following political provisions. This is where he entered into contact with Pareto and started working on the theory of general economic equilibrium under Pareto's direct guidance. In 1906, Boninsegni was appointed to substitute Pareto in the chair of political economy in Losanna. From a theoretical viewpoint, Boninsegni's contribution was modest and not at the level of Pareto's other students (Mornati 1999). Apart from several minor articles, his main publications were *Précis d'économie politique* (1910) and *Manuel élémentaire d'économie politique* (1930). These were mostly popular and educational works with the aim of simplifying Pareto's theory. On the other hand, he carried out a very active role at the university of Losanna and was very much committed to his educational activity. Besides economics, he also taught sociology, statistics and public finance. This variety of interests and competencies will be a characteristic trait of Pareto economists, as they all had a vast range of competencies in the field of social science.

Apart from Boninsegni, Pareto's first true student was Sensini. However, as evident from the correspondence, the latter was soon joined by de Pietri Tonelli, Murray and Felice Vinci. Sensini's role (1879–1958) was particularly important in this initial phase of the school. Sensini graduated in law with a thesis on an economic subject: economic fluctuations in Italy from 1871 to 1900. He then published his thesis as a monograph and sent a copy to Pareto. Sensini was Pareto's favourite student and he remained an always faithful supporter of his teacher's ideas. In 1955, Sensini published *Corso di Economia Pura* drawing on the theory of general economic equilibrium and starting from where Pareto had left off in his *Manuale* (1906). Among Pareto's followers, Sensini distinguished himself for his polemical and combative character. It was also for this reason that he had a difficult academic career, thus interpreting his teacher's iconoclastic spirit. Finally, in 1922, he became full professor of economics at the University of Sassari, although for a short period of time. In 1928, he was called by University of Pisa where he remained until his retirement in 1951 (McLure 2007).

Sensini is the author of the first important work inspired directly to Pareto's theory, *La teoria della rendita* (1912). In this substantial monograph, Sensini faced a classical topic of the economic line of thought – that is Ricardo and Carey's rent theory – and re-interpreted it in modern terms in the light of the theory of general economic equilibrium, basically drawing on the equations of capitalization in Pareto's *Corso*. Apart from the specific content, which consisted in the re-exposition of Pareto's rent theory with very few hints of originality, Sensini's volume is important because it can be considered as a manifesto of the Pareto school, the text which exposed the basic principles and the methodology to follow. Actually, the debate on the rent theory was a pretext to demonstrate the superiority of Pareto's approach not only compared to the classical school, but also to Marshall's theory. This concerned even the rent which, according to Sensini, and contrary to Ricardo's thought, was formed not only in agriculture but also in all the non-competitive markets when the transformation of savings into capital goods did not result immediately but required time. Therefore, according to Sensini, it was possible to divide the economists into two schools: those who used general economic equilibrium and those who, instead, followed other paths. Polemical discussions against literary economists were not lacking, in other words those who besides not using mathematical tools had not understood Copernican's revolution brought into pure economics by the approach of general economic equilibrium. In his words:

> Throughout our study we have opposed – and will continue opposing – literary economics to scientific economics meaning with the latter a social science which aims at discovering the truth following any method whatsoever, in the quickest and safest way possible, similarly to physical sciences. Whereas, with literary economics we mean the discipline which substitutes a rigorous and objective study of economic facts with idle disputations, vague expressions, sentimental phraseologies, infinite metaphysic stuff, fanciful assertions, all qualities typical of the worst kind of literature.
>
> (Sensini 1912: 203)

Moreover, this category of literary economists also comprised those who used a mathematical tool but outside the theory of general economic equilibrium. As Sensini observed in a note:

> It is clear that we are referring here to *mathematician economists* in the true sense of the word, and not to those authors who in order to trace or copy several dozens of diagrams more or less useful. In Italy, for example, the use or rather the abuse of diagrams, was imported from abroad especially owing to Maffeo Pantaleoni, whose widespread fame as mathematician (!) within the circle of literary economists and the vast public, can give an idea of what most people mean with the introduction of mathematics in the field of economics. Now, the diagrammatic school, if we may express ourselves, represents the exact opposite of the synthetic school.
>
> (Sensini 1912: 813)

The contrast between Pareto's approach of general equilibrium and Marshall's approach of partial equilibriums could not have been expressed more clearly. Apart from the use of graphs and equations, the substantial difference concerned the way of understanding the subject matter of the discipline. On the other hand, as mentioned (Magnani 2005), Sensini had the right to be furious for the fact that,

## 12    *The Paretian school in Italy*

in 1907, Pantaleoni had accused him of scarce originality and for the bad outcome of the competition for the position of full professor of political economy at Scuola di Commercio in Genoa.

Sensini's accusations could not be neglected and the answer from Marhall's economists was not long-awaited. It was entrusted to Jannaccone who, in the same year, published a very polemical article in *Riforma Sociale*, entitled *Il Paretaio*. This interesting episode was reconstructed in detail by Magnani (2005). In his article, after mentioning that Pareto had a circle of followers, Jannaccone accused this group of young economists of being sterile and ineffectual imitators of Pareto, students lacking of their teacher's talent who limited themselves in exposing Pareto's theories passively and with a couple of clear plagiarisms. Jannacone included in the *Paretaio* group Barone, Amoroso, Bininsegni, Murray and Sensini, practically all the exponents of the emerging Pareto school. If the criticism against Barone and Amoroso was barely mentioned, Jannacone's attitude towards the other Pareto economists was very different. *Précis d'économie politique* by Boninsegni was considered as a modest summary of *Corso*, and Murray's *Sommarii* were considered simple copies of Pareto's works. The true target of the article was Sensini's *Teoria della rendita* which ruled out the possibility of using Marshall's approach in economics. On the other hand, drawing on several of Sensini's hints, Jannaccone stated that the theory of general equilibrium, even if elegant in its analytical form, had no practical utility and resulted as inapplicable in the real factual world. Amoroso answered Jannaccone in calm tones and even Pareto intervened. In a brief article, Pareto defended the scientific value of his student, reproaching the polemical style and especially the attack against his friend Pantaleoni.

The polemical episode of the *Paretaio*, which took place during the initial phase of the Pareto school, is important because it fuelled a historiographical assessment which was then extended to its mature phase as well. Jannaccone's opinion – at that time easy to uphold – according to which Pareto's students were victims of the greatness of their teacher, became a historiographical cliché that continued to be ascribed to Pareto's followers. For example, Screpanti and Zamangi (2005) in their *An Outline of the Hisotry of Economic Thought*, saved only Amoroso among the members of the *Paretaio*, and did not dedicate a further single line to the development of Pareto's tradition. However, Pareto's school cannot be identified with the *Paretaio*. In the 1920s and 1930s, Pareto's followers demonstrated how the criticisms of scarce originality were totally groundless and that they were able to offer analytical contributions of great relevance, very much appreciated also at international level.

If we leave out Amoroso – whom we will talk about abundantly in the fourth chapter – and Murray – who distinguished himself mainly for his studies in the field of public finance – an exponent of Pareto's first group to take into consideration is de Pietri Tonelli (1883–1952). Graduated in economics at University of Venezia in 1908, he first taught at the Istituto Tecnico Commerciale in Rovigo and then in Ascoli Piceno. After qualifying for university teaching at the University of Bologna, he became professor of economic policy first in Pisa and

*The Paretian school in Italy* 13

then, as full professor, in Venice where he became the director of the laboratory of Political Economy at University Ca' Foscari. In his younger years at university in Venice, he had a lively experience as a militant of the socialist movement. In his scientific experience, his encounter with Pareto was decisive, as witnessed by their correspondence which started in 1907 and lasted until Pareto's death. Following Pareto, de Pietri Tonelli soon abandoned socialist seductions and dedicated himself to the study of the theory of general economic equilibrium.

A first important result of this commitment is evidenced in *Le Lezioni di scienza economica razionale e sperimentale,* published in 1921, with an introduction by Pareto. This work undoubtedly set him among the Italian economists who contributed to the development of economics as a deductive and mathematical science. de Pietri Tonelli remained substantially faithful to this basic approach even when, in the 1930s and 1940s in a totally pioneer way, he aimed at a scientific foundation of economic policy. He was the first to try to analyse, in a rather rigorous manner, the relationships between economics and political science, elaborating a complex theory concerning social relationships. He realized that economic policy could not be considered simply as applied economics, or a residual discipline which dealt with the neglected topics from pure theory such as international trade, the bank system, demographic aspects and much more. In cultivating this prospective, de Pietro Tonelli also wanted to formalize the sociological aspects which Pareto, instead, had included among the non-logical actions, thus excluding them from the economic reasoning. This innovative approach found expression in the volume *Corso di politica economica. Introduzione* (1931) For de Pietri Tonelli economic policy constituted, together with political economy, the science which studied the political restrictions characterizing collective economic choices. The study of political restrictions to economic acts and especially the political transfers of economic resources were objects of economic policy. De Pietri Tonelli only managed to draft this project concerning the construction of a rational economic policy, on the path of general economic equilibrium and Pareto's sociological suggestions. Pursuing this path was quite a problematic feat since the theory of economic policy set out on different roads, first of all that of welfare economics. An explicit political analysis of the economic issues was reached only in the 1970s.

The mature phase of the Pareto school covers a period which goes from Pareto's death (1923) to the Second World War. This is the golden period of the school. Moreover, in those two decades, we also observe the full acknowledgement of mathematical economics and therefore of Pareto's followers' favourite approach. Not only was the formalization of the economic reflection no longer considered with scepticism, when not hindered, but it also became an essential prerequisite for its scientific value. In this period, even the contrast with the economists following Marshall's approach ceased. A division of field took place: they all took care of their own specific topics trying to develop them according to pre-established rules. The period of conflicts and controversies in the attempt to assert one's identity was substituted by specialization; it was accepted that economic theory has many dimensions and each economist

## 14   *The Paretian school in Italy*

is called to give his best in his own field of research. Even the second generation of Pareto scholars was rather numerous and the main protagonists were Arrigo Bordin, Giulio La Volpe, Eraldo Fossati, Emilio Zaccagnini and Giuseppe Palomba.

Since we will cover La Volpe's and Fossati's scientific experiences more in depth in two specific chapters, we here want to provide several bibliographic notes and scientific productions of other exponents of the Pareto school, among whom the most prolific and talented was economist Giuseppe Palomba (1908–1986) from Naples. Giuseppe Palomba was born in the province of Caserta. He graduated in economics in Naples in 1929. He studied with Amoroso, whom he considered his acknowledged teacher. Still very young, in 1935, he qualified for university teaching in political economy, and in particular he dedicated his studies to mathematical economics. In 1939, he started teaching in Catania. In the years following the war he taught in Naples, and at the beginning of the 1970s in Rome.

Palomba was a *sui generis* economist, a great intellectual before being a theoretical economist. He was the prototype of Pareto economists: a scholar who considered the boundaries of the *homo oeconomicus* too narrow and thus pressed into other fields of knowledge such as history of cultures, sociology, philosophy and the study of religions. Palomba started his scientific career as a mathematical economist, following in the steps of his teacher Amoroso. He immediately distinguished himself for his uncommon mathematical talent which found a first expression in the volume dated 1939 *Introduzione allo studio della dinamica economica* (Palomba 1939). In this volume he was the first to introduce the equations of Lotka–Volterra in economics in order to express the relationship between the sector of consumption goods and that of investment goods. This led to extreme consequences: Amoroso's methodological project aimed at highlighting the analogies between economic and mechanical phenomena. In his volume *Meccanica Economica* (1959) he tried to demonstrate how it is possible to use Einstein's relativity equations also in economics in order to analyse pricing in non-competitive markets. Referring to the formalisms of the theory of relativity and adapting them to the economic context, Palomba was trying to demonstrate how large monopolistic or oligopolistic enterprises create a disturbance of the market which is totally similar to a gravitational field. This rather eccentric project of his – that is to surpass the limits of his teacher's dynamic theory following the path of the 1900s physics – did not find any followers in the Italian context and his position remained substantially isolated. Probably his remarkable analytical preparation could have led to other results if he had looked towards the new currents of research that emerged after the Second World War. Said currents required a good mastering of analytical tools, such as the theory of economic growth or the theory of games.

A second current of research carried out by Palomba concerned a classical topic for Pareto economists, that is the relationship between economics and sociology. Palomba was a careful expert of the classical aspects of sociology and he considered the existence of an abstract economy absolutely impossible especially

The Paretian school in Italy    15

separated from the social institutions. From here, his interest in studying the relationship among social classes, structures of power and economic theory which led him to the vast investigations of the history of ideas contained in *Morfologia Economica* (1956) and *L'espansione capitalistica* (1961). He was too eccentric in his theoretical prospective of re-founding economic physics. As a scholar, he also dedicated much energy in studying societies, broadly speaking. Therefore, it is not a surprise that the Neapolitan economist was considered a brilliant outsider, but not a scholar giving fundamental contribution to the economic theory.

A totally different figure was that of Arrigo Bordin (1898–1963). In fact, Bordin did not concentrate only on his scientific activity: after reaching a stable academic position he dedicated himself essentially to his professional activity, and this can explain the non-relevant number of publications. He was appointed with his first university charge in Venice at 32 years old, called by his teacher de Pietri Tonelli. These were the most intense years of his scientific research which led him, in 1935, to win the competition for the chair of Political Economy. He was called to Turin in 1938. Here he put great dedication into his teaching. Then, upon his appointment as managing director of an important mining company, he totally abandoned his research activity limiting himself to educational commitments (La Volpe 1967).

Bordin's most intense period of research coincided with the 1930s. Spurred by his teacher de Pietri Tonelli, he essentially dedicated his time both to improving and developing, in a dynamic sense, Pareto's construction. As regards the first aspect, Bordin realized immediately that it was necessary to overcome the unrealistic principle of perfect information. He put into evidence how every economic agent operates in a context of uncertainty and the consequences of his actions are not known a priori (1939). The topic of expectations, as we will see, was a main topic in the dynamic analysis of the 1930s. However, unlike other followers of Pareto's such as La Volpe and Fossati, Bordin did not reach any formal scheme which could capture this relevant aspect of the economic reality. His theoretical position, as revealed after many years in the article *Equilibrio ed indeterminazione* (1950), turned out to be very similar to that of Knight's as regards the uncertainty which cannot be detected by a statistical measure. Bordin also dealt with the labour market and in particular bilateral monopoly, proposing his view based on the hedonistic strength of contractors. He also introduced the idea of considering the non-negotiation of wages as a damage and thus as a possible element that could contribute in determining the position of equilibrium between employer and trade union (1938).

In the field of dynamics, it is important to mention a vast review which was published in three parts in the Economists' Journal in 1935, entitled *Il significato di alcune moderne teorie matematiche della dinamica*. These three articles in actual fact constitute a monograph which reconstructs precisely the debate on economic dynamics at international level. The article not only discusses the works of Italian authors, but also those of the most important foreign scholars such as Frisch, Tinbergen and Kalecki witnessing the international opening of

16 *The Paretian school in Italy*

Italian authors. In 1939, he gave another remarkable contribution in which he assumed the existence of a *collective function of welfare*, totally analogous to that of the single economic agent. In his view the superiority of corporativism compared to other economic systems, such as, for example, the liberalist one, consisted of the ability to realize an optimal combination of social preferences. Bordin did not study the topic more in-depth as regards the construction of these curves of indifference of the policy maker, but he simply observed that with this tool it was possible to pass to a concept of economic policy capable of claiming the same theoretical rigour of economics.

Another noteworthy contribution of his is dated 1948, in which he very clearly expressed Pareto's followers' viewpoint with regard to the first theory of welfare economics, a topic which became central throughout the years. Actually, Pareto's followers never gave much importance to this result, as they considered it scarcely realistic. In Bordin's words:

> It follows that the statement according to which the subjects of a competition market aiming at the individual maximum utility, *automatically* aim at the collective maximum – conceived as a sum of individual utilities – is purely and simply begging of the question: aiming at the individual maximum simply follows ... the individual maximum, from which a certain profit derives and nothing else. Or, if preferred, it follows the particular collective maximum which regards the specific procedure with which the individual maximums are obtained.... Therefore, the proposition according to which in a competition market of exchange and production the operators aim at the individual maximum, and end up reaching automatically the collective maximum income is a tautology proposition. And it is a proposition which has a remarkable practical relevance similarly to that which tends to deny the utility and the need of every state intervention when this intervention aims at a collective maximum. And this preposition is almost always false when, with that impudence which is common to parrots and those interested, "competition economy" is substituted by the market economy in which a variety of regimes can prosper, which have nothing to do with competition.
>
> (Bordin 1948: 180)

Contrary to what happened in the years following the Second World War, Pareto's followers could not use the first theory of welfare economics to deny the relevance of economic policy, and therefore of the state's intervention in economy. Said theory could only demonstrate that the individual always tries, on the basis of a rational calculus, to reach the best position in consideration of restrictions and preferences. Normally, among said restrictions there is also the fact that the starting point is a specific initial distribution and that there are goods which the market is not able to offer, that is public goods. In other words, the first theory did not constitute for Pareto's followers a topic contrary to the public intervention in economy, but instead this occurred in the following literature.

Emilio Zaccagnini, a student of Bordin's who taught for many years in Turin, falls within the mature phase of the Pareto school with his original contributions. With an education in mathematics, he carried out his activity in Turin where he obtained the chair of economics. Apart from his initial studies dedicated to the derivation of the function index of utility starting from the function of demand, his most original contribution in the theory of general economic equilibrium concerned the so-called theory of simultaneous maximums (Zaccagnini 1947: 1950). It constituted the most ambitious attempt to formulate a general theory of oligopoly within schemes, although simplified, of the theory of general economic equilibrium. What distinguishes a problem of simultaneous maximum from an analogous problem of traditional maximum? In Zaccagnini's words:

> The problems of simultaneous maximum are differentiated by the known problems of maximum or minimum restricted of other functions because the values of the variables have to correspond at the same time to maximum points of a function on the curves (or dimensional varieties) of the other level, and points of maximum of the second on the curves (or variety) of the first level.
>
> (Zaccagnini 1947: 256)

With a modern terminology we could say that the characteristic trait of these problems is the interdependence of the functions to maximize. Therefore, at the point of equilibrium it is not possible to move from the maximum of a function without diminishing the value of the other functions taken into consideration. It is an ambitious attempt to use traditional calculus in order to study strategic behaviour. A typical example of simultaneous maximum is represented by the research of the position of equilibrium in a duopolistic market.

For the economist from Turin the theory of the simultaneous maximums was meant to constitute the general scheme within which non-competitive markets can be analysed: the duopolistic one, the one with $n$ monopolists, the oligopolistic one with $n$ enterprises, the bilateral monopoly with reference to a productive factor. The analytical condition necessary for the simultaneous maximum was found by Zaccagnini in the annulment of Jacob's determinant of the functions to maximize. However, put in these terms, the analytical problem resulted as quite complex and Zaccagnini himself offered a solution only for several specific cases (Zaccagnini 1958). This line of research on the oligopolistic markets was not continued by other authors and remained an isolated case, probably both for the internal difficulties which it presented – some not easily avoidable – and because the study of the non-competitive markets lost its importance in the period taken into consideration. Zaccagnini's writings on this topic can be considered an anticipation of the game theory, where the problem of the determination of the position of equilibrium found a more direct and immediate solution, owing to the use of a different analytical apparatus.

## The Pareto school's core

The previous section took into consideration the main exponents of the Pareto school in Italy which mainly included scholars belonging to the two generations: the Pareto generation, formed by those who entered into direct contact with Pareto, and the post-Pareto generation, constituted by the first generation's students. We are now going to analyse the common scientific and methodological grounds shared by these groups of economists, the individuation of which authorizes us to speak about the Pareto school as a relevant episode of evolution of the economic theory in Italy.

For there to be a school of thought it is necessary to recognize a founder or someone whose work is so relevant as to make a fundamental difference within a discipline. In our case the fundamental point of reference is Pareto's work. Pareto was a complex author who developed many aspects of economic theory, therefore the fundamental question is what part of Pareto's theory did his followers consider as central. There is no doubt that for the economists whom we are considering, the Pareto theory coincided with the theory of general economic equilibrium. Other aspects, such as for example the criticism against the utilitarian view, were pushed into the background. Pareto's followers claimed the approach of general economic equilibrium as their genuine distinctive and unifying trait. They saw in Pareto the economist who accomplished Walras's initial intuition of considering the economic system as if it were made of a network of markets communicating among each other, in which every element and every subject acquires a meaning only in its relation to others. While Walras had limited his analysis to the case of free competition, Pareto had completed the work considering also the non-competitive markets, improving the definition of the methodological aspects. In Sensini's words:

> Scientific economics follows a totally different road. After patient and rigorous investigations, the conclusion is that the only *synthesis* possible up to now, in the world of economic facts, is the one offered to us by the general systems of the equations determining equilibrium. Only these equations finally revealed to us the total impossibility to make any quantity whatsoever, entering the economic problems, rise at the degree of "first cause" of all the others, showing us instead how the ensemble of those quantities forms a single wholeness, intimately connected, so that every attempt of separation cannot lead to other if not gross mistakes and infinite sophisms.
>
> This is one of the main advantages of the synthetic modern economics which appeared for the first time with Walras's important researches, concerning the determination of the economic equilibrium. In the particular case, as much it is very generalised of free competition, Pareto is the brilliant mind that constructed *the general theory of economic equilibrium*, indicating at the same time the main properties of this equilibrium which derive from the theory and that renewed economics in its whole, Pareto himself reconstructing it from the foundations on the basis of new doctrines.
>
> (Sensini 1912: 158)

It is interesting to notice in the above mentioned text that, for Sensini, Pareto's theory is general not because it considers all the markets at the same time, as commonly believed, but because it is directed at all forms of market, the competitive one, even the monopolistic market as well as planned economy. Curiously, a couple of decades later, Keynes also defined his theory generally because he considered free competition as a particular case and the imperfect labour market as a normal case.

For Pareto's followers, the superiority of the approach of general economic equilibrium, at least on the level of pure theory, consisted of the fact that it reunified all the previous theories that could be considered as particular cases. The theory of general equilibrium constituted the more general view – and therefore no longer surmountable – of the determination of the value of exchange or price of goods, one of the main tasks of economics. According to Pareto's followers, a problem often surrounded by linguistic confusion or full of metaphysical elements such as the determination of the exchange value, was brought back to the genuine scientific formulation, that is of the research of solutions of one or more systems of equations. If one of these equations was missing, then the result fell back into the partial view which was typical of the previous theories.

This is how de Pietri Tonelli considered the phases of the development of economic theory. Classical economists Smith and Ricardo, but also Marx, were in error because by considering work only as a source of value they limited themselves to a group of equations which referred to the costs of production, to the sole obstacles, to use Pareto's terms. However, said theories remained standing only if all the other equations of general economic equilibrium concerning consumption were satisfied. The same criticism was made against the Austrian or utilitarian school,

> The utilitarian school – which had numerous followers in different moments and in different countries – by deeming that the values (prices) had as cause (were determined) by utility, it considered a single category of conditions of economic equilibrium. In other words, referring to tastes, they established the equality of the pondered marginal utilities: sufficient conditions to determine equilibrium only in the hypothesis that the other conditions of equilibrium are satisfied.
>
> (de Pietri Tonelli 1921: 330)

Even if economics could obtain a real scientific statute by outgrowing the concept of causality and substituting it with that of interdependence, problems were never lacking, and Pareto's followers were always accused of this, even if they changed in the course of time. In the years we are taking into consideration, the model of general economic equilibrium was put into discussion for its modest interpretative capacity. In fact, the system of equations produced could not be used to make useful economic predictions. This criticism had already been anticipated by Pareto's followers. Sensini had observed that equations of general economic equilibrium could only provide more or less approximate indications of the actual

20    *The Paretian school in Italy*

economic phenomenon for two orders of problems. First of all, the lack of the specific form of functions which appeared in the systems found, which hindered an algebraic solution, besides their numerical solution. Second, the enormous complication faced in the attempt to solve the systems of equations algebraically, due to the high number of equations and unknowns. Therefore, it was a matter of computational difficulty hard to resolve, in Sensini's days as well as a century later. However, there was also a further difficulty, in this case a substantial trait, which derived from the fact that the variables of the economic system were not constant but changed in time, transporting the analysis in the field of dynamics where the analytical difficulties became really insurmountable.

From the equations of general economic equilibrium, according to Pareto's followers, there was supposed to be, at least at a theoretical level, a falsification of the previous theories, considered as necessary conditions in order to reach a new general view of the functioning of the economic system. And Sensini had demonstrated this well in his discussion on the classical theory of rent. According to his opinion, the forming of rent was not a form of income applicable only to fund capitals, but a form of a more general income applicable to all other types of capital. In his opinion, only the theory of economic equilibrium had been able to find a general theory concerning the forming of economic income.

The centrality of the general economic equilibrium approach, both from a methodological and content viewpoint, had two more consequences. The first is that in Pareto's followers' texts we find low interest for the study of the curve of demand and individual offer, with its specific characteristics, for example, elasticity. The texts immediately passed from the equilibrium of the single consumer or producer to the more general study of exchange and interdependence among economic phenomena. In this way, they lost the opportunity to detect very important analytical results, as Hicks's and Allen's studies showed in the 1930s. The second is that they tried to extend Pareto's horizon by including new aspects to be analysed, such as prices dependent on quality or flexible coefficients of production, which had a modest practical meaning but made the mathematical structure of the models more contrived. In 1955, Sensini dedicated a large part in his manual to the exposition of these cases, which however were not able to give real new results.

The possibility of passing from partial equilibrium to general equilibrium, as wished by Pareto's followers, required a further element, that is, the full mathematization of the economic reasoning. It is known that one of the keys to the success of the marginalist approach was the possibility of applying the differential calculus to the economic reasoning. If all the economic measures are quantities, and on the basis of the hedonistic principle every rational agent tends to maximize measures, the use of the mathematical calculus becomes a fundamental tool of the theoretical research (de Pietro Tonelli 1961). For Pareto's followers it was not necessary to formalize the economic debate only to give to the latter greater rigour and more argumentative clarity. Mathematical economics was necessary when considering economic phenomena in their relation of mutual dependence. If mathematics resulted in being useful in the case of partial analysis, it became indispensable in the case of general economic equilibrium. Literary economics, against which Pareto's first students entered into strong controversy, could do without mathematics because it only researched the cause of a phenomenon; but even if they had used mathematics, in the form of graphs or formulas, this would not have produced a scientifically mature result anyway. The aim of mathematical economics for Pareto's followers was not to measure the economic quantities, as many believed back then, but rather to demonstrate how the economic quantities were related to each other. Mathematics was useful to deal with the interdependence among economic factors. In this regard, Sensini observed:

> What perhaps has been detrimental for mathematical economics up to now is the confusion made by almost all of Walras's and Pareto's economists in synthetic theories, with those of Marshall's and Edgeworth's, or even better with those of the so-called Austrian school. The results obtained by the two English mathematical economists are not, generally speaking, comparable to those reached by Walras and Pareto, since the former mainly limited themselves to single expositions. In said cases, although the use of analysis can lead to interesting results, generally speaking it has scarce utility. Therefore, literary economists rightly observe that one could do without it, whereas the others demonstrated that the use of certain fields of mathematics is absolutely indispensable for the expositions of general cases of economic equilibrium.
>
> (Sensini 1912: 158)

Therefore, Pareto's followers were the first to highlight the fundamental relation between analytical instrument and economic content, at least in the field of pure economic theory. Not only was mathematics useful for a more in depth understanding of the economic phenomena, but it became the essential tool of investigation in the field of general economic equilibrium. Although they were identified as mathematical economists, at least in the Italian context between the two wars, they never stopped highlighting how mathematics was only an instrument for economic investigation. Actually, when in the years following the Second World War it was clear that the mathematical aspect would have surpassed the economic aspect, they did not keep quiet and made their criticisms heard.

A third element which united the economists belonging to the Pareto school was the clear distinction between pure or rational economics on one hand, and the theory of applied or experimental economics on the other. Despite the emphasis given to the use of mathematics, the economists from the Pareto school remained faithful to their teacher's belief according to which every science, and therefore also economics, had to have an experimental character, and, therefore, be based on observation. This is why they committed themselves with the same energy on one hand to pure economic theory, and on the other to the attempt of finding empirical proof. This strong dichotomy was the re-proposal within the economic theory of Pareto's scheme of the difference between logical actions and non-logical actions. Pure economics proceeds quickly without being concerned if its

22   *The Paretian school in Italy*

abstractions have or do not have an actual empirical corroboration. It mainly deals with the homo oeconomicus' actions, a useful abstraction created to isolate some relevant aspects of the economic behaviour. However, with Pareto, the metaphor of the homo oeconomicus is only a first approximation of the individuals' behaviour and has to be integrated with knowledge in other disciplines, such as sociology or ethics. Thus, it is up to applied economics to overcome the theoretical bindings set by rational economics in order to offer a complete explanation of economic facts.

The awareness of the ontological limits of pure economics led Pareto's followers in two directions for research. The first was to use statistical data when possible. Pareto's followers were the first to emphasize the importance of empirical researches in the field of economics. It is not a coincidence that Amoroso in his *Lezioni di Economia Matematica* dedicated an entire paragraph to the experimental determination of a function of utility, considering several statistical series on family budgets in Germany. Pareto himself dedicated most of his *Manuale* to applied economics, reserving only an initial part to pure economics. The desire to find data led some followers of Pareto's to set up laboratories of experimental economics, such as for example de Pietri Tonelli in Venice and Fossati in Genoa. Moreover, it often occurred that they held courses on methodological statistics. Again, an example can be found in Fossati who was the first in Italy to offer to his students a course in econometrics. The second path towards applied economics can be found in the broad sociological investigations offered by Pareto's followers. The field of non-logical actions was determining, and Pareto's students did not disregard carrying out incursions in sociology or in political science. They were interested in the social processes leading to the origin and formation of economic institutions in the broadest sense of the term. From this point of view they were very eclectic authors who dealt with a vast series of topics, not only economic.

There is a last methodological element which unified Pareto economists. They followed the same aim which was to make economics a scientific discipline on the model of natural science, and in particular rational mechanics. The latter, with its rigid division between statics and dynamics, with its subdivision between pure and applied mechanics, provided a formidable methodological model to which Pareto economists tried to conform. This inclination towards natural sciences was very strong in the first generation of Pareto's followers. de Pietri Tonelli and Amoroso constitute an example of this desire to imitate mature sciences. In time, however, even Pareto's followers realized that economic phenomena could not be read as analytical categories of rational mechanics. The analogy between economic and mechanic phenomena gradually lost importance among Pareto's second generation followers, with the sole exception of Palomba.

## The Pareto school's main research programmes

The period between the two World Wars has been defined with a happy metaphor by Shackle (1967) as the *Years of High Theory*. A period in which several lines

The Paretian school in Italy   23

of research were confronted, all united by the attempt to overcome the rigid schemes of the theory of general economic equilibrium and the unrealistic underlying hypothesis. The economic reality was a lot more complex than what was stated by the traditional scheme of choice in the condition of full perfect information. The theory of general economic equilibrium gave an optimistic representation of reality: perfect competition would have led naturally to the full allocation of resources and the disappearance of unemployment. The difficult years that followed the First World War did not live up to this optimism and required other answers both as regards the theory and the provisions of economic policy.

The group of Pareto's followers concentrated their theoretical efforts basically on two areas of research: the formal construction of economic dynamics and the theory of non-competitive markets. Less relevant, instead, were their contributions in other ambits of economic theory, such as the monetary one. In Italy this was a very active field of research in which the protagonists were authors belonging to Marshall's school, such as Del Vecchio and Fanno. The unresolved problem was to integrate the monetary theory within the theory of general economic equilibrium in order to overcome the naïve view of money as a simple tool of exchange. Pareto's followers, especially in the second half of the 1930s, developed a third research programme which we could define as an attempt to offer a scientific basis to the claims of corporative economics. The theory of corporative economics, besides the petitions of principle on the need to overcome the individualistic paradigm in economics, had remained a frame void of contents. The project matured only in the 1930s, led first of all by Amoroso. The aim was to offer a scientific basis to planned economics, considered as the third path between economic liberalism and planned economics of a socialist nature.

The dynamic theory which originated between the two World Wars was a genuinely new path. The core of the marginalist economic theory was essentially static and formed a complete theoretical system in its essential elements. This was obvious for Walras, but in a certain sense also for Marshall. As observed by Schumpeter it was time to cross the Rubicon, that is to elaborate a dynamic theoretical system in which statics could be considered a particular case. In this regard, the most important contributions were provided by those who looked at the analysis of the statistical data as a source for the construction of models of economic dynamics, such as Ragnar Frish (1933; 1936) and Jean Tinbergen (1934; 1935). This empirical approach is what mostly drew the historiographical attention (Weintraub 1991). However, next to this statistical course there was another approach which found its full development only in the years following the Second World War, and was mainly interested in mathematical aspects. This course was started in the 1920s by two American mathematicians, G. Evans and C. Roos, and in the following decade it was resumed and developed with original contributions in Italy by the economists belonging to the Pareto school.

Among the founders of marginalism, the problem of the scientific construction of dynamics was felt especially by Pareto, but also by Pantaleoni. However, as we will see, an adequate theoretical solution was not found. In *Manuale* (1906) after 20 years of research in various directions, we find this lapidary statement of

## 24 *The Paretian school in Italy*

Pareto's, "The theory of statics has greatly progressed; successive equilibrium is very rarely or scarcely mentioned; apart from a special theory, that is economic crisis, nothing is known concerning dynamic theory" (Pareto 1965: 96). The initial attempts offered by Pareto to construct economic dynamics on schemes of rational mechanisms was totally abandoned. As we will see in the following chapters, the task faced by Pareto's followers was to try to develop the construction of economic dynamics. In syntony with their teacher's indications, they pursued different paths in search of the definition of formal models capable of interpreting the evolution of historical series. This approach of dynamic equilibrium will constitute a possible alternative compared to the approach advanced by Frisch and Tinbergen, a sign of the theoretical pluralism which characterized the 1930s.

A second research programme which the Pareto economists worked on concerned the theory of non-competitive markets. Generally speaking, the beginning of this research at international level is identified with Sraffa's publication of an article dated 1926, *The Laws of Returns Under Competitive Conditions* (Shackle 1967) in which the Italian economist criticised the frail basis of Marshall's theory. As known, the article closed with the exhortation to abandon the path of free competition and turn in the opposite direction, that of imperfect competition. What we are interested in is that Sraffa's criticism against perfect competition was not an isolated reflection in the Italian context, and actually we can even say that it represented the common position among economists. The fact that perfect competition was incompatible with the growing efficiencies of scale had already been mentioned in *Lezioni di Economia Matematica* by Amoroso in 1921. The most interesting part of the lessons is substituted by an in-depth exposition from the analytical viewpoint of the form of oligopolistic market, or of *n* monopolists, to use the language of those years. Therefore, renowned economists in Italy had clear in mind both the theoretical and interpretative limits of the hypothesis of perfect competition, which they considered a pure school case. In 1930, Amoroso published an important essay entitled *La curva statica di offerta* in which he discussed pricing in an oligopolistic market, placing price in function of the number of agents. Perfect competition resulted as a special case in which the number of enterprises tended to infinite. Moreover, Amoroso himself anticipated the famous index of Lerner, a measure which ties the market power of the single enterprise to the elasticity of demand. This contribution was published only in Italian and almost passed unnoticed at international level.

If the market of goods was very distant from the conditions suggested by perfect competition, the same situation was found in the labour market which could be assimilated to a form of bilateral monopoly between the entrepreneurs' associations and the trade unions. The topic of the functioning of the labour market was greatly covered in literature in the 1930s. Concerning the issue of the labour market and wages, the theoretical marginalists had some difficulties which were not easily surmountable. Although the main principle was represented by the idea that wages could be measured by the marginal labour product, this assumption seemed very distant from the economic reality of those days and therefore of scarce utility. The starting point of the review of the traditional theory can be collocated in the last part of Pigou's *The Economics of Welfare* (1920) which he dedicated to an examination of industrial conflict and how this could affect collective welfare. On the basis of the evidence of the facts, Pigou argued that the labour market had by then completely lost the characteristics of a competitive market, and was very close to resembling a bilateral monopoly, in which the negotiation was carried out between trade unions and the employers' organizations. This new prospective, found by Marshall's successor, led to a result which was well known on the theoretical level: the solution of the equilibrium resulted as indeterminate. Since the negotiation concerned both the wages and the number of those employed, neither the trade unions nor the employers had any inclination to insist for economic claims beyond a certain limit. Therefore, a zone of non-determination was found comprised between a maximum limit and a minimum limit within which the wages, and consequently also employment, could vary due to the relevant strength of the agents. Since the conflict which led to the determination of the actual wages resulted often as very expensive for the contracting parties, and especially determined a loss of welfare for the community, the English economist proposed that the controversies on wages be entrusted to a judge who could be voluntary or imposed by law. Pigou's conclusion on the topic of wages was quite clear: the theory according to which wages were determined by the marginal labour product had to be surpassed and wages were usually found above or below this value as regards the state of industrial relationships. This position of Pigou's constituted a decisive parting from the traditional systems, and was resumed and confirmed by Hicks in his *The Theory of Wages* (1932).

The Italian situation was well aligned with the said thought. The fascist regime had intervened on this issue once again with law n. 56, dated 3 April 1926. The bases of the new authoritarian regulations of the labour market were as follows: suppression of free trade unions, creation of a *Labour Court*, effectiveness *erga omnes* of the collective employment contract. The first corporative economists, Gino Arias, Filippo Carli, Massimo Fovel, Spirito tried to elaborate a theory of wages in line with the new indications of the regime. They proposed the notion of corporative wages, a new way of defining the remuneration of the employee in order to overcome class conflict. This theory of corporative wages soon became vague and ambiguous because each one of the authors who dealt with it offered a different definition. If for Arias it was supposed to be connected to a Tomistic origin of the right price for labour, at the opposite extreme we find Breglia's position for whom corporative wages corresponded to the neoclassical notion of wages of perfect competition, which in the new monopolistic context could be guaranteed only by the state. In his report presented at *Il Convegno degli Studi Sindacali e Corporativi* in 1932 in Ferrara, Masci stated openly that with the law dated 1926 on the collective employment contract, the fascist regime had actually regulated industrial relationships in a new way, according to the model of bilateral monopoly. The arbitrary function, made necessary by the presence of a zone of indeterminateness of the variables involved, was carried out in Italy by

## 26 *The Paretian school in Italy*

the Labour Court which made sure that contracts were complied with, and it carried out preventive actions in order to prevent trade union conflicts. This assimilation of the employment collective contract to the contract among monopolists unfolded two problems which Masci highlighted without adding a solution. The first was represented by the fact that the number of workers could not be considered an exogenous datum, that is the unemployment issue remained open. Second, if wages moved away from the marginal product it became possible to move the equilibrium by introducing "political, national, moral criteria, and so on, which however did not enter in the traditional framework of economic science" (Masci 1932: 166). Contrary to other corporative economists, Masci suggested not to abandon traditional economics completely, but to consider its theories based on the individualistic view being valid only with first approximation, trying then to introduce in the investigation new hypothesis and conditions responding to the reality to theorize. Among Pareto's followers, as already observed, Bordin was mainly the one who intervened in this debate with an article dated 1936, *Alcune generalizzazioni di un caso di monopolio bilaterale*, and with a following one entitled *Un caso di monopolio bilaterale* (1938). He faced the problem of indetermination of the point of equilibrium introducing the concept of hedonistic strength of the agents as an objective criterion to determine the particular wages which will be formed, including the maximum limit and the minimum one.

A third important research programme can be found in the *corporative turning point* of the Italian academic (and liberist) economists collocated in the mid-1930s. Amoroso was the one who broke the ice on the theoretical level. He was certainly the most renowned economist at international level, and in 1934 he wrote an article with De Stefani entitled, *La logica del sistema corporativo*. In this work the two authors strongly stated that the corporative economic theory was not a new theory denying the traditional approach, but a new approach which constituted its natural development in the epoch of monopolistic capitalism. On the other hand, in the same year, with the creation of the *Corporazioni* provided for in 1926 but never implemented, the corporative structure abandoned the merely doctrinal debate. The *Corporazioni* were to constitute the main institutional innovations of the regime in the field of economic policy, and this required some scientific interpretation exactly on behalf of the economists. This attempt to graft corporative topics into the traditional economic theory had an immediate return even at academic level. In fact, starting in the mid-1930s, the official denomination of the courses in economics was changed by decree, thus becoming courses in economics and corporative economic policy. Even the university manuals were adequately changed for the new historical needs. In some cases, said changes concerned simple, but relevant, integrations (Papi 1934a; Amoroso 1938), in other cases the interventions were more substantial (Fanno 1936; Masci 1941–1942). However, we have to take into consideration that corporative economics did not have a totalizing approach and that the economists had a discrete freedom of thought. In 1936, La Volpe, Pareto's follower, published his remarkable monograph on dynamic equilibrium which had nothing corporative and was reviewed correctly in the *Journal of Political Economy* as a work apparently belonging to the Pareto tradition.

The comparison with the economic theory of corporativism concerned the main traditions of thought in Italy, both Marshall's and Pareto's. The former was mainly represented by Del Vecchio, Papi, Fanno and Masci. The first did not produce anything important in this field if we exclude a comment to the Carta del Lavoro in 1927, widely quoted (Del Vecchio 1934). The more substantial contributions were provided by Papi (1934a, b), Fanno (1936), and Masci (1934a, 1934b, 1941–1942). Papi tried to integrate corporativism in his theory of economic fluctuations adding a final part on the corporative system in the third volume of his *Lezioni di economia generale e corporativa* (1934), which however did not integrate well with the part preceding it. Fanno and Masci produced the more organic attempts, even if introductive, looking at economic corporative theory from the point of view of economics. Fanno, encouraged by Einaudi, in 1936 printed the definitive version of his book, *Introduzione allo studio della teoria economica del corporativismo*, of which a lithographed version had been circulating for some time. A further influential attempt to integrate corporativism in the economic theory can be found in *Lezioni di Economia corporativa* by Masci (1941–1942), the volume being published after the author's sudden death in 1941. The exponents of the Pareto school were definitively those more convinced in supporting corporativism, although with clearly different characteristics, starting from the main exponent Amoroso. Pareto's followers, on the basis of an approach which referred to Pareto, strongly posed the problem of the dichotomy between the economic aspect and the political-collective aspect of the economic action. They all searched for a synthesis between orthodox theory and corporative system with quite different results, as we will try to highlight.

# 2 Pareto's legacy in economic dynamics

## Introduction

Apart from a few remarkable exceptions, especially represented by A. Marshall and J. Schumpeter, the first generation of marginalists mainly concentrated on the theory of value and distribution, that is, on the static aspects of economic theory. Consequently, some of the fundamental topics of the classical school, such as the analysis of the causes of economic growth, were no longer on the economists' agenda, not being in step with the new epistemological view of economics. In fact, the latter was establishing itself definitively as a science of the allocation of scarce resources.

In this setting, even Pareto ended up turning to static analysis. In fact, the parts of his work explicitly dedicated to dynamic analysis occupy a position of modest relevance, with the exception of the theory of economic fluctuations, which, however, he collocated in the field of applied economics and not in that of pure economics. As a matter of fact, in collecting his fundamental results in his first work of synthesis, *Corso* (1896/1897), he relegated the discussion on economic dynamics to a few paragraphs (especially in the notes) with the aim of indicating possible directions of research more than presenting complete and definitive results, as occurred instead for the static theory of economic equilibrium. With the new approach based on the subjective theory of value, the static part basically came to light already complete of all its elements, whereas the construction of the dynamic part resulted in a problematic field of research for several generations of economists.

This simple consideration enables us to understand why this part of Pareto's theory was disregarded for a long time, to then become the object of in-depth analysis only in relatively recent years (Donzelli 1991, 1997; Tusset 2004). This research has provided a clear and complete picture of Pareto's theoretical position in the field of dynamics as well as the evolution of said position: from his first attempts to apply the principles of rational mechanics to this field, up to his abandonment of the formal economic schemes and definitive passing to sociology. Therefore, we will limit our discussion to the theoretical elements which were resumed and developed by his followers and students. Actually, we will see how the exponents of the Pareto school closely followed their teacher's indications in the field of dynamics, some developing them along the original lines of research (Amoroso 1939; La Volpe 1936), others simply reasserting them even after several decades (Sensini 1955). In order to rebuild the events that characterized the development of his students' modelling, it is necessary to start from Pareto's writings, and specifically from the concept of dynamic equilibrium which played such an essential role.

## Dynamic equilibrium: first and second order dynamics

Within Pareto's vast production, there are not many references to economic dynamics. Therefore, considering the aspects in which we are interested, these can be easily and precisely identified in several paragraphs of *Corso* and in a brief article dated 1901. Pareto's illusion to be able to create a rigorous and formal economic dynamics, on the basis of what had been possible for statics, lasted only a few years. In paragraphs 585–587 and 928 of *Corso*, we can find a first outline of his approach towards the issues concerning dynamics, still linked to the schemes of rational mechanics. A second and totally different discussion, instead, is present in the appendix of the article dated 1901, *Le nuove teorie economiche* entitled, *Le equazioni dell'equilibrio dinamico*, in which he used a more traditional scheme and referred to Walras in the attempt to dynamize directly the equation of general economic equilibrium. None of the two attempts produced the hoped for results, nor were they considered satisfying by Pareto who abandoned this field of research to dedicate himself to sociological studies. According to Pareto, economic dynamics is a small part of the broader social dynamics which is dominated by non-logical actions, thus difficult to explore. In the following paragraphs we will take into consideration the position expressed in the pages of *Corso.*

*Corso* is a voluminous treatise divided into two parts. The first is shorter and dedicated to pure theory: in this part Pareto presents Walras's theory of general economic equilibrium. Besides the presentation, which results to be clearer and more organized, Pareto's scientific contribution also consists in broadening Walras's theory to monopolies. The presence of monopolistic markets does not alter the pure economic theory of mutual relationships among markets, even if it affects the results in terms of collective welfare. The second part, much larger, is dedicated to applied economics. Pareto never stopped reasserting the importance of the distinction between pure and applied economics, which actually constitutes one of the characteristics of his methodological approach. In the first chapter of his second book, dedicated to the analysis of the economic organism, Pareto discusses economic dynamics for the first time. The chapter is entitled *Principi generali della evoluzione sociale*, and before confronting Darwin's theory of evolution Pareto dedicates several pages to the importance of the paradigm of rational mechanics also in economics. We here find the famous tables that put economics and mechanics in comparison. Economics can be considered as the mechanics of economic behaviour in which the concepts of force, space and constraints turn into those of goods, marginal utility and income. Pareto reasserts

## 30 *Pareto's legacy in economic dynamics*

an important aspect of his view of economic theory: when considering economic equilibrium in a precise moment, it is necessary to compare the economic system to a system of material aspects. Instead, when studying the evolution of a society and its institutions, a biological comparison with living organisms is to be preferred. Pareto also outlines a theory of natural selection: he asserts that the economic and social institutions that survive changes are those which better adapt to an environment in continuous evolution. However, even from the collocation of the analysis, it is clear that according to Pareto the dynamic of the economic system and that of the society cannot be separated. In dynamics, even more than in statics, the non-logical actions play a determining role. Economic dynamics is therefore a subset of the broader, and more interesting for Pareto, society dynamics.

Pareto started his analysis of economic dynamics in paragraph 585, which he significantly entitled *L'equilibrio economico e l'equilibrio sociale*. In his words:

> § 585. *Economic equilibrium and social equilibrium.* Generally speaking, the conditions of a society change very slowly. Any society usually offers a rather considerable resistance against internal or external forces which tend to modify it. The accidental motions that are produced in society are neutralized by the opposite motions which they cause; finally, the latter end up dying out and society returns to its initial conditions. Society can thus be considered in a state of stable equilibrium.
>
> § 586 Actually, in this case it is not a matter of static equilibrium, but of dynamic equilibrium, because the society in its whole is hauled by a general motion which slowly modifies it. Generally speaking, this motion is identified with the term evolution.
>
> In mechanics, d'Alembert's principle enables us to carry out a complete study on the dynamic state of a system. For the moment, we are not able to distinguish an analogous principle in economics, nor in social science. In both these sciences, we are obliged to substitute the consideration of dynamic equilibrium with the consideration of a series of static equilibria.
>
> (Pareto 1971: 641)

These paragraphs are fundamental as regards Pareto's observations on dynamics for several reasons. First of all, they reassert the centrality of the concept of equilibrium also in dynamics. It is not a static or stationary equilibrium, a situation in which quantities do not change in time. This concept, so important for economic statics, occupies a central position also in dynamics. Pareto offers a heuristic definition: equilibrium becomes dynamic when changes take place slowly, thus without altering the structure of the system. In analytical terms, equilibrium is dynamic when the change of the variable results in a continuous function of time, assumed as an exogenous variable which can incorporate all the factors of change, both the economic and the extra-economic ones. It is a very general definition which in the beginning may seem difficult to apply.

*Pareto's legacy in economic dynamics*    31

Initially, the idea of dynamic equilibrium can appear as an oxymoron. Perhaps this is why Pareto used the famous metaphor of the man coming down the snowy slope. It is a metaphor which he used to introduce the distinction between first order dynamics – still linked to Walras's schemes – and second order dynamics – exempt from the limits of the first. In Pareto's words:

> To give a rough but eloquent idea of the issue, let's suppose that a man in a sledge is coming down a slope. Another man is coming down the same slope on foot, stopping after every step. The two men start off at the same time. They proceed constantly together and reach the foot of the slope at the same time. Their movement, therefore, is *more or less* the same. But the motion of the man in the sledge is a continuous motion: the relative study implies a problem in dynamics. The motion of the man coming down on foot represents a series of consecutive positions of equilibrium: he passes from one to another in a discontinuous manner. This is exactly what we can study in economics: a series of consecutive positions of equilibrium.
>
> (Pareto 1971: 643)

In this passage, Pareto establishes an important distinction in dynamic analysis which constitutes a sort of methodological watershed. Pareto's followers, but not only as in the case of Pantaleoni, clearly distinguished a first order dynamics and a second order dynamics, where the first should constitute a propaedeutic phase for the second. First order dynamics is defined by the fact that the dynamic equilibrium is constituted by a series of consecutive positions of equilibrium. General economic equilibrium constitutes a great allocative mechanism which at the end of each period establishes the position of equilibrium for the economic variables: the succession of these optimal equilibria constitutes first order dynamics. This definition is very close to that of Walras's.

Second order dynamics is Pareto's specific contribution, at least in the initial phase, to the solution of the problem concerning dynamics which Walras had left unresolved. It is not only a matter of temporal intervals becoming so small so as to be able to pass from a discrete case to a continuous case. Actually, it is a matter of passing to a different methodological paradigm, that of rational mechanics. This discipline is traditionally divided into two parts: statics and dynamics. Both the first and the second have been studied for centuries, therefore the analytical apparatuses are well developed and consolidated. The logical scheme of reference is the same: both the static position and the motion of the system of material points derive from the contrast between the forces which act upon the system and the constraints. Pareto's initial idea is that the same methodology can be applied to economics as well. This analogy produced excellent results in statics, reducing the problem concerning the economic agent to a problem of maximum constrained. It was a matter of extending this line of reflection also to dynamics.

The importance of this distinction in dynamics was reasserted a couple of decades after the publication of Corso by de Pietri Tonelli, one of the most

## 32  *Pareto's legacy in economic dynamics*

faithful followers and interpreters of this distinction. In the introduction to his *Lezioni di scienza economica razionale e sperimentale* dated 1921, he observes:

> Rational economics can be divided into three parts. A first part includes static economics which studies the positions of equilibrium not keeping into account the variable of time. A second part includes dynamic economics, in which the positions of equilibrium are studied keeping into account the variable of time. When considering discontinuous variations and studying series of consecutive positions of equilibrium, this leads to first order dynamics. When considering continuous variations and studying the motions of the economic phenomenon as regards the series of consecutive positions of equilibrium, this leads to second order dynamics.
>
> (de Pietro Tonelli 1921: 42)

Similar to Pareto, de Pietri Tonelli also dedicated his voluminous text of lectures to the theory of general economic equilibrium only considering statics. His references to economic dynamics were very brief since at the beginning of the 1920s it was not clear how to develop second order economic dynamics. This distinction led to consequences even within the Pareto school. Its exponents such as Amoroso, La Volpe and then Palomba concentrated on the mathematically more interesting developments of second order dynamics. First order dynamics aroused less interest. Fossati, Sensini and, to a lesser extent, Vinci, remained faithful to the scheme of the succession of equilibriums with less innovative results.

### Second order dynamics in *Corso*

The first aspect which Pareto outlined in *Corso* concerned the characteristics of second order dynamics; only afterwards, in the article of 1901, he passed to first order dynamics. This change of perspective indicates how second order dynamics presented problematic elements which could not satisfy Pareto's positivistic approach.

In a dense note in § 587, as mentioned in the previous section, Pareto discusses the basic reason why the scheme of rational mechanics, which in economic statics became the contrast between tastes and obstacles, cannot be applied to dynamics. On the basis of Pareto's observations, passing from statics to dynamics in rational mechanics is guaranteed by d'Alembert's principle, thus he wondered if this principle could be applied in economics as well. The fundamental equation, which in analytic mechanics enables rigid bodies to pass to dynamic analysis, is obtained by using Newton's second law and keeping in mind the actions of constraints. The fundamental equation of dynamics is as follows:

$$\sum_{i=1}^{n}(F_i - m_i a_i)\delta_i = 0 \qquad\qquad [1]$$

*Pareto's legacy in economic dynamics* 33

where $F_i$ represents the force applied to the body, $m_i$ its mass, and $a_i$ the relative acceleration, while $\delta_i$ is the infinitesimal displacement. The term $m_i a_i$ represents the forces of inertia, therefore on the basis of [1] the motion of a material system is re-conducted to the action and reaction of the operating forces: both the active forces and the passive ones. From a mathematical viewpoint, [1] defines a system of second order differential equations, the solution of which is determined by calculus of variations.

In the note in paragraph 587, Pareto applies the equation [1] directly to the consumer's behaviour, where $F_i$, as in the case of statics, are marginal utilities associated to the consumption of different goods. The resulting equation is exactly analogous to [1] and is as follows:

$$\left(\varphi_a - \frac{\delta x_a}{\delta r_a}\right)\delta_a r_a + \left(\varphi_b - \frac{\delta x_b}{\delta r_b}\right)\delta_b r_b + \dots = 0 \qquad [2]$$

where $\varphi_i$ are the marginal utilities of the single goods, whereas $\frac{\delta x}{\delta r}$ represent the forces which act in the opposite direction, thus the resistance to the variations of consumption, analogously to the forces of inertia $m_i a_i$ of the equation [1]. However, these purely formal passages do not seem to satisfy Pareto, who observes:

> In case of a material system, equation [2] is simply the one given by the principle of virtual movements combined with d'Alembert's principle. Instead, in case of an economic system, we are blocked because we ignore not only the value but also the actual nature of the functions,
>
> $$\frac{\delta x_a}{\delta r_a}, \frac{\delta x_b}{\delta r_b}, \dots \qquad [3]$$
>
> For a material point, instead, we can consider $\varphi$ as the forces that stress it and thus the functions [3], with a minus sign, are the forces of inertia, and are as follows:
>
> $$\frac{\delta x_a}{\delta r_a} = m\frac{d^2 r_a}{dt^2}, \quad \frac{\delta x_b}{\delta r_b} = m\frac{d^2 x_b}{dt^2} \qquad [4]$$
>
> where $dt$ is the time during which the material point goes along the line whose components are $dr_a$, $dr_b$, $dr_c$. These equations are analogous to those which would need to be found for an economic system.
>
> (Pareto 1971: 643)

Pareto provided an example in a second mathematical note in § 928 of *Corso*, but then he did not continue his research as regards the form of the inertia equations in economic behaviour, as mentioned by Sensini (1955: 250). Therefore, we can say that Pareto's view is less mechanistic than what is generally considered, especially in the field of economic dynamics.

## 34   *Pareto's legacy in economic dynamics*

A thorough discussion concerning the difficulties in interpreting dynamics according to the schemes of rational mechanics is offered by Donzelli (1991). The basic reason owing to which it is not possible to pass from the dynamic schemes of mechanics to those of economics consists in the fact that the relationship between space and time in economics is not the same found in rational mechanics. The rational choice theory implies two distinct concepts of time: the time of the choice and the time of the realization, whereas this distinction has no meaning in the case of motion of material bodies in which these two aspects coincide instantly. This explains Pareto's inability to obtain an expression for the forces of inertia (Donzelli 1997). The problem concerning the analogies with rational mechanics is reflected in a further issue. The equations of rational mechanics are second order differential equations which somehow have to be obtained from the basic model. This is why Pareto, but as we will see Sensini as well, is obliged to interpret in a different way the consumption that in the case of dynamics becomes the velocity of consumption, that is variation in time. This ambiguity in considering economic quantities as finite values or as variations depending on the scheme of reference, be it that of statics or dynamics, constitutes a second element which highlights the difficulty in lining up dynamics with rational mechanics on conceptual schemes.

With this brief mathematical note, Pareto concludes this first draft of second order dynamics which, actually, will no longer be taken into consideration. A final reference to this purely formal formulation will be found only in the last part of an article dated 1906 which, however, was Sensini's translation of an article written in German several years before:

## Dynamics

Up to this point we have taken into consideration the static aspect of the problem. The dynamic aspect has been discussed very little, and has originated mostly imperfect and obscure works, with the exception of the theories of crisis. It has not been possible to find in the results of the experience regarding equilibrium a quantity of the total ophelimity $\Phi$ or of its partial derivatives To determine these functions, it is necessary to pass to dynamic viewpoints, just as form is measured through acceleration in mechanics. The analogies between mathematical economics and rational mechanics are numerous and deep-rooted; one of the fundamental equations of mathematical economics is simply the equation of virtual velocities. A specific part of dynamic economics, that which deals with *crisis*, has led to important and accurate studies, which are mostly empirical. From these studies, however, we can see that the economic circulation presents phenomena analogous to those of inertia in mechanics. Probably one day mathematical economics will be able to use a principle analogous to that of d'Alembert's. However, it is preferable not to anticipate events. For now, only economic statics has been developed scientifically and has given useful results.

(Pareto 1906: 449–450)

Therefore, right after a first drafting, Pareto completely abandoned the perspective of second order dynamics, that is, the idea of being able to obtain, through a close analogy with rational mechanics, the laws of the variations of economic quantities depending on time. The scheme obtained from rational mechanics regarding the comparison of tastes and obstacles shows its epistemological limits. If in the case of statics it was possible to create tablets showing the analogies between economic concepts and those of rational mechanics, in the case of dynamics this transposition resulted as totally problematic because no reasonable economic concept corresponded to the concept of mechanic inertia. This insurmountable conceptual difficulty was mentioned once again by Pareto in a letter to a young Amoroso in 1907:

> The difficulty is not in recognising that the habit corresponds to inertia, which I find to be likely at the least; the difficult aspect is in finding what corresponds economically to the mechanic mass, and what corresponds economically to the mechanic acceleration multiplied the mass. If this is not known, if we do not know in economics what relationship there is between force and acceleration, we cannot write the equations of economic dynamics.
>
> (Pareto 1973: 594)

Therefore, it is not an analytical or a formal obstacle which the economist has to face. The economic phenomena in this field are too complex to be investigated through differential equations of rational mechanics, which had had such great success in statics. Moreover, their study cannot be separated from that of a general view of evolution of the society in its whole which can be obtained, according to Pareto, only coming out of the rigid chains of pure economics. It will be necessary to look in other directions and especially to have at our disposal a different mathematical formalism capable of transforming a dynamic problem into an economic problem.

## Second order dynamics as economic cycle dynamics

In the last pages of *Corso*, Pareto offered an example of how it was possible to develop second order dynamics, and once again he did so in a note in a chapter dedicated to economic crisis, which according to Pareto is the first form of continuous dynamics. At the beginning of the chapter, he observes that the economic phenomenon is not a static phenomenon, but rather dynamic. Thus, from his viewpoint, economic crisis is not to be considered as an accidental event which disturbs the equilibrium of the variables but rather their normal state. A prosperity phase is followed by a period of depression which in turn prepares for the following wave of optimism and prosperity. We will consider Pareto's theory of the economic cycle, and of its following developments, in Chapter 8. Two main elements characterize Pareto's view of the economic cycle. First of all, he

## 36    *Pareto's legacy in economic dynamics*

considers the economic cycle as a phenomenon of equilibrium and not of lack of equilibrium. This means that in real life economic variables move slowly in time following a law which is the economist's task to determine (de Pietri Tonelli 1921: 23). Second, the oscillatory motion of the variables, which is the peculiar characteristic of the economic cycle with its phases of expansion and contraction, depends on forces endogenous to the economic system and not on exogenous elements, as for example monetary perturbations. We here want to highlight Pareto's analytical contribution provided once again in a note in paragraph 928. This note is important because it contains the first, and for what concerns Pareto also the last, explicit formulation of a mathematical model of economic cycle (Boianovsky and Tarascio 1998).

In this note Pareto considers the simplest case, that of a single individual who every day receives a certain amount, $r_a$, saves a part, $r_e$, and consumes the rest purchasing a single good, $a$. Later on, even Pareto rejected this mathematical example. In paragraph 172 of *Manuale* we find the following note: "Note 2 in paragraph 928 is based on erroneous considerations and is to be totally modified." Pareto had noticed several inaccuracies in the mathematical part. The first to notice them had been Wicksell in 1899 in the review to the second volume of *Corso*, about which though Pareto was in the dark. It was therefore a brilliant error.

Pareto wanted to show in the note that even this simple behavioural scheme is capable of generating a cyclical trend and therefore certain economic dynamics. The initial equations are the following:

$$\frac{1}{p_a}(\psi_a - f_a) = \psi_e - f_e \qquad r_a p_a + r_e = r_s \qquad [5]$$

The first expresses the optimality condition, while the second is the budget constraint. Pareto then assumes that the expenditure for goods fluctuates around a constant value, according to the expression $r_a = a + x p_a$, from which the quantity of saving becomes, $r_e = r_s - p_a(a + x)$, where $x$ represents a small variation of the quantity purchased. Pareto's intuition is to develop the equation of equilibrium [5] in one of Taylor's series, obtaining the following expression:

$$\frac{1}{p_a}(f_a - f_e) = \frac{1}{p_a}(\psi_a(a) - \psi_e(e)) + \frac{1}{p_a}(\psi'_a(a) - \psi_e'(e))x$$

$$+ \frac{1}{p_a}(\psi''_a(a) - \psi''_e(e))x^2 \qquad [6]$$

To reach a closed and thus operative formula, it is necessary to give a precise form both to the function of marginal utility and to that which expresses the resistance to change. Pareto proceeds with power functions, obtaining $f_a = A(\frac{dr_a}{dt})^2$ and $f_e = B(\frac{dr_e}{dt})^2$. Inserting the functions within Taylor's expression we finally obtain the final equation:

$$\left(\frac{dx}{dt}\right)^2 = k^2(1 - h^2 x^2)$$ [7]

The latter is a second order differential equation, of which the solution is a trigonometric function, where $k$ and $h$ are the constants that depend on the parameters.

$$x = \frac{1}{h} sin(c + kht)$$ [8]

Pareto can therefore conclude that consumption fluctuates around parameter $a$. He then observes:

> The easiness with which the general equations obtained for the economic aggregate are suitable for representing all the phenomena that the observation reveals, is absolutely remarkable. After all, this is the best proof of the utility of this system of representation and of its complete harmony with the nature of things.
>
> (Pareto 1971: 756)

Equation [8] is of great relevance because it expresses the structure of the continuous dynamic equilibrium from a mathematical viewpoint. The value of the variable depends only on time, as in rational mechanics which studies the motion of bodies. This functional dependence of an economic variable on time will be the distinctive trait of this approach to economic dynamics. In *Corso*, Pareto was satisfied with the example expressed in the note, and therefore dedicated the whole paragraph to a description of the main causes and phases of economic fluctuations. These are triggered by endogenous causes, such as variations in the consumers' preferences, or by exogenous causes, such as technical progress; the ascending movement must necessarily stop and actually proceed in the opposite direction. Pareto excludes categorically that the reason can be monetary or financial since the crisis would occur even if the credit did not exist. This example will not be re-proposed in *Manuale*, a sign that Pareto's research had already changed direction, as highlighted in the article of 1901.

## First order dynamics in the article dated 1901

Abandoning the main but not very fruitful road of the analogy with rational mechanics, Pareto offered a second attempt for a way towards the construction of economic dynamics in the brief but dense appendix to the article dated 1901, *Le nuove teorie economiche*, with a meaningful title, *Le equazioni dell'equilibrio dinamico*. These few pages seemed to be opening a new research programme, but the project was not developed in Pareto's following works. Nonetheless, we can notice how this short note was considered important since in another article dated

## 38  *Pareto's legacy in economic dynamics*

1930 Demaria considered the mathematical appendix dated 1901 as Pareto's mature position in dynamic analysis.

With this article, Pareto wanted to probe the possibility to formalize first order dynamics or successive equilibria, and therefore returned to a more traditional ambit. The analytical expedient used by Pareto in this appendix to dynamize the theory of general economic equilibrium consists of assuming that all the economic transactions are referred not to a single instant of time, but to a generic temporal interval $dt$ of arbitrary amplitude. For the remaining part, the formal scheme does not change even if it is no longer possible to maintain the division of the static equations into three main groups: exchange, production and capitalization equations. In dynamic analysis the phenomenon of exchange cannot be separated from that of production; in fact, it is the latter which provides the society with the goods object of exchange in time. Apart from this formal modification (the introduction of a new variable $dt$), the system of general economic equilibrium, with its different systems of equations, remains similar to what found in statics, with the sole difference that the solutions will not be values but functions referred to the intervals of time considered. What mainly interests Pareto is that even in the new analytical context the system of equations obtained results perfectly determined. If, for simplicity, the quantity of individuals, goods and assets are considered constant, all elements which in a dynamic context could change, the number of the unknown variables of the dynamic system is equal to that of the equations. Actually, the only dynamic variable of the model is saving, which in fact is represented as a first derivative. However, this brilliant solution also seems to lead to more problems than those it actually resolves. The note concludes with Pareto's following observation:

> We have thus obtained the equations of dynamic equilibrium. Now it would be easy to work out the ones which refer to at least the main oscillations. However, if we want more particulars from our equations, they will become more complicated, which they are already enormously. Therefore, for the moment, a totally different road needs to be pursued: instead of complicating the equations, we need to find a way to simplify them, even at the cost of sacrificing many particulars of the phenomenon.
>
> In the system of equations exposed, there is a system of simultaneous differential equations, and in general it will be impossible to integrate them except by approximation. And this is also the only method that can be pursued to resolve the equations of the system.
>
> (Pareto 1901: 259)

Among Pareto's followers, Sensini was the only one who pursued this second road proposed by Pareto. In fact, Sensini dedicated the second part of his lessons, *Corso di Economia Pura* (1955), to the exposition of this part of Pareto's theory on dynamics. Among Pareto's students, Sensini was the most uncompromising critic concerning the analogies between rational mechanics and pure economics.

*Pareto's legacy in economic dynamics* 39

If this finds some application in statics, for Sensini it could not be applied to dynamics. In 1955 he observed:

> The danger to be avoided is to want to build economic dynamics on models of mechanic dynamics (D'Alembert's principle), just as economic statics was built on the models of mechanic statics (equation of Lagrange). In statics there is full analogy between economic phenomena and mechanic phenomena, which also explains Pareto's success in his static-economic investigations, considering his expertise in mechanics. In dynamics there is no analogy between the above mentioned phenomena, which explains the lack of success of the economic-mathematical theories which were based on d'Alembert's principle.
>
> (Sensini 1955: 220)

In order to understand what Pareto had in mind in his article of 1901, it is useful to follow the detailed analysis that Sensini carries out in his lectures. Pareto's student, first of all, considers the side of consumption. The system of consumption equations can be made dynamic through two tactics. The first consists in the fact that both sides of consumers' budget constraint are considered within a specific arbitrary interval of time, $dt$. Second, saving is introduced in differential terms as a derivative as regards time, even if the form of this function is not specified. During the interval of time taken into consideration, the equation of each single consumer's budget is as follows:

$$\left(p_s r_s + p_t r_t + ....\right)dt = \left(p_a r_a + p_b r_b + ... + \frac{dr_e}{dt}\right)dt \qquad [9]$$

The solution of this first system referred to the consumer's behaviour requires, as usual, that the marginal utilities of the different goods be levelled, exactly as in statics, with the only difference that now the single curves of demand will depend also on a differential component, that is saving. The system of [9] referred to the whole of consumers and goods enables to obtain the totality of the demand curves. The same procedure, adding the temporal interval on both sides of the equation, is applied to the other systems of equations which form the structure of general economic equilibrium. For example, in Sensini's lectures the system of capitalization equations is as follows:

$$\frac{dR_e}{dt} dt = \Pi_s \frac{dQ_s}{dt} dt + \Pi_k \frac{dQ_k}{dt} dt + .... \qquad [10]$$

$$\frac{p_s}{\Pi_s} dt = \frac{p_k}{\Pi_k} dt = .... = idt \qquad [11]$$

In the equation [10] the term on the left represents the share of saving allocated for the production of new capital goods, and the term on the right represents

## 40 *Pareto's legacy in economic dynamics*

the total masses of the goods produced, where $\Pi_s$ indicates the production cost of every single good. In [11] the interest rate results from the relationship between the price of the service of the capital good and its cost, exactly as in statics; in a condition of perfect competition this value must be the same for all capital goods. An analogous line of reasoning can be followed for the remaining two blocks of equations: the one concerning equality between the costs of the single goods and their price, and the one concerning the full use of the resources available.

Therefore, similar to Pareto, Sensini, a couple of decades later, is also content with a pure formal solution of the problem, that is the theoretical possibility to write the equations of dynamic equilibrium. However, it is a solution with scarce practical relevance because these equations are almost impossible to reach. He observes:

> 6. It is necessary to highlight the impossibility to integrate all these differential equations which appear in the systems described in the previous paragraphs. In other words, the totality of the above mentioned equations could be considered as a single system of first order simultaneous differential equations, to then pass on to their integration through methods provided by Mathematical Analysis. It is superfluous to add that, due to the great quantity and complexity of said equations, and due to the lack of a large quantity of data which would be necessary, it is impossible to pursue such path.
>
> (Sensini 1955: 320)

Therefore, the dynamic of successive equilibria, even in its formal elegance, could not resolve many problems. First of all, there was a problem linked to the heuristic value of the theory of general dynamic equilibrium. If statics was already considered by its critics as an empty box, the construction of dynamic equilibrium seemed even more abstract. Second, there were mathematical difficulties in finding a solution to a system of dynamic equations made of many equations and many variables. Lastly, there was an even more fundamental criticism which concerned the actual nature of this approach to dynamics. This criticism is expressed clearly in the initial part of a long article (1935) prepared by Vinci, entitled *Il significato di alcune teorie moderne della dinamica economica*. With reference to Pareto's position, he observes:

> The principle that regulates this construction, and that of the enterprise – which we here omit for sake of concision since it would add nothing to the matter we are studying – is still the principle of statics. However, the aggravating circumstance is that, if the period for the realization of solutions in statics is indeterminate, that for the realization of solutions in dynamics is determinate; and if in the first case there can be certainty in the verification, in the second case said certainty of verification is basically inexistent. Not only: since the solutions at the end of the first interval consist in the

*Pareto's legacy in economic dynamics*   41

successive data and so on, if the first is missing so is the second, and the whole system strays from reality, without any possibility whatsoever of contact even of first approximation.

(Bordin 1935: 14)

Bordin was sharp in observing that even in first order dynamics it was impossible not to consider statics, or comparative statics, because the inter-temporal link among the variables was not expressed. Pareto's fundamental principle in dynamics concerning the interdependence among the economic variables showed all its theoretical weakness. After every short interval, the economic system, perturbed by whatever factor, would find a new point of equilibrium without being able to say which was the determining factor. A true analysis of economic dynamics required the reintroduction of the principle of causality, which however the Pareto school had put aside.

## Pareto beyond Walras

After examining Pareto's theory concerning dynamics, it is almost natural to compare it with that of Walras's. It is known that the two economists from the school of Losanna shared the same logical approach towards economic problems and considered the theory of general economic equilibriums as the most complete expression of economics in the field of statics. We still have to take into consideration, though, the relationship between these two economists in the field of dynamics.

As observed (Donzelli 1997), Walras's dynamic analysis and that of Pareto's do not present marked differences at first sight. In fact, they both tend to explain the temporal evolution of an economic system as a series of equilibria in succession in time. In fact, the method which Walras proposed of mobile equilibrium, even if in embryo, is what Pareto called first order dynamics. As highlighted in the previous section, the limitation of the method of the successive equilibria consists of the fact that a position of equilibrium is independent from the previous one since the disturbing elements can be the most different and disconnected among each other. In order to overcome this difficulty and reach a methodology which enables to understand the temporal evolution of the economic quantities, Walras turns to the mechanism of *tatonnement*, an element which distinguished him from Pareto. According to Walras every dynamic procedure passes through various phases. In his words:

It is possible to clearly distinguish the following three phases, especially if considered as consequent. The phase of the preliminary attempts to establish equilibrium in theory. The static phase of the actual determination *ab ovo* of equilibrium concerning the delivery of the productive services during the period of time taken into consideration, the conditions agreed upon, without any changes in the data of the problem. A dynamic phase of continuous

## 42  *Pareto's legacy in economic dynamics*

disturbing of the equilibrium with changes of the data and the re-establishment of the equilibrium disturbed.

(Walras 1974: 438)

According to Walras there is a very quick mechanism of adjustment in economics which, through purely ideal modifications, can lead to a position of equilibrium. He believes that perfect competition is the actual mechanism which guarantees the reaching of this position. In a first phase, all the quantities are constant and the variations that intervene are purely virtual, and therefore not observable. This first phase is followed by the concrete phase of the actual choice of individuals' action plans, and therefore the static phase is accomplished. It is at this point that there is room for dynamics. It is generated by the fact that in time the data change and therefore new equilibriums take place, which in their totality constitute what Walras calls mobile equilibrium, while in the 1930s Hicks will call it temporary equilibrium because it referred to each and every single temporal interval. Thus, for Walras, as for Pareto, the main problem of dynamics does not lie in the analysis of the adjustment processes towards equilibrium, but rather in finding the positions of equilibrium which, however, are not constant in time because the data of the system change. Walras observes:

> First of all we will establish equilibrium in line of principle theoretically, then mathematically, and then practically on the market. At that point, our society will be ready to function, and if desired, we can pass from a statics viewpoint to a dynamics viewpoint. To do so, it will be sufficient to assume the data of the problem, the quantities possessed, the curves of utility or of need, etc., variants in functions of time. Fixed equilibrium will transform into a variable or mobile equilibrium, which re-establishes itself on its own as it is being disturbed.

(Walras 1974: 322)

Of course Walras is well aware of the fact that the hypotheses on which he is basing his method of analysis are ideal hypotheses, which generally speaking do not correspond to the prevalent conditions in real economies. In a well-known passage, he affirms that in reality equilibrium is never reached, because the data change continuously and prior to the process of adjustment. However, this way of considering dynamics does not seem to entail significant distortions compared to the empirical reality where changes are quick enough to enable the system to reach its equilibrium.

This being said, the differences between Pareto's and Walras's approaches do not derive from basic theoretical divergences, but reflect a different degree of trust towards an analytical model which is the same for both, that of equilibrium. As regards first order dynamics, Pareto differently from Walras in the article of 1901 tries a first formalization, considering the economic quantities as velocities and no longer as single values. However, the result which was confirmed once again by Sensini's analysis (1955) was modest. Even Pareto's first order dynamics did not come from statics since it lacked of a real intertemporal analysis and the evolution of the economic system was traced back to a simple succession of instant equilibria. Pareto and his followers searched for the answer in continuous dynamics or that of second order. It was not only a matter of making the temporal distance of periods infinitesimal, that is to pass from discrete to continuous, but rather to find the fundamental dynamic principle which could explain the evolution of a phenomenon. However, also this attempt of Pareto's, as mentioned, was soon abandoned. Basically we can say that Pareto's attempt to go beyond Walras's approach in the path of rational mechanics was not successful. Despite the former's higher analytical ability, the attempt to dynamize economic equilibrium had to pursue a totally different path.

## First and second order dynamics in Pareto and Pantaleoni

Pareto's distinction between first and second order dynamics leads us to a confrontation with an analogous comparison carried out several years later by Pantaleoni. Right when Pareto was completely abandoning the certainties of pure economics, in 1909 Pantaleoni published an article entitled, *Di alcuni fenomeni di dinamica economica*, which remains his main contribution in this field (Bellanca and Giocoli 1998). The long text is divided into two clearly distinct parts: the first, theoretical, aims at offering a general scheme so as to define his overall view of economic dynamics; whereas the second, in line with the ideas of the Italian economists, shows the utility at an interpretative level considering several practical cases.

Pantaleoni starts out accepting the traditional definition of the concepts of equilibrium, statics and dynamics. From these definitions he intends to show how Walras's and Pareto's approaches do not exhaust the range of dynamic phenomena to be taken into consideration. According to his opinion, economic science is first of all the science of laws of economic equilibrium, brought to perfection in statics by Pareto. Instead, an analogous layout lacked for dynamics, and this was even more serious since according to a definition which will be very fortunate, he believed that static economics was a particular case of dynamic economics. Lacking this part of economics theory, the whole structure of economic science resulted seriously inadequate.

Compared to Pareto and Walras, Pantaleoni takes into consideration a much broader set of phenomena to be investigated in dynamics which studies in general the variations of the economic system when disturbing forces intervene. Since he intends to provide a general classification of phenomena in dynamics, that is a classification valid even outside the condition of equilibrium, he considers three forms of dynamics: a) dynamics which brings the economic system back to its previous state of equilibrium, b) dynamics which leads the system towards a new equilibrium, c) dynamics which does not lead the system back to any equilibrium whatsoever. In his words:

## 44  *Pareto's legacy in economic dynamics*

> The aim of this note is to call the economists' attention on three different forms of phenomena in dynamics. Two of these forms are very similar, that is they can be treated as such: in fact, after the occurrence of these forms of dynamism, the economic system goes back to its previous position of equilibrium or rests on a new position of equilibrium. When they meet, if the economic system is subject to the third form of dynamism, it does not go back to a position of equilibrium, but continues to be disturbed. And this can happen for a period of time which surpasses that within which a reasoning has sense, as well as it be undefined, or that an economic social system is substituted by a non-economic social system.
>
> (Pantaleoni 1909: 75)

First and second order dynamics are very similar because their systems return to a position of equilibrium, the one they had in the beginning, or enter into a new final position. Pantaleoni calls these two forms first order dynamics. It is easy to recognize in first order dynamics the method of comparative statics. At every variation of parameters, on the basis of the economic postulates – for example, those of hedonistic behaviour and free competition – the system reaches a new position which will be maintained until new facts arise. The third form is absolutely peculiar and is called second order dynamics. In this third case the system does not go back to "a position of visible equilibrium, or foreseeable equilibrium as effect of the phenomena in dynamics" (Pantaleoni 1909: 78). Pantaleoni observes that economists mainly and limitedly studied the first order dynamics, that of comparative statics. The few who ventured in second order dynamics sought refuge in analogies with biology. Pantaleoni mainly studies second order dynamics which, from his viewpoint, is a step forward compared to Walras and Pareto, and he does so in a descriptive manner highlighting several cases in which this radical dynamic manifests itself.

Pantaleoni identifies four causes of second order dynamics. The first is determined by the fact that often the economic agent strays away from the paradigm of rationality. It is the case in which the action of the *homo oeconomicus* is restricted or conditioned by ethical motivations which make the final outcome of the action not totally foreseeable. The second cause is linked to the demographic factor, always considered with great interest by Italian economists. With the third cause he goes back to a purely economic explanation of second order dynamics since Pantaleoni takes into consideration the analysis of the variations of the relationship between general expenditure and specific expenditure, that is the variation of the average cost. In this category, Pantaleoni includes different economic phenomena such as the dimensional growth of enterprises, the expansion of the public expenditure, the passing from a market economy to a planned economy. This aspect will be studied by Masci in the 1930s as he will develop Pantaleoni's observations leading them to the distinction between fixed capital and variable capital. The fourth factor is a specification of the third since Pantaleoni considers the case of the decreasing curves of cost. In this case, every position of equilibrium

*Pareto's legacy in economic dynamics*  45

is purely temporary and unstable since it depends on the structure of the demand. The increase in demand generates a reduction of the single cost which in turn leads to a further expansion of the first, generating a characteristic process of cumulative causation. These two last factors are for Pantaleoni the base on which second order dynamics is founded. It concerns those transformations which irreversibly change the physiognomy of the economic system and leave a door open to following changes. Following a biological analogy, the system interacts continuously with the environment, and the structural changes trigger relationships which impede the system to return to the primary equilibrium position.

This brief description of Pantaleoni's view enables us to make a comparison with Pareto. Actually it is Pantaleoni himself who helps us in this sense when he states, as regards the decreasing curves of average cost, that "they are extremely interesting curves under many aspects, especially for the phenomena of first order dynamics, which as we can see, are also the only ones that Pareto discusses in his *Manuale*" (Pantaleoni 1909: 124). Therefore, Pantaleoni had his friend's lesson well in mind, but he confined them in his first order dynamics. Pareto's dynamics in its two forms – that of the series of successive equilibria and continuous dynamics – certainly belonged to the first order dynamics because in both cases the hypothesis was that motion intervened maintaining the fundamental conditions of the economic system unchanged. First order dynamics develops within an unvaried economic structure, in other words structurally stable. Pareto did not ignore the second order dynamics in Pantaleoni's sense, but this perspective meant exiting the economic ambit to enter into the sociologic consideration. For Pareto the extra-economic factors could be essential, but they could not be included in the economic sphere, thus showing a greater methodological awareness. Pareto's analytical observations and those of his followers had difficulty in adhering to a view of dynamics which could not be formalized in an analytical scheme.

However, there is also another difference: Pantaleoni's dynamics, even in its most traditional form, is still a dynamics of disequilibrium. This is an element which clearly distinguishes him from Pareto. Economic dynamics remains the study of motions in a position of disequilibrium which then reach positions of equilibrium. While for Pareto dynamics is the study of different equilibrium positions in time, for Pantaleoni dynamics also concerns, and perhaps mainly, how to pass from a position of equilibrium to another. Pantaleoni observes:

> Let's suppose that an economic equilibrium whatsoever has been reached: this equilibrium will be a static position. When the motions meet, this will constitute dynamic phenomena. These motions may be those which take place so that equilibrium may be reached, or those which take place when equilibrium is bothered so that it may be re-established, or also so that a new position of equilibrium may be reached.
>
> Therefore, economic statics is the study of the positions of equilibrium, whereas economic dynamics is the study of motions manifesting positions of lack of equilibrium which lead back to positions of equilibrium
>
> (Pantaleoni 1909: 80)

46   *Pareto's legacy in economic dynamics*

This step marks a further distance between the two economists. For Pantaleoni first order dynamics is essentially a dynamic of disequilibrium since he is more interested in the actual carrying out of the process which recovers its position of rest. In Pareto and his followers this dynamic of disequilibrium is completely absent and the variables adjust instantly to the changes of the parameters of the surrounding conditions. Today we could put it in the following words: Pareto's analysis is interested in long-term periods, in the determinations of the laws of motions of the economic variables which do not change in time, whereas Pantaleoni is interested in the short-term periods, and thus in the dynamics of adjustment towards secular tendencies.

Therefore, even if Pantaleoni used Pareto's distinction, he then offered a different content. Although he accepted Pareto's and Walras's schemes, Pantaleoni tried to broaden them so as to reach a more open view of economic dynamics, closer to a historic dimension in which change is marked by the irruption of new facts which determine new paths that were not foreseeable in advance. In Pantaleoni's dynamics, time plays an essential role as a powerful factor of structural change. Pareto's time instead is the logical time of rational mechanics, that is when the system moves according to its internal laws once the forces involved are depicted. It is not a coincidence that Schumpeter praised Pantaleoni as the neoclassic author who had come closer to his view of creative destruction. Paretian authors remained rather indifferent to Pantaleoni's formulation which instead was criticized by la Volpe. He will find followers in Italy only in Demaria who in the 1930s proposed a strongly vitalist view of dynamics, in which the weight reserved to new facts led to a complete abandonment of the residual analogies with mechanics. Also for Demaria, as for Pantaleoni, the paradigm of dynamics lay in the idea of change and not in that of equilibrium.

## Pareto's legacy

As seen in the previous paragraphs, Pareto's dynamic analysis remained at a first draft level and did not find further adequate development, also because Pareto himself abandoned the schemes of pure economics to dedicate himself to sociology. In his *Manuale* we find an open acknowledgement of the fact that dynamic analysis is a chapter of the economic theory which still has to be started, if it is true that "the study of pure economics is divided into three parts: a part dedicated to statics; a part dedicated to dynamics which considers the successive equilibriums; a part dedicated to dynamics which studies the movement of the economic phenomenon" (Pareto 1906: 95). Pareto then continues observing that "The theory of statics has made great progress; there are very few or scarce mentions to the theory of successive equilibriums; with the exception of a special theory, that of economic crisis, nothing is known about the dynamic theory" (Pareto 1906: 96). Consistently with this drastic initial judgement, the only reference to dynamics can be found in paragraphs from 73 to 88 of Chapter 9 *Il fenomeno economico concreto* dedicated to the analysis of economic crisis. Moreover, in discussing this topic, Pareto renounced to the formal elements which he had presented in *Corso* ten years before. In this timeframe, not only no progress had been made, but Pareto's observations show clear signs of withdrawal: contrarily to statics, dynamics did not reserve immediate success but remained a problematic field of investigation.

Pareto's draft in dynamics was a step forward compared to Walras. Dynamic analysis is essentially an intertemporal analysis of how the economic variables are linked throughout the various periods. Pareto's answer to this problem was the introduction to the idea of dynamic equilibrium, that is of the need to find a behavioural rule or law which would show the trend of the economic variables in time. The model to which Pareto initially referred was that of rational mechanics which however after an initial enthusiasm seemed to be unsatisfying. Also the consideration of Walras's schemes in intertemporal terms, with the introduction of the saving equation, remained at a purely preliminary stage. Therefore, basically we can say that Pareto's project to create a formal dynamics remained at an initial stage and is one of the main issues which Pareto's school left unresolved. However, Pareto indicated a very precise path in a scientific climate at the beginning of the twentieth century, in which the interest for dynamic economics was characterized by a great variety of theoretical and methodological approaches which referred to cultural influences such as organicism, evolutionism and historicism. As seen in Pareto the biological metaphor and the concept of historic time as an irreversible quantity which characterizes economic phenomena in their becoming played an essential role.

It was a difficult task for Pareto's students to elaborate on the schemes of continuous dynamics once the first order dynamics had been excluded because it kept the analysis within statics, even if comparative statics, and once Pantaleoni's great dynamics had also been excluded as it could be better studied by sociology. Until the end of the 1920s the situation did not seem promising. As observed by Amoroso in 1929, economic dynamics seemed to be a totally exhausted research field from a mathematical viewpoint. At international level, as we will see in the following chapter, the only economist who tried to dynamize Walras's equations from the very outset was his student Moore who, however, pursued a statistic path not very congenial to the Italian economists. Since Pareto and his followers considered themselves first mathematical economists, the construction of second order dynamics, outside the inadequate schemes of rational mechanics, needed to find different analytical grounds which were prepared by two American economists, G. Evans and C Roos. In fact, they showed the utility to apply a new mathematical tool, the functional calculus, to economic theory. Only this new mathematical tool will be able to show the fruitfulness of the approach of dynamic equilibrium. Pareto's economists were the first to use it at length even if their contributions, firstly due to the linguistic barrier and then for the emerging of a new view of dynamics linked to R. Frisch, did not obtain the importance they deserved. The anticipating role of the Pareto economists of the 1930s will be clear only in the 1960s with the definitive introduction of the functional calculus in dynamics and in the more simplified form of optimal control.

# 3 Dynamic equilibrium in the international context

## Introduction

As it has been pointed out by historical critics (Ingrao and Israel 1990), the 1920s were a period of stagnation for the theory of general economic equilibrium. Focusing on the complex interactions of interdependence between markets did not seem a promising way to advance economic theory. Beyond a small circle of mathematical economists, this approach faced much opposition. In France, Walras did not have many followers, and in England, the theory of general economic equilibrium came rather late and did not stimulate many contributions before the writings of Hicks in the second half of the 1930s. The only remarkable exception was represented by Italy, the only country in which Pareto's thinking had strongly taken root.

The initial roadblock for the theory of general economic equilibrium was due to two different reasons. The first reason was internal and regarded the logic of the model itself. Even Pareto, despite his solid mathematical background, in order to simplify the theory of general economic equilibrium did not go beyond the simple tests of equality between the number of equations and the number of unknowns. Given these analytical premises, from a mathematical point of view, the theory of general economic equilibrium seemed rather rudimentary and could hardly be deemed satisfactory. It offered a fascinating vision of the operation of market economies as a coherent set of relations but its analytical advances had been modest and they had not grown in step with economic intuition. Some more mathematically interesting aspects, like the study of the conditions of existence and uniqueness of the equilibrium achieved, were ignored and those who had brought them up, like the young Italian mathematician Scorza, attracted the anger and ridicule of Pareto. As it is known, for further discussion of more formal aspects of the theory of general economic equilibrium, the economic theory would have to wait until the 1930s and the results of the meetings of the Vienna Circle (Ingrao and Israel 1990).

In the 1920s few economists, even those more mathematically inclined, were drawn to the study of these internal issues with the model. Even Paretian economists, on the frontier in this field of research, looked with much skepticism, upon the purely formal developments of the theory of general economic equilibrium.

And, except for an important piece, that could have opened considerable research possibilities, by Amoroso in 1928, "Discussion of the system of equations that define the consumer's equilibrium," published in the *Annali di Economia*, they did not contribute to this field which was considered beyond the interests of economics as a scientific and, above all, empirical discipline. The Paretian economists were well aware of the debate on these mathematical issues but they did not find it important. Also in 1936 [1963], in a long article dedicated to the developments of this theory de Pietri Tonelli, the most authoritative Paretian, along with Amoroso, critically observed that:

> The studies done by those mathematicians (as opposed to economists) departs from Walrasian analysis, and by focusing on the existence and uniqueness of economic equilibrium, oversimplify them and the hypotheses on which they are based.
>
> (de Pietri Tonelli 1936: 156)

Although Paretian economists were always described as true mathematical economists, they maintained a correct distance from the easy and immediate application of mathematics to economics.

The second reason that can explain the lack of interest in the theory of general economic equilibrium in the first post-war period was its essentially static character. And also, the first drafts of a dynamics theory that we have seen in Walras and Pareto, in the face of the long waves of the post-war economic crisis, were completely unsatisfactory. There was a desire for something more from economic theory than simply a reassuring scientific representation of the world; there was a desire for answers to the serious economic issues of the time – the great unemployment which was followed by the *Great Depression*. To transform the theory of general economic equilibrium from a simple mathematical tool to a productive economic theory it was necessary in other words to go from a static approach to a dynamic approach that was able to capture the evolution of economic facts. As Del Vecchio, the leading exponent of the Marshall tradition in Italy, observed, in 1925 in Italy all the theoretical economists were still concerned with the problem of the scientific construction of economic dynamics. On one hand there was the intense debate over the causes and the consequences of the economic cycle, and therefore a very limited aspect to economic dynamics, and on the other hand there was the need to ground dynamics on rigorous and solid bases like those of statics, rooting it in the work of Walras and Pareto. In the field of dynamics, the significant formal developments that we encounter will be marked by the ambition to increase the explanatory content of the theory, to bring the theory closer to economic facts, unlike the approach adopted in the 1930s in which the main goal was to achieve a rigorous mathematical foundation.

In the years that followed the First World War the economists who were interested in the developments of the theory of general economic equilibrium concentrated essentially on the issue of its transformation in the dynamic sense. Research on the international level went in two directions: one statistical and one more

## 50 *Dynamic equilibrium internationally*

mathematical. The protagonist of the statistical shift was undoubtedly H. L. Moore, an American student of Walras, who tried to dynamize general equilibrium equations through empirical means. His articles, especially his 1929 volume *Synthetic Economics*, resonated greatly on the international level. The economic theory of Moore was *synthetic*, a term already used by Pareto, in that it combined theoretical and empirical aspects, leading to a complete vision of the economic phenomenon. This approach evoked great interest in the Italian context as well (e.g. in Demaria, Masci, Del Vecchio, De Pietri Tonelli), where Moore's approach was carefully evaluated, albeit in a critical vein. In fact in the 1930s academic distinctions were not rigid and it was quite possible for a professor of economics also to teach other disciplines such as finance or statistics; therefore in addition to the theoretical interest there was also an educational interest.

A considerably more relevant development that had long-lasting results was the mathematical approach that first took hold in the United States in the 1920s and was then resumed in the following decade in Italy. In the United States it was developed a few years earlier thanks to the contributions of two American mathematicians, G. Evans (1924, 1930) and his student C. Roos (1925, 1927, 1934). In Italy dynamic equilibrium found fertile ground in the Paretian school of thought. Through the application of functional calculus in economics they clearly showed the way for the creation of economic dynamics, both in the case of a single market, and in that which most interests us of general economic equilibrium.

## Dynamic equilibrium as *mobile equilibrium*: H. L. Moore

A student first of Menger in Vienna and later on of Walras, Moore can be considered the only American economist to have made a significant contribution in the first phase of general equilibrium theory. From the very beginning he was attracted by empirical analysis and tried through a series of contributions to examine various aspects of marginalistic theory in a statistical light. For our purposes, the most important essay is *Synthetic Economics* of 1929, in which he aimed to dynamize Walras's general economic equilibrium equations through empirical means.

Moore's writings were well known and appreciated in Italy through timely reviews and numerous critiques (e.g. Demaria 1930). Many Italian economists expressed their opinion, even the most critical, on this approach to the dynamics of general economic equilibrium that evidently was considered with great attention. Among those who deeply studied Moore's theory, surely Guglielmo Masci is worth pointing out. Masci was an economist who, though not within the small circle of Paretians, was still a staunch supporter of the theory of general economic equilibrium. He discussed the works of Moore in some methodological essays (Masci 1934b) and most importantly wrote a thorough presentation in his volume of *Lezioni di statistica* from 1933, the second part of which is dedicated to the statistical analysis of economic dynamics, i.e. Moore's theory.

Moore's stated purpose was to build economic dynamics by introducing the element of time in the theory of general economic equilibrium of the static type introduced by Walras (Demaria 1930). In the natural sciences the analytical

*Dynamic equilibrium internationally* 51

instrument with which one switches from the static to the dynamic consists of the use of difference equations or differential equations relative to the variables considered. This is the direct method that shows how variable change happens over time. Moore, however, followed a different route. He sought to introduce time in economic variables implicitly, correcting each variable of the dynamic factors that affects its behaviour. Moore's dynamics turned out to be very similar to that of the successive equilibria derived by statistical means.

Moore was not very interested in the purely analytical part of the theory of partial equilibria, as he was in general equilibrium theory, but he focused his attention on the issue of determining the empirical forms of demand and supply functions, in relation to their development over time. To do this, Moore resorted to the technique of considering two values of individual economic variables: the historical, real value, found in a single period and a second value which was found by interpolation of its secular trend obtained by statistical interpolation. Each variable, such as the price or the amount of a particular good, was then redefined as the relationship between its value in the short and long term, the exact one and the one achieved by interpolation. In this way Moore believed he could free the individual variables from the accidental and extraneous factors that could influence the development in the short term. Because of how the time series was created, the most likely value of the variables turned out to the secular one. Therefore Moore was able to affirm that its demand curves were no longer static but rather moved around a trend that represented the dynamic equilibrium or, to use his expression, the *mobile equilibrium*, a term taken from Walras.

Technically Moore used a method of analysis called *trend ratios* where he replaced each variable, for example the price $p_i$, with the relationship $p_i / \bar{p}$, where $\bar{p}$ the long-term price was obtained by interpolation and therefore $\bar{p} = f(t)$ . Using this relationship the influence of the dynamic factors, which manifests itself in the long-term value, was largely eliminated. For example, following his line of reasoning the traditional demand function became the following:

$$D_i = a \frac{\bar{D}_i}{\bar{p}_i} p_i + b \qquad\qquad [1]$$

where $\bar{D}$, with $\bar{D} = f(t)$, represented the value of the trend of the demand amount and $\bar{p}$ that of the price. The equation [1] simply indicates the variation of the demand amount with respect to its normal value in time $t$; it captures the oscillations of the economic system around its long-term trend, so to speak. In Moore's model the economic system tends toward a point of equilibrium which is given by its secular value, and for this reason, the trend line represents, therefore, the trajectory along which the dynamic equilibrium of the entire system is achieved. This long-term trend is determined by external factors such as demographic growth, the evolution of tastes and needs, and technical progress. The equation [1] has been criticized by Italian authors, above all, due to two aspects. First, it depends on the choice of the temporal interval. Depending on the number of years taken into account, the value of the trend changes and therefore also that of the

## 52 *Dynamic equilibrium internationally*

dynamic demand curve that is derived from it. Second, it appeared arbitrary to refer to every single year for the demand curve obtained for the whole period.

What interests us is that Moore also extends [1] to the case of general economic equilibrium. He goes back to Walras's system and considers specific functional equations for the supply and demand curves, together with availability constraints. The new variables are always obtained by comparing annual variables to their historical trend. For example, the generic function of demand for good $b$ in Moore's model became the following:

$$\frac{D_b}{\overline{D}} = \left(\frac{p_b}{\overline{p}_b}\right)^\alpha \left(\frac{p_c}{\overline{p}_c}\right)^\beta \left(\frac{p_d}{\overline{p}_d}\right)^\gamma \dots \qquad [2]$$

where the variables with the hyphen represent the long-term historical values. A similar reasoning also applies to the supply curves. If we add to these two systems of equations the equilibrium conditions relative to costs and to the complete use of factors, as in the traditional Walras system, the system is defined by when the number of equations, $2m + 2n - 1$, is equal to that of the unknowns, the quantities and prices of goods consumed, the quantities and prices of the factors used.

According to Moore in this way a system of equilibrium was created, no longer abstract, but real inasmuch as it was based on empirical data; and no longer static but mobile and dynamic because it occurs along the line of the trend or secular movement. The arithmetic mean of the relationship between the actual values and the secular ones is equal to the unit. It therefore follows that the most probable value to assign to the real value is the trend value. So, according to Moore, every real value of economic variables tends toward a point of equilibrium that is given by the secular value and the trend line represents, therefore, the path along which the dynamic equilibrium of the system occurs.

Italian economists considered Moore's model a remarkable breakthrough in the theory of general economic equilibrium. For the first time there was a departure from the vagueness of implicit functional expressions to arrive at demand and supply functions that were well defined at the analytical level. Second, they were put to the test of experience, and this was much respected by Italian economists. Despite this progress, the statistical approach was criticized because it remained on a purely descriptive level and did not address the causes that could explain the long-term trend. This last point was considered an external variable, introduced simply for analytic convenience but without an appropriate explanation. In the words of Masci:

> The new dynamic economy is thus more than anything else, a statistical method, difficult to apply and based on a set of arbitrary assumptions: a method has the dual purpose of adapting the generic and abstract functional correlations of the general static equilibrium to the mobility and fluidity of economic life, and to introduce numerical data instead of the abstract symbols of static systems. Except that, outside the field of statistics, the central problem of dynamics would be for the economy to determine the factors which in general depends on the shape of the centennial movement.

The economy, in short, does not concern not so much because the line of dynamic equilibrium is what is in that place and at that time: .... Economics concerns itself with finding a universally valid explanation of dynamic movement: to build, in short, one or more theoretical schemes, that may are of a kind that the economic reality can develop. Then we will be able to say what are the factors, the fundamental and essential causes determining each type of dynamism, and will be able to claim that we have achieved a rationally valid formulation of the laws of the dynamics.

(Masci 1934: 221–222)

For the reasons indicated by Masci, and widely shared by other Italian economists, this empirical approach to dynamic equilibrium had little following in Italy, where those dealing with these issues, primarily the Paretians, were more attracted by mathematical formulations than by statistical generalizations. For Demaria, too, the system created by Moore could only constitute a valid point of departure in order to understand the forces of the economic movement, what it came to lack was the explanation of the centennial tendency of the variables that was viewed simply as an external trend. Now the purpose of dynamics, according to Italian economists, was not to describe phenomena but rather to offer a valid explanation of the forces in play. For Italian economists who worked on these issues, statistics was not the most suitable tool for constructing economic dynamics, because purely empirical conclusions could not have that necessarily logical character that belonged to the sphere of scientific reasoning.

## Evans and the birth of economic dynamics

Despite the important contribution of Weintraub (1998), much remains to be analysed in regard to Evans's role in the birth of economic dynamics. For my purposes here, a brief outline will suffice. First, Evans was a pure mathematician who dealt with economics in the first phase of his outstanding academic career. And his articles on economics were published in journals of mathematics, not of economics. After the 1930s he abandoned economic theory and returned to his studies in physics and mathematics.

His initial interest in this field, and especially in potential theory, led to a doctorate at the Rice Institute (Texas) awarded for a thesis on Volterra's integral equations in 1910. Because at that time completion of a doctoral programme required a period of study in Europe, Evans obtained a scholarship to continue his studies on applied mathematics in Rome under Volterra himself from 1910–1912.Subsequently he was offered a position at the Rice Institute, where he remained until 1932, in which year he was appointed to a chair at Berkeley, where he was given the task of reorganizing the Department of Mathematics.This first phase of Evans's research had two main features: one concerning content, the other concerning method. As for the former aspect, Evans built his reputation among American mathematicians as an expert in the field of functional calculus and for this reason, in 1918, was invited to present this topic to the association of American mathema-

## 54 *Dynamic equilibrium internationally*

ticians. In a formative period of this branch of mathematics, Evans realized its great potential. As for the second feature, Evans was interested above all in the possible applications of this new theory, not so much in its abstract or strictly theoretical aspects. This was an attitude entirely different from that of the search for axiomatization that would prevail in economics during the post-war period.

Evans' approach to economics came about in stages. His first article was published in 1922 – "A Simple Theory of Competition" – and it contained a still static analysis of the oligopoly theory. Its innovative aspect consisted in its rigorous, but not formalistic, approach. Evans in fact took for granted the existence of a well-defined quadratic cost function, $TC = Aq^2 + Bq + c$, and a well-defined market demand function, $Q = ap + b$. He addressed the problem of the determination of the equilibrium price and quantity with variance in the number of firms. His analytical approach was the same as that adopted in the physical sciences: it started from a certain functional structure and then determined the unknowns, without any interest in other general properties of the problem. Evans used the same non formalistic approach in his first contribution to dynamic economics contained in his 1924 article, "The Dynamics of Monopoly," which was also published in a mathematics journal, *The American Mathematical Monthly*. In a period of strong price turbulence like the 1920s, Evans was the first to consider a demand function which depended linearly on price variation ($\dot{p}$),

$$Q = ap + b\dot{p} + c \tag{3}$$

The term $b\dot{p}$ can be seen as introducing a speculative factor, according to which the quantity demanded increases when price is increasing. In light of equation [3], the monopolist's problem becomes that of maximizing the flow of profits on an interval of time $(t_1, t_0)$, by choosing a function of time $p(t)$. After the substitutions, the expression of profits depends at each instant on two magnitudes, the level of price and its variation,

$$\int_{t_0}^{t_1} \pi(p, \dot{p}, t) dt \tag{4}$$

Evans observes that the maximization of equation [4] does not depend explicitly on time and it is a problem that pertains to the field of calculus of variations. The solution leads to a second order homogeneous differential equation that, in this simple case, can be solved and brings us to the following general dynamic equation

$$p(t) = \bar{p} + C_1 e^{mt} + C_2 e^{-mt} \tag{5}$$

where the two constants $C_1, C_2$ are determined by means of the boundary prices, $p_0, p_1$.

Equation [5] can be considered the first explicit formulation of the *dynamic equilibrium* of one economic variable, in this case the price, and we shall see similar ones later. The equilibrium obtained in [5] is dynamic in two respects. It is so in descriptive terms because the price is a continuous function of time. The solution is not a single value but a path in the given interval. And it is dynamic also in a normative respect because equation [5] arises from an optimization process where $p(t)$ denotes the optimal trajectory. This equation prompts a further comment. In the discussion of the solution Evans point out the fact that the Cournot solution, the static one, can be considered a particular case when the equation of demand does not involve $(\dot{p})$. Hence dynamic equilibrium, in this peculiar context, can be considered as a generalization of the static equilibrium. Evans's 1924 article contains his crucial contribution to the birth of dynamic economics in the modern sense. Subsequent minor studies (1925, 1929) were collected in the 1930 book, *Mathematical Introduction to Economics*, but they did not bring any new results to the field of dynamic theory.

With his brief article of 1924 Evans opened the way for the mathematical theory of dynamic equilibrium. For the first time an economic problem in the field of dynamics was analysed with the appropriate mathematical tools, which were highly advanced not only for the economists of the time but also for the mathematicians. The calculus of variations furnished the instrument appropriate for the purpose of building economic dynamics. It was possible to go beyond the static state because the solution of equilibrium was itself a function of time. In the following years Evans' approach was resumed and extended beyond the monopolistic case in the direction to render general equilibrium truly dynamic by his student at the Rice Institute, C. Roos.

## Roos and the dynamics of general economic equilibrium

Also Roos was less an economist than a mathematician in the first phase of his research, and subsequently a statistician. He had a decidedly greater influence than Evans. Unlike the latter he did not choose a university career and his name is associated with being the first scientific director of the *Cowles Commission* and one of the founders of the *Econometric Society*. In 1937 he established the *Econometric Institute* in New York, of which he was director until his death in 1957. His writings on economic theory belong to the first part of his professional career.

Roos' first but important contributions constitute an extension of the line of inquiry pursued by Evans, his mentor at the Rice Institute.Also these articles appeared mainly in mathematics journals, which testifies to their dense analytical content. The first of them, "Mathematical Theory of Competition" (1925), appeared in the *American Journal of Mathematics*. In it Roos extended the analysis developed by Evans in the previous year to the case of several firms, using the same analytical scheme. Evans' dynamics of monopoly became Roos' dynamics of oligopoly. In the second part of the article Roos takes a step forward and generalizes Evans's differential demand equation. This was made possible by the fact that a linear differential equation of second order can be expressed in the form of Volterra's integral equation (Arfken and Weber 2001). By operating in this way Roos introduced the following new demand function:

## 56  *Dynamic equilibrium internationally*

$$Q(t) = ap(t) + b + \int_{-\infty}^{t} \varphi(t-\tau)p(\tau)d\tau \qquad [6]$$

The meaning of [6] is as follows: the quantity demanded $Q(t)$ depends on the current price $p(t)$ but also on all past prices, weighted according to a function that decreases in time $\varphi(t-\tau)$. Also in this more complicated case Roos is able to obtain the necessary conditions for the solution, and the price results in a very complicated function of time, involving a continuous time lag structure derived from the equation [6].

Roos extends the dynamic model to the general equilibrium in the article published two years later, "A Dynamical Theory of Economics" (1927). The purpose of this article evidenced by its title was ambitious, for Evans intended to construct a dynamic scheme for the general economic equilibrium, thus accomplishing a project in which both Walras and Pareto had failed. He wrote in the introduction: "Let us replace the static general equilibrium of Walras and Pareto by a dynamic one in an attempt to show the relationship existing between the problem of competition and the theory of economic equilibrium. In developing this new theory we shall show that the theory of Pareto is incomplete in several respects and endeavour to complete this theory" (1927: 647).

Construction of the general dynamic equilibrium required some further extensions. The first concerned the equation of demand. Roos assumed in the paper that the total demand was a function of the rate of change of price, but also depended upon the rate of production and the acceleration of production. The total demand function could be written as

$$Q = q_1 + q_2 + \dots q_n = Q(q_1, \dots q_n, \dot{q}_1, \dots \dot{q}_n, \dot{p}, p, t) \qquad [7]$$

Also the cost function will be a function of the rate of production, the price and the acceleration of production,

$$CT_n = CT_n(q_1, \dots q_n, \dot{q}_1, \dots, \dot{q}_n, p, \dot{p}, t) \qquad [8]$$

In this case the profit $\pi_k$ of each producer for the period considered will be given by the integral

$$\pi_k = \int_{t_0}^{t_1} (pq_n - CT_n)dt \qquad [9]$$

As can be seen, [9] is a generalization of Evans's [4]. Maximization of equation [9] is a very complicated mathematical problem, but Roos is able to demonstrate that it is possible the determination of the $n+1$ functions $q_n(t)$ and $p(t)$ in terms of time and the initial given conditions.

In the second part of his article Roos considers the dynamic equilibrium of the entire economy. The scheme is the Paretian and Walrasian one, in which there are now $m$ commodities and $n$ firms. The quantities consumed and supplied depend on all prices and on the rates of production. The novelty introduced by Roos is that at the usual group of static equations descriptive of a general equilibrium (Ingrao and Israel 1990), he adds $n$ equations of profit [9], one for each commodity. With this assumption the problem is reduced to a case in the calculus of variations and it is possible to determine the rate of production $q_n(t)$ and the path of prices $p_n(t)$. Using the concept of maximum profit Roos was able to pass from the dynamics of monopoly to the dynamics of general equilibrium, realizing the Paretian project advanced in the 1901 article. He writes: "The time variable has been introduced directly into the equation defining general equilibrium, and it is shown that a dynamic equilibrium exists. If we added the equation $t = t_0$ the equations defining dynamic equilibrium they become equations defining static equilibrium at the time $t = t_0$" (Roos 1927: 655). Obtaining an operational result from this purely mathematical construction would require defining the form of all the functions concerned. This is what Roos would do in his 1930 essay on the theory of the economic cycle.

In the 1930s Roos abandoned this mathematical view of the dynamic equilibrium and returned to analysis of partial equilibrium relative to the empirical estimation of the demand curves. His last important theoretical contribution was his 1934 book *Dynamic Economics: Theoretical and Statistical Studies on Demand, Production and Prices*. As apparent in the title, Roos' interest had by now entirely moved to statistical inquiry. In the second chapter we still find treatment of the demand curve in the form of a Volterra integral, but this serves only as the theoretical basis for analysis of statistical data in function of time lags.

Roos' writings of the second half of the 1920s constitute the most ambitious attempt to dynamize the Walrasian theory. However, the results were ambiguous and they induced Roos to switch largely to empirical analysis. The complex mathematical construct was not so useful without the exact definitions of the functional forms involved, as Pareto had pointed out two decades previously. In general economic equilibrium the use of functional calculus had not led to the greater realism that its introduction should have yielded. Moreover, still to be analysed was the problem of the microeconomic foundations of the demand and cost functions; a problem ignored even by Evans. All these issues were addressed during the 1930s by the Italian economists belonging to the Paretian School.

## Dynamic equilibrium in the Pareto tradition: general aspects

As we have observed, the contributions of Evans and Roos were published in mathematics journals and not economics journals. Given their elevated analytical content, they circulated more amongst mathematicians than amongst economists. In the 1920s the United States context was still largely dominated by institutionalism and its empirical analysis and there wasn't much room for mathematical economics. Even Evans's 1930 volume passed entirely unnoticed (Weintraub 1998)

The situation did not even change in the next decade when the first contributions of Samuelson on economic dynamics begin to appear, such as the article

## 58 *Dynamic equilibrium internationally*

"The Stability of Equilibrium: Comparative Statics and Dynamics," published in *Econometrica* in 1941. Instead of building on the well-known contributions of Evans and Roos, Samuelson would go a different route, as indicated by Frisch and his definition of economic dynamics. And even in the definitive work, *Foundations* of 1947, which ends with two chapters devoted to economic dynamics, there are very few references to the work of Evans and Roos, who were completely marginalized for a long period in the economic debate.

Samuelson dedicates a short paragraph to a critical argument of Moore's concept of dynamic equilibrium, asking if it can be considered an adequate generalization of the concept of the stationary state. The answer is negative. Even Samuelson first notes that this representation of equilibrium of a statistical type depends on the length of the time series considered and therefore does not have general validity. Second, the dynamic equilibrium from a mathematical point of view leads to the creation of an equilibrium that lacks the criterion of uniqueness because it comes to depend on several parameters that can be chosen arbitrarily. Samuelson concludes: "Therefore I refuse the method of approximation outlined here as defining an equilibrium of unique movement, although it may be appropriate to achieve specific solutions" (Samuelson 1947: 358). But Samuelson's critique is aimed mainly at the form of dynamic equilibrium that he calls historical equilibrium. In such a system time becomes essential in the sense that the value of a variable depends not only on the knowledge of initial conditions but also on the date that the initial conditions are assigned. Curiously he even comes to say that such a system may not even be considered dynamic. Samuelson observes:

> Based on this definition, the historical movement of a system might not be dynamic. If one year there is a large harvest due to favourable climactic conditions, and the next year's is low, and so on, the system will be static, though not stationary. The same is true for a system that shows an increase or a continuous tendency, if the centennial movement is taken as data, and if the system adapted instantaneously.
>
> (Samuelson 1947: 440)

On the basis of this severe critique by Samuelson, the idea of dynamic equilibrium will disappear from the scene for a few decades before reappearing in the 1960s in the form of growth theory. For a decade dynamic analysis will be confined to researching the conditions of stability of equilibrium, and will be set aside as a theory of change and of evolution of economic systems. It was not by chance that Samuelson only sporadically dedicated himself to the analysis of long-term economic phenomena.

The Evans/Roos theory of dynamic equilibrium had a greater resonance in Italy where mathematical economics had greatly developed, both in the Marshall tradition (Ricci and Fanno) and in the Pareto tradition. In the 1930s the dynamic equilibrium approach developed by two American mathematicians became the preferred field of research of followers of the Pareto school. All its major representatives, Amoroso, La Volpe, Palomba, Fossati, Vinci made significant

*Dynamic equilibrium internationally* 59

contributions in the field of dynamic research, following different research directions but with the same approach, as we will try to show.

The Italian approach to the creation of dynamic equilibrium possesses some different characteristics with respect to that of the two American mathematicians. We have seen how both Evans and Roos, when building their dynamic models, always began, rather pragmatically, with well-defined cost (and supply) and demand functions, considered as an initial point. The approach of Italian economists is very different on this point because they take as a starting point a more fundamental element of economic reasoning, that of the intertemporal utility function. Pareto's students prove less resistance than their teacher to using the utility function, considered simply a necessary analytical instrument. The fact that the Paretians openly considered a utility function of this type to study economic dynamics derived from the fact that they felt they were economists first and mathematicians second.

In Amoroso, La Volpe and Fossati, the decision to use the utility function in order to include the element of time occurred essentially by following the Austrian tradition, as indicated, for example, by Rosenstein-Rodan in his *The Role of Time in Economic Theory* of 1934. In this viewpoint, the economic agent aims to plan his/her action within a specific amount of time that might also coincide, as in the case of the consumer, with his entire existence. In analytical terms it was about introducing an intertemporal utility function in relation to the amount consumed in the different periods in which the period taken into consideration was divided. Adopting this model and thus viewing economic trends in light of such a temporal continuum, according to the Italian authors, the typical consumer would try to maximize the following expression:

$$U = \int_{t_0}^{t_1} U(c)dt \qquad [10]$$

and a similar function would characterize the behaviour of the firm. Equation [10] tells us that in an intertemporal context a rational agent will try to maximize the utility as a sum of the utility obtainable in individual sub-periods. To make this expression manageable analytically both La Volpe and Amoroso suggested that utility was separable over time, an assumption that we will see taken up again in all subsequent literature. Fossati, however, preferred to remain on a more traditional path without applying functional calculus, dividing the function of utility in sub-periods, each one characterized by a condition of optimality. Therefore the Italian economists have situated themselves on a much more general and intuitive path from an economic point of view, which was that of the consumer's (as well as the manufacturer's) intertemporal choice.

As it is known, the equation [10] was introduced by Ramsey in the article in 1928, "A Mathematical Theory of Saving," and attracted little attention from economists, despite the fact that it was examined in depth in Allen's 1938 book (Duarte 2009). Aside from the circle of Paretians, we do not see this analytical

## 60 *Dynamic equilibrium internationally*

structure again until Cass's theory of optimal growth (1965). This article was well known to the Italian economists, and often cited, but does not seem to have had a great influence. The main reason lies in the fact that it was a contribution to macroeconomics that was outside of the theory of general economic equilibrium. Second, even the mathematical formulation had been reworked by Ramsey due to the concerns about using the social utility function. From Italian economists we do not find any reference to the saturation point, or 'bliss', which does have an important role in Ramsey's model. The next problem will be to characterize the structure of intertemporal utility function, the new goal of dynamic theory. Amoroso will choose his preferred route of analogy with rational mechanics, faithfully referencing Pareto, introducing a factor of inertia in consumer behaviour. La Volpe will rely on a more modern vision of Austrian origin explicitly introducing the action of expectations and arriving at the definition of temporary equilibrium before Hicks did. Fossati would try to introduce, though in an elementary way, the dimension of risk and of uncertainty in the intertemporal context.

A second aspect, connected to the first, concerns the type of mathematics used in the solution of the problem of construction of economic dynamics. The Paretians fully apply the new techniques of functional calculus, adapting them to the economic context. They bring more suitable solutions to the economic argument than those created by Evans and Roos. A fundamental problem in this approach is the definition of initial and final value of variables involved. We have seen how the two American mathematicians proceeded in a rather simple way, imposing an initial and final condition on the prices. But this solution does not mean much from an economic point of view, inasmuch as the final choice must be the goal of the optimal choice. La Volpe will resolve this difficult analytical problem by introducing a new condition of transversality related to the final wealth. This will be the solution also adopted by the 1960s literature on optimal growth. Amoroso will follow the rules of rational mechanics and will use as an initial condition both the value of the variable and the function of its initial variation. From the Italian authors we do not see any further reference to Volterra's integral equation, which was Roos's main tool. The issue of intertemporal optimization was resolved in the most simple and natural way by directly applying the techniques of the calculus of variations. The Volterra equation was a rather complex and sophisticated mathematical tool, but not necessary when the analytical framework was changed.

A third element that characterizes the Italian tradition in this field is that it, from the beginning, situates itself in the area of general economic equilibrium. The frame of reference is always one of the interdependence of the economic actors who interact with each other through a variety of markets. Consequently, the discussion will also follow the same structure: first the demand equations will be obtained, then the supply equations, and ultimately the compatibility of this whole set of conditions. No more can be done in the field of dynamics, where to get more concrete results, more drastic hypotheses would need to be made, such as adding a representative agent, as will occur in subsequent literature.

## The synthesis of de Pietri Tonelli

It is de Pietri Tonelli, who in a long and detailed article prepared for the ten-year anniversary of Pareto's death, published in two segments in the *Rivista di Politica Economica* in 1935, took it upon himself to analyse the results obtained by the Pareto school. The chapter that interests us the most is the central one, Chapter 7, entitled "The Fruitfulness of Pareto Theories," dedicated to examining the subsequent developments of the Pareto theory and in particular the developments in the field of dynamics. Indeed, from his point of view it was precisely in the field of dynamics that Pareto's input yielded the greatest results. De Pietri Tonelli never dealt directly with economic dynamics as his field of research was the scientific foundation of economic policy. So it is even more interesting that he accurately analysed the state of dynamic theory in the mid-1930s in the Pareto environment.

First and foremost, as a Paretian, he does not fail to observe the essential link between the development of the mathematical tool and progress in economic science. Just as infinitesimal calculus had been the basis of the achievements of modern science, thus

> the period of development of the infinitesimal calculus and of the natural sciences which applied them, corresponds to and is followed by, for a certain period of time, the period of development of the political economy that culminates in Pareto. The period of sistematizing infinitesimal calculus is followed by Cournot and, considerably later, by Walras. The period of improvement of the infinitesimal analysis is followed by the work of Pareto
> (1961: 75)

However, like many other Paretians, de Pietri-Tonelli warns against excessive confidence in using the analytical tool as an end unto itself. Indeed, we must not confuse economic reasoning with mathematical formalism. These two elements are complementary rather than substitutes. He observes:

> It has been shown that to address the economy, a person can be a good mathematician without being a good economist, while perhaps the opposite is perhaps not true: a good mathematical economist has to be good mathematician and good economist, since it is obvious that the real requirements of the economic theories must not be sacrificed to the theoretical requirements of mathematics. There is no doubt since the economy involves mathematics, what interests an analyst and what interests an economist can be different. A mathematician might be interested in certain economic analyses, of no practical significance and of no importance for the economist, while the economist might be interested in certain mathematical analyses, of no interest to the pure analyst.
> (1961: 76)

To go from the static to the dynamic requires, according to de Pietri-Tonelli, a new development in the formal tool, represented in this case by the substitution of infinitesimal calculus with functional calculus, where the aim is not to find a

## 62 *Dynamic equilibrium internationally*

single optimal value, as in traditional calculus, but rather the entire optimal path of the variable which continually depends in this way on time.

De Pietri Tonelli does not fail to observe how this research on dynamic equilibrium had been started already in the second half of the 1920s by Evans and Roos who were the first to extensively use calculus of variations to dynamize the consumer demand function, making it depend also on expectations, formally represented by the first derivative of price with respect to time. This dynamics formulation had been presented in a complete way by Evans in his *Mathematical Introduction to Economics* in 1930. Roos (1934) expanded it even more since the demand function was made to depend not only on present prices and expectations on future ones, but also on past ones, using the integral-differential equations of Vito Volterra. De Pietri Tonelli further noted:

> With the inherited nature of economic models coming into play, differentiated equations and those of the partial derivatives were no longer sufficient to resolve problems, otherwise the data would determine the future. The functions that depend on other functions lead to integral equations and integral-differentials, into which integrals figure, which translate the sums of elementary functions, corresponding to the hereditary actions; these hereditary actions contain the characteristic parameters of the system, its functions and the time, during the period immediately previous to the one being taken into consideration, indefinitely or up to a given point in time. Moreover, more general types of equations have been introduced into functional derivatives, in order to express more generally the hereditary action, which depends on all the values of the time function, in the hereditary duration. Therefore, in general terms, the inheritance problems enter in the functional analysis them. And, while the algorithm that presides the mechanics and classical physics is constituted by differential equations, the algorithm of heretidary mechanics and physics is constituted by integral-differential equations and by functional calculations.
>
> (1961: 78)

This long quote shows how the analysis of dynamic equilibrium required an advancement in analytical tools, which, moreover, was within reach. In reality, then, between the two mathematical tools indicated by de Pietri Tonelli, integral-differential equations of Volterra and functional calculus, only the latter was actually developed, while the former was never explored. It is interesting to note that when de Pietri Tonelli wrote these lines, Paretian economists had not yet achieved the key results that came a few years later; so he pointed to a direction of research that actually seemed more promising. He would rather defend the new approach from eventual criticism than depart too much from Pareto's theory. He further observed:

> However it cannot be said that the new directions in economic theory oppose Paretan theory, inasmuch as Paretan economics is static, not taking into

consideration the time variable, and the new directions are dynamic, considering the economic variables in function of the time. The new directions and Pareto's vision constitute two different ways of viewing economic transformations.

(1961: 84)

De Pietri Tonelli's review also could not avoid an assessment of Moore's moving equilibrium theory. Even for an economist in the Paretian tradition, the statistical way was not the best for constructing genuine scientific theories, in that, in accordance with the opinion of the other Italian economists, purely statistical conclusions could not have that degree of evidence and logical necessity that belonged to a real scientific law.

## Towards dynamic analysis

Within the Pareto school, the challenge of the formal construction of dynamic equilibrium using functional calculus was taken on by two scholars: Amoroso, mathematician and direct collaborator of Pareto, and his young pupil, La Volpe, an economic historian by training but who could count on the help of valid members of the Neapolitan school of mathematics. In 1936 La Volpe published an essay for the university professorship, "Studies on the theory of general economic dynamic equilibrium," whose main contribution is in the theoretical field, and is probably the highest point reached in the Paretan school. Eraldo Fossati, preferred to follow a more traditional route instead, still in an intertemporal framework.

So we can say that in the mid-1930s the Italian school, and in particular the Pareto school was on the frontier of international research. The Italian economists were well established, they published in international journals and were called to found the *Econometric Society*. In this period the best results were obtained, which for a number of reasons remained confined to the national context. The scientific climate in Italy then changed towards the end of the decade. Many economists, both in the Marshall tradition and the Pareto tradition, abandoned theoretical analysis and went towards corporatism, in the belief that an analysis of economic institutions could give a greater realism to economic science. But this wholesale shift, with the exception of Amoroso, led only to confusing descriptive analyses that contributed to the isolation and marginalization of Paretian economists in the changed post-war cultural context. In the climate of revenge that followed the Second World War, the false ideological pretensions of corporatism were removed but also the considerable analytical results that had been achieved in the field of economic theory.

# 4 Dynamic equilibrium and economic mechanics in Luigi Amoroso

## Introduction

Luigi Amoroso can be considered one of the most important Italian economists of the first half of the twentieth century, certainly the one with the best preparation in Mathematics. He was more well-known in the mathematical field than among the economists, and his many works not only contributed in a decisive manner in developing economic science in Italy, but they also became known outside the national territory (Guerraggio 1990). Amoroso belonged to that nucleus of Italian economist-mathematicians who participated actively in the foundation of the *Econometric Society* at the beginning of the 1930s (Brandolini and Gobbi 1990). Given these preliminary aspects, it is even more surprising that after the Second World War a veil of oblivion fell over this author (as, however, over many other exponents of the Italian Pareto tradition). It is likewise surprising that his works, apart from several remarkable exceptions, have been considered of scarce relevance or even ignored, and included in a general dismissive judgment on the theoretical modesty of corporative economic observations. In Amoroso's case, this evaluation is totally reductive and misleading because his analytical contributions were top level and went way beyond the ideological veil of corporative economics contributing to defining several important elements within the Italian tradition of economics. Only recently historiographic critiques have brought attention back to Amoroso's observations due to the contribution he gave in the development of economic science in Italy between the two wars (Keppler 1994; Giva 1996).

Amoroso was born in Naples in 1886. He started his studies in Mathematics in Pisa in 1903 and attended the Scuola Normale Superiore in Pisa for two years. He completed his studies in Rome, where he graduated in Mathematics in 1907 with a thesis on the theory of complex variables. He started his university career in 1908 as Giulio Castelnuovo's assistant holding the chair of analytical geometry, but after following Pantaleoni's lessons in Rome his attention turned to economics, which directed him towards Pareto and the Paretian theory. In 1907 Amoroso started an epistolary relationship with Pareto with whom he remained in contact throughout the years, as witnessed by the many letters exchanged (Pareto 1973). Pareto immediately recognized his student's skills and encouraged him from the

## Dynamic equilibrium and Luigi Amoroso    65

very outset to dedicate his studies to mathematical economics, even if his interest was totally directed towards sociological studies. In 1910 Amoroso was appointed as professor of economics, and in 1914 of mathematical physics. In 1914 he become professor of financial mathematics at the Istituto Superiore del Commercio in Bari and then he moved to Naples to teach economics. In 1926 he was called to Rome where he was given the course of economics at the Department of Political Science. In 1956 he retired from teaching. Amoroso did not limit his activity to the academic environment, but like many other Italian economists he covered different institutional charges especially during the 1930s: he was governmental councillor of the Banco di Napoli, managing director of Assicurazioni d'Italia, and member of the board of directors of Istituto Nazionale per le Assicurazioni (Giva 1996). He died in Rome in 1965.

## From statics to dynamics: Amoroso's research programme

As mentioned (Giva 1996), Amoroso's scientific activity shows a strongly unitary character, focusing in its maturity phase around the development of dynamic analysis in all its possible aspects, from the formulation of an original theory of the economic cycle to the dynamization of the theory of general economic equilibrium. Actually, it is possible to distinguish two very distinct phases in Amoroso's research. The first period, from his activity at university as assistant to the 1920s, is strongly marked by the influence of his renowned teacher, Pareto. During these educational years, Amoroso published several articles, mainly of a few pages, which were published in *Giornale degli Economisti*. His aim was to defend, on one hand, and to divulgate on the other, Pareto's theories and particularly the theory of general economic equilibrium (Amoroso 1909, 1910, 1911). His efforts, carried out under Pareto's guidance, aiming at giving a complete mathematical setting to the economic theory found application in the volume *Lezioni di Economia Matematica* (1921). This text not only established him as one of the main exponents of the Pareto school, but for many years it also remained the point of reference for this discipline in Italy. His observations in the field of static economics, apart from a few minor articles, provided two important contributions. In the article *La discussione sul sistema di equazioni che definiscono l'equilibrio del consumatore* dated 1928, he anticipated in a certain measure the axiomatic turning point of the theory of general economic equilibrium. Shortly afterwards, with a second article, *La curva statica di offeta* (1930), he gave an original contribution to the study of equilibrium of an oligopolistic market, one of the main topics of the period running between the two World Wars.

The second phase, the one scientifically more mature and richer in results, went from the 1930s to the first years of the 1940s and saw Amoroso committed to constructing equations of general dynamic equilibrium. His role as main exponent in the modelling of dynamics in Italy was highly recognized in the fact that he was entrusted with the task of covering these topics in an essay entitled *Contributo alla teoria matematica della dinamica economica* (1932), published

## 66  *Dynamic equilibrium and Luigi Amoroso*

in *Quinto Volume* of *Nuova Collana di Economisti Italiani e Stranieri*, edited by G. Demaria, dedicated to economic dynamics. In the 1930s, Amoroso pursued two different research paths. At the beginning of the decade he proposed an interesting theory of real economic cycle, thus intervening in the intense theoretical debate which the *Great Depression* had generated (we will cover Amoroso's theory of the economic cycle in Chapter 7). In the second part of the decade, he went back to his ambitious project of his youth years to dynamize the equations of general economic equilibrium. This project found its first expression in an article dated 1938, *La teoria matematica del programma economico*, and a complete development in the volume *Meccanica economica* dated 1942, in which he collected all his lectures given during the academic year 1940–1941 at Regio Istituto di Alta Matematica of Rome, created in 1939.

From an epistemological viewpoint, Amoroso's line of thought shows great consistency and a precise basic viewpoint. Pareto had widely used analogies with rational mechanics to provide a solid theoretical foundation to the economic issue, at least up to the sociological turning point, however, this aspect is even more evident in Amoroso's writings. The references to rational mechanics, as a paradigmatic model to follow, are quite numerous and widespread throughout all his writings, from the initial ones on the Pareto theory to the ones written more in his mature years. In his youth years, Amoroso sees a full analogy between the methods of rational mechanics and those of economics. In his short essay *L'applicazione della Matematica all'Economia Politica* dated 1910, he states

> The application of infinitesimal procedures to social science has been carried out mainly, not to say exclusively, in *Mathematical Economics*. Pure economics – as Mr. Volterra said in an inaugural speech at our University several years ago – was modelled on mechanics, using its procedures and methods, and arriving at analogous results.....
>
> Just as flexible and inextensible threads, surface without friction etc. are considered in Mechanics ideal and schematic beings, which are the material points without extension, likewise the notion of homo economicus has been introduced in Economics. The concept of force in mechanics corresponds to the concept of ophelimity in Economics.
>
> (Amoroso 1910: 362)

This close analogy was resumed in the comparative schemes between rational mechanics and pure economics in the final paragraphs of *Lezioni di Economia Matematica* dated 1921. On the basis of this analogy the concepts of space, force and constraints in rational mechanics become concepts of wealth, utility and income in economics. From this discipline Amoroso also derived the possibility to pass to more refined analytical tools, more fit to capture the variations in time of the quantities taken into consideration, such as the calculus of the variations which he widely used. In a retrospective contribution prepared to celebrate the centenary of Pareto's birth, he observed:

*Dynamic equilibrium and Luigi Amoroso*  67

It is extremely difficult to pass from Statics to Dynamics. It implies the construction of a theoretical process analogous to what has been developed in Mechanics in the line that goes from Galileo to d'Alembert and which is based on the consideration of the *forces of inertia* of the system. In Economics there is something analogous to the inertia resistances present in Mechanics. It is necessary to evaluate these resistances and however represent them with adequate algorithms. Recently, this is what has been done continuously of Pareto's work.

(Amoroso 1948: 13–14)

The epistemological reference to rational mechanics, which is mentioned continuously in Amoroso's writings, on one hand provided him with innovative analytical tools; on the other hand, though, it confined his view to a nineteenth-century epistemological perspective which considered natural sciences as the privileged methodological model to follow. This research of connections between the physical world and the economic world will never cease in Amoroso, and will actually tend to increase. During the last part of his scientific activity, he abandoned all fanciful ambition to find in economics something resembling the force of inertia, and took into consideration the action of the elastic forces in order to study the monetary phenomena. However, he did not find many followers in this field.

### Lezioni di Economia Matematica and the article La discussione sul sistema di equazioni che definiscono l'equilibrio del consumatore

In 1921, Amoroso established his reputation as an economist publishing *Lezioni di Economia Matematica*. This text became, in actual fact, one of the few textbooks on mathematical economics – or pure economics as it was called back then – available also at international level, and was promptly reviewed positively by Edgeworth in 1922. Edgeworth started out in his review stating that "the high reputation earned by the Italian school of mathematical economics will be enhanced by this publication" (1922: 400). Nonetheless, there were also some criticisms since Edgeworth considered the extension of Cournot's model on the case of monopoly to that of duopoly not totally legitimate. The work was not translated into English due to the fact that many mathematical economists knew Italian, even if the official languages for economists at international level were French and German.

The correspondence with Pareto shows the genesis and the aims of this first important publication. Amoroso started his epistolary relationship with Pareto in 1907. In that period, Pareto's interest in political economics was diminishing, but he immediately understood his interlocutor's potentiality. The exchange of letters, which continued until Pareto's death, mainly concerned issues on mathematical economics, besides the teacher's interest in following his student's academic vicissitudes. Pareto entrusted this young mathematician with a strategic

## 68   *Dynamic equilibrium and Luigi Amoroso*

task: to promote mathematical economics also at educational level as an autonomous discipline, detached from economics. This field of studies was absolutely congenial to Amoroso who did not disappoint his teacher's expectations, even if it took him a while. Pareto immediately encouraged Amoroso to prepare a volume on mathematical economics. The starting point was the mathematical appendix of *Manuale*. Instead, Amoroso wrote several minor essays on the Pareto theories and did not seem to proceed in that direction. In a letter dated 1911, Pareto mentioned the matter again inviting him to resume the initial project and write a book on mathematical economics. A first version was finally ready in 1916 and was immediately sent to Pareto for his opinion which was very positive. The volume that Pareto received was entitled *Economica matematica* and it contained Amoroso's lectures held at the Istituto Superiore di Studi Economici e Commerciali in Bari. These lectures then became *Lezioni di Economia Matematica* which for several decades became the text of reference on mathematical economics, at least in Italy.

*Lezioni di Economia Matematica* was written with a double aim. The first was openly educational: to explain the Pareto theory concerning general economic equilibrium in a clear and accessible way even to non-mathematical readers. Second, Amoroso gave some original inputs mainly concerning the theory of non-competitive markets. Pareto had studied monopoly for a long time but had not covered in depth other forms of imperfect competition. This aspect makes Amoroso's text different compared to the text published the same year by de Pietri-Tonelli, *Lezioni di teoria economica razionale e sperimentale*, whose aim was mainly educational.

*Lezioni di Economia Matematica* is a very innovative text in many aspects and it depicts the matter in a new way, that which will become the normal way of discussing the issue after the Second World War. Apart from an introduction on money circulation, the text is divided into three parts. The first part concerns the theory of the consumer, the second part concerns the producer, and the final part is on general economic equilibrium. This division of the matter in itself marks a distinction from the more popular manuals of the time, such as *Principi di economia* by Graziani, which maintained the traditional division starting with production and finishing with the distribution of wealth. In the part concerning the consumer the main novelties concern the broad use of the function of logarithmic utility and especially the use of Lagrange's multipliers to define the consumer's equilibrium. Amoroso is one of the first economists who uses this methodology to analyse the problem of the consumer from a mathematical viewpoint.

Even more interesting is the part concerning the theory of production, in which there is a modern viewpoint of the theory of costs (Keppler 1994). After introducing the distinction between unitary cost and marginal cost, in paragraph 28 there is an in-depth discussion on the conditions of stability of the enterprise's equilibrium. Amoroso clearly distinguishes two kinds of equilibrium: a stable equilibrium and an unstable equilibrium. The first case corresponds to a situation in which production decreases and therefore the unitary costs increase, while the second case corresponds to a situation in which the production increases and unitary costs decrease. According to Amoroso, this is the most noticeable case in the economic reality of that time, characterized by many industrial and bank mergers. As regards the case of increasing returns, competition equilibrium results as impossible and all the enterprises are concentrated in the hands of a sole producer. This is an important anticipation of Sraffa's thesis several years later. A significant chapter is the one dedicated to the analysis of the behaviour of $n$ monopolists (today we would say of the oligopolistic market). Amoroso correctly finds that the oligopolistic equilibrium is in general unstable, since the total profit is a decreasing function of the quantity produced by each enterprise.

His Lessons in the volume of 1921 close with paragraph 66 dedicated to the acknowledgement of economic dynamics. After two decades from the publication of Pareto's *Manuale* the situation had not changed, and even Amoroso could state that "*Economic dynamics* and its laws are still unknown at the current stage of science" (Amoroso 1921: 463). However, while Pareto had turned to sociology, Amoroso believed that rational mechanics was still the field of studies to turn to. He observes:

> It is evident how the laws of economic dynamics are still unknown. Moreover, it is also evident in which direction it would be necessary to go in order to trace the first lines of said laws: the path set by the founders of Mechanics can serve as guideline.
>
> Classical Mechanics is based on two fundamental principles: the principle of inertia and the principle of D'Alembert. In order to determine the laws of motion of a material point, the first principle is sufficient. Whereas, the second principle is necessary to pass from the motion of a point to a motion of a system. We need to see if it is possible to introduce in Economics something analogous to the principle of inertia, from which we can work out the laws of economic motion of an isolated individual.
>
> (*Lezioni* 1921: 460)

The path towards the analogy between mechanics and economic dynamics was not realized immediately, and only during the second half of the 1930s Amoroso wrote the dynamic equations which he had been researching since his youth.

As regards statics, from his mathematical mind-set Amoroso could not avoid thinking about the fact that the mathematical model of the theory of general economic equilibrium resulted as quite elementary from an analytical viewpoint. In general, it was possible to determine the necessary conditions, such as the equality between the quantity of equations and the quantity of the unknown factors, but this result could not be considered satisfying. Said criteria could satisfy the economist, but not certainly the demanding mathematician. This kind of issue, internal to the construction of the mathematical models, was faced partially by Amoroso in 1928 in an article entitled *Discussione del sistema di equazioni che definiscono l'equilibrio del consumatore,* unfortunately published only in Italian but whose relevance was clear to Schumpeter who mentioned it specifically in his *History of Economic Analysis*. This article is

## 70    *Dynamic equilibrium and Luigi Amoroso*

especially relevant because it represents a first remarkable anticipation of the axiomatic approach to the theory of general economic equilibrium which will be developed during the second half of the 1930s. Amoroso's article starts out focusing on the problem:

> The traditional theory of the consumer's behaviour in the well-known formulations of Walras, Edgeworth and Pareto, and expressed in my *Lezioni di Economia Matematica*, is not complete. Actually, reducing the problem to the research of a maximum, it requires that the quantities found must satisfy certain conditions which are sufficient, but not *necessary and sufficient* for a maximum. It is necessary to carry out an analysis of the system, which shows that the solutions exist, as their quantity, etc.... The aim of this note is not to provide such analysis.
>
> (Amoroso 1928: 31)

The aim of the article is the following:

> Our aim is to demonstrate that – under certain conditions which we will specify in the following paragraph – the system of the consumer's equilibrium always provides for one single solution which actually corresponds to the condition of maximum as postulated by the hedonistic principle, and therefore represents the only solution of the problem concerning the consumer.
>
> (Amoroso 1928: 33)

Amoroso's demonstration proceeds in a rigorous manner according to the mathematical style, using different lemmas which enable the solution of the problem. These lemmas are necessary to demonstrate that if a solution to the problem of the maximum of the consumer exists, then it can be the only solution possible and internal to the set of given resources. Nothing is said concerning stability. The rigorously deductive procedure through which this result was obtained made Guccione and Minelli (1999) observe how this article can be considered as one of the first examples of the axiomatic method applied in economics. The conditions which guarantee what Amoroso calls the "fundamental theory" of the equilibrium of the single consumer are those which are usually found in the structure of the function of utility, the decreasing of the marginal rate of substitution. As a follower of Pareto's, Amoroso is not satisfied with the enunciation of this proposition, but he reasserts that it is in line with the experimental data, remaining faithful to his positivistic approach. Even if very significant, this was a partial theoretical result because it exclusively referred to the case of a single consumer.

In the years that immediately followed, Amoroso did not continue along this path of research, but changed direction dedicating himself to dynamics. The following year he published a first contribution which had a note of originality, *Le equazioni differenziali nella dinamica economica* (1929). In his lessons collected in *Meccanica Economica* dated 1942, he mentions the problem

*Dynamic equilibrium and Luigi Amoroso* 71

concerning the existence and uniqueness of the solutions. Explaining the theory of the consumer, Amoroso reasserts the validity of the result obtained 15 years before,

> It is hereby demonstrated that under certain conditions, which substantially are those indicated in lesson II as regards the curve of the index of ophelimity, the system formed by the equation $p_1 x_1 + p_2 x_2 + ... + p_n x_n = R$ and by the equation $\dfrac{1}{p_1} \dfrac{\partial \Phi}{\partial x_1} = \dfrac{1}{p_2} \dfrac{\partial \Phi}{\partial x_2} = ... = \dfrac{1}{p_n} \dfrac{\partial \Phi}{\partial x_n}$ generally allows one single solution: therefore it determines unequivocally the unknown $x_1, x_2, ..., x_n$.
> Without expatiating in giving a demonstration of this general theory, we want to show the validity in the specific case should the function of utility take on the form
>
> $$\Phi = A x_1^a x_2^b ... x_n^k,$$
>
> $A$ being a positive constant; and $a$, $b$, ..., $k$ being also positive constants, the sum of which is inferior to a unit.

(Amoroso 1942: 22–23)

If the problem of the existence and uniqueness of the choice of the single consumer is well supposed, doubts can arise in case of the presence of more consumers, therefore, in the general case of the equilibrium of pure trade. The problem in this case is to establish the solutions of a system with $mn + n$ variables, $n$ being the number of goods and $m$ that of consumers. In this case, certainly more complex, Amoroso, following his typical style, chooses a constructive reasoning: he does not stop to define axiomatically the conditions which guarantee the result searched for, but demonstrates that under realistic hypotheses a solution does exist and is unique. In his words:

> It is likely that the conditions postulated in due time for the functions indexes of the ophelimities are sufficient to ensure that the system, generally speaking, always admits one single solution. The issue is still unresolved. We do not intend to face it at this time and we will only demonstrate how the theory is true in the particular case that the functions indexes of ophelimities take on the simple form,
>
> $$\Phi = A x_1^a x_2^b ... x_n^k,$$
>
> $A$ and $a, b, ...., k$ being positive constants.

(Amoroso 1942: 38)

Then Amoroso proceeds with the actual calculus of the solutions. At this point Amoroso's approach is clear: he totally abandons the course started in 1928 as regards the axiomatic demonstration of the properties of the solutions of equilibrium, and he sets out on a totally different path, that is, to build particular

## 72  *Dynamic equilibrium and Luigi Amoroso*

examples which would somehow be derivable from the empiric experience. Amoroso, and others among Pareto's followers as well, never really showed great interest in purely mathematical issues that could derive from the economic reflection, which nonetheless had to be rigorous and formalized. This non-axiomatic approach to mathematical problems in economics was typical of Pareto's approach, more careful of the realism of hypotheses than to their formal rigour. In conclusion, Amoroso's position on the matter of the existence and uniqueness of equilibrium can be considered as the paradigmatic position within Pareto's school, keeping in consideration also the fact that some of those who worked assiduously in this field such as G. Sensini, never felt the need to intervene on this point (Sensini 1955), considering the matter totally unimportant.[1]

### From the theory of the economic cycle towards the dynamic theory of general economic equilibrium

The 1930s were years of intense research in which Amoroso was mainly busy constructing economic dynamics. However, it is important not to forget an article which made him known at international level, *La curva statica di offerta*. In this article, Amoroso anticipated the famous index of Lerner, a measure which links the market power of the single enterprise to the elasticity of demand.

At the beginning of the decade, Amoroso was dedicated to studying the mathematical theory of the economic cycle. The turning point was represented in the article dated 1929, *Le equazioni differenziali della dinamica economica*, in which Amoroso was favourably impressed by the concept of the differential equation of Roos' demand. It is also interesting to notice the moment in which Amoroso seems to declare the turning point of his research. The article begins in the following way:

> Several years ago, mathematical economics seemed at a dead end. After Walras's and Pareto's general arrangement, which collected all the ideas on the theory of equilibrium in a single synthesis, it seemed that the last word had been given, at least pro tempore, and that the new method had produced, for the moment, all the fruits of which it was capable. This did not mean that new mathematical problems were not at the horizon; but rather that their solution seemed to be beyond the strength of human intellect... The idea was a transformation from the static theory to a dynamic theory, but the way towards this solution was not visible. The interference of the strictly economic phenomena with the political and social ones, on the other hand, in the dynamic field, seemed so strict that a strictly economic analysis seemed void of meaning. Economic dynamics seemed to get lost in the wider sea of Sociology and Politics.
>
> (Amoroso 1929: 68)

*Dynamic equilibrium and Luigi Amoroso*  73

However, Amoroso continued by stating that, owing to Evans, this dead-end situation had been definitively overcome due to the fact that the dynamic problem had been traced back to the calculus of variations.

Amoroso's first works on economic dynamics concerned the theory of the economic cycle. Towards the end of the 1920s and the first years of the 1930s, Amoroso tried to elaborate a mathematical model of the economic cycle, exploiting the introduction of the differential equations of demand. These first contributions to dynamic analysis are summarized in the essay dated 1932, *Contributo alla teoria matematica della dinamica economica*. The essay covers a very wide range of topics, from the dynamization of the offer curve, to a non-monetary theory of the economic cycle, up to the actual study of demographic dynamics. Breaking away from the main opinion of the Italian economists who looked at the monetary disturbance, Amoroso proposed a real theory of the economic cycle to which also other followers of Pareto's turned. This aspect is covered in detail in Chapter 7.

Another stage in the construction of Amoroso's dynamic theory is represented by the article dated 1933 entitled, *La dinamica dell'impresa*. It is a short technical contribution that examines the problem of the maximum of a monopolist when there are adjustment costs. This article, a note of a few pages, no longer published in *Giornale degli Economisti* but in *Rivista Italiana di Statistica, Economia e Finanza*, is important because for the first time Amoroso uses the calculus of variations. As usual, he develops the theoretical part and then offers a calculus example. The basic model is that taken from Evans and consists of considering the single monopolistic enterprise's optimal choice process. The offer curve becomes dynamic making the production cost depend not only on the quantity of the factor purchased but also on its variation. Amoroso observes:

> We will be able to show the enterprise's dynamism, thinking that the total cost is the function not only of the quantity produced, but also of the rhythm with which the production varies in time. That is the function of $x$ and $\dot{x}$, where $x$ indicates the quantity produced and $\dot{x}$ the derived of $x$ compared to $t$.
> Being $\theta$ the total cost, then the marginal cost will be
>
> $$d\theta = mdx + nd\dot{x}$$
>
> $m, n$ being partial derivatives of $\theta$ compared to $x$ and $\dot{x}$. We can call $m$ the static coefficient and $n$ the dynamic coefficient of the marginal cost. The first measures the difficulties which have to be overcome in order to reach a specific dimension of the enterprise; the second expresses the fact that said difficulties worsen when the velocity with which the motion proceeds varies.
>
> (Amoroso 1933: 444)

With plant adjustment costs introduced in linear form, the problem required for the entrepreneur to maximize not only present profits but also discounted future

## 74   *Dynamic equilibrium and Luigi Amoroso*

profits. This, according to Amoroso, entailed that the function to be maximized was the following:

$$J = \int_0^\infty (xp - \theta)e^{-it}dt \qquad\qquad [1]$$

Amoroso was now able to apply the method of the calculus of variations to produce an expression comprising a new term which represented the system's force of inertia, which vanished, as it must, in stationary state. This expression assumed the general form of a differential non-linear equation of second order in the unknown function $x$, which Amoroso solved by hypothesizing that the elasticity of demand was constant. Overall, therefore, given the position, and at the initial velocity, it was possible to determine the quantities produced at a certain moment of time as functions not only of price in that instant but also of the entire succession of prices from that initial instant to the one considered. Amoroso thus concluded that it was a *principle of heredity* whereby the present is conditioned by the past. The 1933 essay constituted the crucial advance towards dynamic equilibrium. Amoroso was able to demonstrate the fundamental analytical instrument of functional calculus by offering a reasonable economic interpretation of it: the dynamic of production depends, through resistances and frictions, on the entire preceding process.

It is during the second half of the decade that Amoroso returns to his initial project of his youth: the dynamizing of the equations of general economic equilibrium. Using his terminology, Amoroso had by now completed the corporative turning point and it was a matter of building a theory of mathematical dynamics in line with the new role given to the state in the economic life. The first important contribution is an article dated 1939 entitled *La teoria matematica del programma economico*, followed shortly after by an article published in *Econometrica* in 1940, *The Transformation of Value in the Productive Process*. Its dynamic conception will find full expression in the text dated 1942, *Meccanica Economica*, which collects the rich lessons held at Alto Istituto di Matematica in Rome, which we shall now take into consideration.

## The theory of general dynamic equilibrium of consumption

The volume *Meccanica Economica* constitutes the final result of Amoroso's observations carried out for about 30 years. In this work he makes a fundamental step towards the generalization of Pareto's equilibrium, which was static or stationary. In the introduction, Amoroso clarifies that "these lessons reconnect directly to Pareto's theory of general economic equilibrium and precisely to the mechanic representation which he presented in *Manuale* published in 1906" (Amoroso 1942: vi). Even after many decades, it was a matter of going beyond Pareto's draft by integrating statics with dynamics. For this reason, the lessons are divided into two parts: the first draws on the static theory of general economic equilibrium entirely formulated already in 1921, whereas the lessons from the

*Dynamic equilibrium and Luigi Amoroso* 75

twelfth chapter on are totally new and dedicated to general dynamic equilibrium. In the context of the evolution of the economic theory, even Pareto's, this passing from statics to dynamics is crucially important:

> If there is something that characterises the economic life, especially in the modern form of industrial civilization, this is the continuous development of plants and capitals, which together form the tool by which man dominates nature. However, the new capitals are created with saving: whence the place which rightly is given in the economic theory to the saving process.
>
> The representation of this process results to be mutilated in the theory of equilibrium. In fact, if the movement is supposed as stationary, this means that it is supposed that the existent positions are maintained indefinitely and therefore the mass of saving remains unvaried, not only in its complex and the individual shares, but also in the single uses pro tempore; it also means that new capitals are not created, if not within the necessary limits to reintegrate exactly what has been destroyed or which however deteriorates. A different representation would be in contrast with the prerequisites.
>
> This mutilation is serious, such to reach the conclusion that in this sector the theory of equilibrium is by nature incapable of representing the main part of the actual phenomenon.
>
> (Amoroso 1942: 119)

Therefore it is necessary to integrate Pareto's system with a theory of saving and accumulation, coming from the stationary representation in which the quantities always take on the same value in favour of a more realistic description of the economic life. As already observed by de Pietri Tonelli, it was a great mistake to consider Pareto's system static simply on the basis of the fact that the quantities did not refer to a certain temporal interval. Instead, he observed that Pareto's equilibrium could be considered as a stationary equilibrium, a condition in which the quantities do not change with the varying of time (de Pietri Tonelli 1961: 84). Amoroso intends to go beyond this merely defensive position to demonstrate that it is possible to build a real dynamic equilibrium in which the economic quantities depend explicitly on time.

The broadening of the temporal horizon of the investigation, passing from a single period to more periods, requires the introduction of new analytical tools which enable us to represent adequately the inter-temporal relations which are thus determined. The economic choice is carried out at the beginning of the period, but it has to keep into account what happens in all the following intervals in which the action plan of the economic agent is divided. From this viewpoint, the crucial innovation consists in the substitution of the infinitesimal calculus with the functional calculus, as La Volpe had already done. In a genuinely inter-temporal context it is no longer sufficient to have the usual techniques of static optimization, as Evans and Roos had already demonstrated, but it is necessary to use a more refined mathematical tool which can enable to determine the entire

## 76  Dynamic equilibrium and Luigi Amoroso

optimal path within a given temporal interval, as required by second order dynamics. The optimal solution of the economic agent, be it the consumer or the producer, will no longer be a point in the space of choices, but rather a function which describes the optimal trajectory. The calculus of the variations imposes itself as a privileged mathematical tool in the field of dynamic optimization. In this way, Amoroso was the forerunner, by about 20 years, all the literature on optimal growth which flourished in the 1960s, and he did so with a more mathematical awareness than his student La Volpe.

Amoroso dedicated *Lezioni XII* and *XIII* to the study of the theory of the consumer's behaviour and *Lezione XIV* to that of the producer's. The general theoretical scheme is the one typical in Pareto's followers: he tried to demonstrate that in the new analytical context, certainly richer and more complex, the number of quantities to determine, the unknown, would be equal to that of the functional relations, thus guaranteeing the internal consistency of the economic system. Neither Amoroso nor the other exponents of Pareto's school went beyond this to further investigate the problems linked to the conditions of existence, uniqueness and stability of the solutions found, elements which instead became a crucial test of the theory of general economic equilibrium of the years following the Second World War. This certainly critical aspect of Pareto's followers' approach, on one hand, refers to the typical characteristics of Pareto's second order dynamics which is a dynamic of instantaneous equilibrium, while on the other hand it results linked to a problematic concept which Pareto's followers had concerning the relationship between economic reflection and mathematical tool. This is an element which emerged, as we will see, in Eraldo Fossati, Pareto's only follower who analysed the mathematical developments of the theory of general economic equilibrium.

In Amoroso, the novelty within the theory of consumption is represented by the explicit introduction of a principle analogous to that of inertia in mechanics, according to the project manifested in 1921. In general, as observed by Amoroso, the quantity consumed of a specific good, $c_i$, in a certain temporal interval is itself a function of time and represents the velocity of the flow in consumptions. In turn, its derivative with regards to time, $\dot{c}_i$, can be interpreted as the acceleration, assessed algebraically in value and sign, of this flow of consumption. For Amoroso, if we want to give a realistic description of the consumer's behaviour it is necessary to keep in consideration the weight of habits and the psychological resistances which can accelerate or slacken the variation of the expenditure for consumption. In formal terms, the function of utility becomes as follows:

$$U = U(c_i, \dot{c}_i) \qquad\qquad [2]$$

Amoroso gives to [2] the name of Langrange's ophelimity in order to distinguish it from that of Pareto. For construction, it can be considered an extension of the latter since if the resistances against change are null, when $\dot{c}_i = 0$, the two functions of utility coincide and there is the return to the static case.

*Dynamic equilibrium and Luigi Amoroso* 77

The rational consumer will try to determine the maximum value of the trajectory of consumption represented by [2] in a fixed temporal interval. From a mathematical viewpoint, the problem is well determined since it means finding the optimal trajectory of the following functional:

$$\int_{t_0}^{t_1} U(c_i, \dot{c}_i) dt \qquad [3]$$

We are in the presence of a typical problem of calculus of the variations whose necessary conditions – but also sufficient – for the kind of equations that Amoroso has in mind,[2] are represented by Eulero's equation:

$$\frac{\partial U}{\partial c_i} - \frac{d}{dt}\left(\frac{\partial U}{\partial \dot{c}_i}\right) = 0 \qquad [4]$$

Amoroso calls this expression Langrange's marginal utility. The first term of [4] represents the marginal utility in a traditional sense, while the second, which captures the dynamic element, constitutes the loss of utility originated by the presence of habits (inertia of the system), and lastly, the costs associated to changes. Should the consumer have to divide the income among more goods on the basis of the income (*Lezione XIII*), this condition of equilibrium implies that the total utility becomes maximum when the value of Langranges' marginal utilities considered are the same, exactly as in the static case.

Basically, for Amoroso the dynamization of the theory of consumption takes place through the extension of the marginal principle introducing a relation which expresses the psychological resistances to change. There is full analogy with rational mechanics, expressed not only at an interpretative level but even more so on the analytical level since through [4] the consumer's dynamic behaviour is traced back to a second order differential equation, exactly as in the case of the motion equations of analytical mechanics. The summing of the single individual demands leads to the market demand for each single good. In Amoroso's words:

> Patrimony, saving, velocity and accelerations of consumptions for the entire community are the sum of all the corresponding quantities relevant to all the subjects present: thus they too are *functionals* of the prices and of the interest rate. The equations which express this dependence are the equations of demand and of offer – for the services provided – and are written as follows:
>
> $$X_i = F_i(p_1, p_2, \ldots, p_n, i)$$
>
> $X_r$ being the *collective* demand (or offer, if negative quantity).
>
> (Amoroso 1942: 143)

78 *Dynamic equilibrium and Luigi Amoroso*

Summarizing, by applying the calculus of the variations and assuming that the choices of consumption in time are not instantaneous but characterized by a psychological resistance, Amoroso believes to have given a fundamental contribution to the construction of second order dynamics. The optimal consumption of every single good varies on a continuous basis depending on the relations defined by [4]. Some problems can be posed from a mathematical viewpoint since the system is composed of a high number of differential equations whose solutions is not always possible if not in some special cases. However, from a theoretical viewpoint nothing hinders to obtain the usual functions of demand, as he himself demonstrates with the particular specifications concerning the form of the function of utility (Amoroso 1942: 143–145).

## General dynamic equilibrium of production and the energy viewpoint of the productive process

Throughout his research, Amoroso remained a nineteenth-century economist who tried to base the scientific claims of the economic investigation on analogies with natural sciences.[3] This epistemological project found its most complete expression in the interpretation, in energy terms, of the productive process contained in the text dated 1942. According to Amoroso, the similitude between mechanic and economic phenomena is complete: even in the sphere of production it is possible, keeping into account the interpretative differences which nonetheless exist, to find the principle of energy conservation at work, one of the basic principles of classical physics, in the form of the minimum means principle; with the only difference that while in nature it derives from the experimental evidence but we do not know the origin, in economics it is the intentional outcome of a rational behaviour. We can follow Amoroso's line of reflection introducing the part on dynamic equilibrium concerning the enterprise's behaviour and thus production.

The mathematical nature of the problem concerning the producer is totally analogous to that of the consumer, once the production is made dependent not only on the quantity of the factors used but also on their rate of variation (*Lezione XIV. La dinamica dell'impianto industriale*). In this case the total revenue ($T$) and the total production cost ($\Theta$) are represented by the following expressions

$$ T = pz(x, \dot{x})e^{-it} \qquad \Theta = qxe^{-it} \tag{5} $$

where $p$ represents the price of the product, $q$ that of the productive factor; $x$ in turn, indicates the flow of productive investments and $z$ the quantity of product supplied in a specific temporal interval. It is important to notice how the dynamic element of the model is constituted by the fact that the total revenues do not depend only on the intensity of the investment but also on its variation ($\dot{x}$), exactly as in the case of the dynamic choice of the consumer.

*Dynamic equilibrium and Luigi Amoroso*  79

The entrepreneur's aim is to maximize the accumulation of profits within the interval $t_0 \leq t \leq t_1$,

$$\int_{t_0}^{t_1} (T - \Theta) dt \qquad\qquad [6]$$

In this regard, Amoroso observes,

> With this hypothesis we can admit that the producer inspires his action to the principle of maximun return , which thus appears formally analogous to the principle of minimum action. With this fundamental difference: the principle of minimum action represents a law of nature, while the principle of maximum return, expression of the general economic principle of minimum means, represents a principle of conduct.
>
> (Amoroso 1942: 150)

The application of Eulero's equation leads to the following relation (called by Amoroso, Langrange's production equation),

$$\frac{\partial T}{\partial x} - \frac{d}{dt}\left(\frac{\partial T}{\partial \dot{x}}\right) = \frac{\partial \Theta}{\partial x} \qquad\qquad [7]$$

This equation constitutes a reformulation from a dynamic viewpoint of the condition of optimum static determined by the equality of the marginal revenue, which now depends also on the variation rate of the factor, with the marginal cost. Besides the stationary case, there is a new term, $\dfrac{d}{dt}\left(\dfrac{\partial T}{\partial \dot{x}}\right)$, to which Amoroso offers the following interpretation:

> [...] if the regime is not stationary, the maximum return is conditioned by the forming of a gap between value and marginal cost of production. This gap can be positive or negative: it is positive when the forcing of time would imply a cost not adequate to the return ; negative when the loss for a below-cost marginal production is inferior to what would result from a further disinvestment of the productive factors. In both cases it is the expression of *losses and latent profits*, represented by inertia resistances.
>
> (Amoroso 1942: 155)

Exactly as in the case of the dynamic treatment of consumption, Eulero's equation leads to the formulation of a system of second order differential equations also in that of the industrial plant, equations which in turn determine the unknown functions, the quantities of factors used $x_n$, considering $2n$ arbitrary constants which can be determined imposing the starting and final configurations, or assigning starting configurations and initial velocities. In the first case, which Amoroso considers the most interesting, it is possible to find a theory of economic

## 80 *Dynamic equilibrium and Luigi Amoroso*

programme, which he will indicate as one of the highest theoretical moments of corporative economy. In *Lezione XVI* the scheme of general economic equilibrium is completed with the determination of the system of prices through the criterion of the balancing of demand and offer on all markets, exactly as in the static case, with the only difference that in this case consumption and production are in general functionals, explicitly depending on *t*.

The productive process from an energy viewpoint derives from a particular interpretation of (7), developed in *Lezione XV, Meccanica ed Economia*. Amoroso observes that the term on the left can be considered as a sort of kinetic energy, even if this analogy is purely formal since the function is neither quadratic, nor homogeneous. Instead, the term on the right can be analysed in general terms as a fall of potential energy which derives from the use of resources $d\Theta = -dV$. When production is null, this energy is at its max and reduces as the productive process takes place. If the economy is in a stationary condition, the equation (7) can be written in the form of principle of conservation of energy, $dT + dV = 0$, which in general terms becomes

$$T + V = Cost. \tag{8}$$

For Amoroso this equation indicates that in the competitive case – a situation in which the price is equal to the marginal cost – it is necessary to consider the theory of energy conservation since the sum of the value of the total product and the costs borne is equal to a constant. The value of production represents kinetic energy, while the total cost can be interpreted as a form of potential energy. Likewise, in the field of economic processes it is possible to find the general principle of energy conservation which was very important in the mechanics of the nineteenth century. In Amoroso's words:

> If the prices are supposed to be invariable and if the effect of interests is neglected, the transformation in value which is affected in the productive cycle may be interpreted in the sense of the sum of the values expressed by the potential energy of the plant and of the kinetic energy. This means that all variations of cost up or down must find their exact equivalent in the increase or in decrease of the latent product (marginal cost).
>
> (Amoroso 1940: 9)

In Amoroso's strongly positivistic view, the principle of equality between marginal cost and marginal revenue is not only the expression of a rational behaviour, but it indicates that in the process of transformation from one form of energy to the other, the actual nature operates as a producer, which in a situation of stationary state is animated by the intent to give the maximum return (in terms of energy) to production. The principle of minimum action can, therefore, be interpreted as a principle of minimum cost in the sense that the transformations of energy which are produced in nature take place in such a way as to present, in terms of energy, a minimum cost.

*Dynamic equilibrium and Luigi Amoroso*   81

This energy interpretation of the economic theory of production will find eco in Samuelson and Solow's article dated 1956 in which the two authors proposed to demonstrate the correspondence between the principle of energy conservation and the optimal theory of capital. Further episodic references can be found in literature concerning the optimal growth towards the end of the 1960s (Shell 1969), but this topic on the analogy between economic and mechanic phenomena, typical of the first generation of marginalists, will no longer be covered.

## Amoroso corporative economist

The scientific profile that we have depicted of Amoroso would not be complete without considering his reflections on the corporate theory which he started developing during the second half of the 1930s. It has been observed how corporatism cannot be considered as an organic doctrine but rather as a wide cultural container, scarcely homogeneous (Faucci 1990). This consideration is valid also for what concerns the specific element of the economic theory of corporatism. Despite the imposing quantity of publications on corporatism during the second half of the 1920s (for a good overview see Bruguier Pacini 1936), at the beginning of the new decade its original scientific nucleus was not yet clear, besides the generic criticism to individualist hedonism of the traditional theory and the project of a re-foundation of economic sciences on new basis.

Amoroso was one of the economists who from the very outset took sides with the fascist regime for ideological reasons which had very little to do with the economic theory of corporatism. In fact, Amoroso was conservatory and openly critical towards any kind of democratic thought, and remained deeply bothered by the social disorders which followed the First World War. He considered the authoritarian regime the proper tool to regain social peace and the affirmation of conservatory values which he saw being put into discussion. This position of his was clearly expressed in an article dated 1930 entitled *La visione economica del fascismo* in which he justified his support of the corporative system on the basis of the practical failure of economic liberalism witnessed by the social disorders of the first half of the 1920s. The fascist regime became in his eyes the political tool essential to reconcile private interests with the collective ones, even if coercively. He observed:

> Fascism, in Italy, overturned a situation which seemed desperate in just a few years. It made trains move, workers work, it brought back peace in factories and fields, it restored order in all the sectors of economic activities.
>
> (Amoroso 1930: 264)

This convinced adhesion to fascism on an ideological level, but also on a moral and religious level, did not lead to any specific contribution in the field of economic reflections, though. Amoroso remained distant from the discussions

## 82 *Dynamic equilibrium and Luigi Amoroso*

on economic theory of corporatism and on the need to rebase economic science on a new basis at the end of the 1920s. He remained an economist with a marginalist approach who worked on completing Pareto's theory.

It is during the 1930s that Amoroso worked on the project to build an economic theory of corporatism which aimed at having the same characteristics of formal rigour of the theory of general economic equilibrium. These new analytical results are at the base of the statements made in his essay dated 1934 *La logica del sistema corporativo*, written with De Stefani. In this work he outlines his ambitious research programme which aimed at demonstrating how corporatism does not constitute a rift with the traditional theory but rather its synthesis and surpassing. The theoretical system of the classical economists, for Amoroso, had been overcome for the fact that it was not capable of interpreting the new economic phenomena, characterized by processes of concentration both in the productive and in the bank fields. Amoroso observes:

> The process of inversion is the consequence of two converging forces. On one hand, there are the needs of industrial techniques which prolong the productive cycle, enlarge the dimension of the enterprises through the production in series, require more capitals for plant and execution. They thus produce inequalities among competing enterprises, creating a hierarchy of costs, making it impossible to reproduce favourable circumstances, which theory postulates as a necessary condition, so that enterprises can be sent back into the condition of minimum cost. On the other hand, the single units, no longer cells but groups, expression of financial and industrial interests, animated by a will to dominate, are increasingly led to substitute the action of *homo oeconomicus* with that of *homo politicus*. In other words, they are led to direct action not towards the achievement of a maximum of utility, as regards the existing political and economic situation, but towards the aim to modify for its own advantage the juridical and political situation.
>
> The price – which in theory seemed sovereign dominating the life of enterprises and which is not dominated – now becomes a tool of manoeuvre on behalf of groups which control production. Whereas the commands are no longer automatically interlocked in the system of prices, but are manoeuvred by the political and financial forces involved. The process of inversion which finds its first reason to be in the needs of technique, accelerates its course under the pressure of political forces. Competition degenerates in industrial and financial plutocracy.
>
> (Amoroso and De Stefani 1934: 154–155)

For Amoroso, the crisis of liberalist economy was irreversible and it was necessary to find a new way to reconcile private interests with those of the community. This third path, between liberalism and socialism, was found in corporatism. For Amoroso there was no break with the previous economic thought but actually a development in the sense of a greater realism. In his words: "In this synthesis, the corporative system overcomes the previous three currents of thought: the

*Dynamic equilibrium and Luigi Amoroso* 83

naturalistic current of classical economics; the historical current; the political current represented by mercantilism, protectionism and socialism" (Amoroso and De Stefani 1934: 163). In this peculiar interpretation, the corporative state is not in contrast with the theory of general economic equilibrium, on the contrary it was supposed to integrate the individual initiative. Amoroso remained a neoclassic economist as regards the theory of pure economics, and became a corporative economist with reference to applied economics.

This attempt to offer a scientific foundation to corporatism is well expressed in an article dated 1939 *La teoria matematica del programma economico*, the first contribution in which Amoroso completely developed his view of economic evolution. The contrast between the individual levels and the collective aims is resolved by the concept of economic planning through the application of the calculus of variations. The marginalistic view of the optimizing behaviour of the single individual is not abandoned but is subordinated to the economic plan, to the general aims which the political actor proposes. Dynamic equilibrium becomes equilibrium of programming, a situation in which the scarce resources are continuously adapted so as to reach the pre-established aims. The corporative element is represented by the fact that the aims of the programme are not chosen by single individuals but indicated in an authoritarian manner by the State. According to Amoroso it is up to politics to indicate the aims which economics will then be in charge of reaching with the minimum price. The article finishes peremptorily:

> Mathematical economics is Logic and not Politics, and its duty is not to provide an aim but to enlighten the path to pursue as regards the aim given. Thus, far from being incompatible with the idea of corporative mystic, the mathematical method is a tool for the coordination of action directed to the achievement of those aims.
>
> (Amoroso 1939: 144)

In other words, for Amoroso the encounter between corporatism and economics takes place subordinating the latter to political choices. In this way the marginalist economist saves the autonomy of his scientific discipline, but at the same time corporatism becomes the mathematical theory of the economic programme. Therefore, Amoroso's economic theory basically has nothing of corporative and it is for this reason that it maintained its scientific value, besides the ideological interpretations that he himself proposed.

## Final observations

After considering how Amoroso developed his proposal for the construction of second order dynamics in Pareto's ambit during the 1930s, the question that remains open is why this project remained an isolated contribution with a modest influence.[4] The answer can only be articulate because, when considering the undoubted elements of genuine scientific progress, Amoroso's proposal presented strongly problematic aspects which established its decline.

## 84 *Dynamic equilibrium and Luigi Amoroso*

Considering the innovative and progressive aspects, it is undeniable that from an analytical viewpoint Amoroso reached his purpose, which was to extend Pareto's categories also to dynamics. Widely using the calculus of variations, he was able to define Langrange's two twin notions of utility and productivity which constituted a theoretical enrichment that enabled him to take into consideration, at least in formal terms, the temporal dimension of the economic choices. The values of equilibrium of the variables were no longer constant measures but rather functionals that depended explicitly on time. Moreover, the microeconomic scheme remained intact in Amoroso, on the basis of the single individuals' behaviour and their interactions in a context of general economic equilibrium.

However, these acquisitions, even if remarkable, were not able to counterbalance the limits of this approach to the construction of the economic dynamics. The first limit is epistemological, deriving from the intrinsic problem in building economic dynamics on the basis of analogies with the categories of rational mechanics. Besides the difficulties from an interpretative viewpoint – the assimilation of the economic behaviours when the forces of inertia are operating can cause more than one criticism – the essential point is that the analytical categories of the latter have a rather modest role outside the condition of stationary state. The analogy with the principle of conservation of energy requires that the system is in a state of rest, but this is in contradiction with the project to determine a dynamic model.[5] Just as Pareto had imagined, the analogies with rational mechanics can be deviating or of scarce utility in the case of dynamic analysis.

A second weakness in Amoroso's perspective, linked to the first, consists of the fact that the international research was going in a different direction, that of the centrality of the role of expectations, as La Volpe's elaborations will witness, as well as those of Fossati. On the contrary, besides the simple formal reference to directive forces, which often appears in his writings, Amoroso never developed this perspective, remaining linked to his mechanist view of the weight of forces of inertia.

It is likely that the main reason for the crisis in which Amoroso's perspective ended up, can be found in the fact that it never was transformed into a theory of accumulation and economic growth, elements which will become the distinctive traits of the dynamic theory after the Second World War. While Amoroso moved in the direction of extending Pareto's categories in a dynamic key through the functional analysis to have a general picture of the evolution of the economic systems, international research was developing successfully in a totally different direction, as indicated by Tinbergen (1934) and Frisch (1936). According to these two authors, the analysis becomes dynamic not because the measures depend generically on the time factor, but rather for the fact that the variables taken into consideration refer to moments in time different among each other but connected. According to Schumpeter this approach was more fit for an analysis of dynamic phenomena also because it was more congenial to the analysis in aggregated terms which was affirming itself with detriment to the disaggregated one (Schumpeter 1960: Part V, chap. 4). Lastly, it is important not to neglect the ideological aspects of Amoroso's concept. In his essay dated 1938, *La teoria del programma economico*, he tried to demonstrate how the dynamic theory could be considered as the scientific part of corporative economics. The state's role was to determine the aims of collective action while the economic theory was to establish the optimal use of the resources through the finding of the optimal programme. With the fall of fascism, even this state-controlled interpretation of economic dynamics was totally ignored, to then be widely reconsidered in the 1960s at international level in the literature on optimal growth. From these general characteristics, it is no surprise that Amoroso's ingenious system was considered more a refining of Pareto's system rather than a tool which could offer new possibilities of development for dynamic analysis. For this reason he was no longer mentioned, with the sole exception of his student Palomba (1959), who probably did so more out of a sense of gratitude towards his teacher than due to a deep conviction.

## Notes

1  Amoroso's position concerning the analytical matter of the existence and uniqueness of equilibrium did not characterize only Pareto's school, but constituted the scheme of reference also for other authors of the post-war period. For example A. Graziani in his essay, *Equilibrio Generale ed Equilibrio Macroeconomico* (1965), seems to reach a similar position, even if no longer referring to Pareto's theory but rather to Walras's. For Graziani the requisite of uniqueness is the characteristic of all the systems with functions of productions with flexible coefficients, since the functions have the necessary requisites of continuity and convexity (Graziani 1965: 43–44).

2  As an example of a function appropriate for the purpose, Amoroso indicates, $U = \log x - e^{-\dot{x}}$, from which it is possible to derive Eulero's equation as follows, $x\ddot{x} + e^{\dot{x}} = 0$

3  This convincement is reasserted by Amoroso in the article dated 1957, *Modelli meccanici e modelli economici*, in which the force of inertia is substituted with the elastic force.

4  Among the sporadic references to Amoroso's works we here highlight the content in *Storia delle dottrine economiche* of *Dizionario di Economia Politica* edited by Claudio Napoleoni (1965), prepared by Siro Lombardini.

5  This internal criticism was developed accurately by Dominedò in an article prepared in 1942 but published only in 1966.

# 5 Dynamic equilibrium and expectations in Giulio La Volpe

## Introduction

Together with Giuseppe Palomba, Giulio La Volpe (1909–1996) can be considered the main exponent of the second generation of the Pareto school in Italy. After graduating in Economic History at the Naples Regio Istituto Superiore di Scienze Economiche e Commerciali in 1930 with a thesis on the economic reforms of the Murat government, he concentrated on pure theory in the 1930s focusing in particular on the theory of economic dynamics. After obtaining a teaching position in 1937, the following year he was called to Venice by Alfonso de Pietri Tonelli where he was to remain until 1972 when he moved to Rome University's Faculty of Political Science until he retired. La Volpe was very active in Venice not only in the academic sphere but also organizationally. Like other Paretians, such as Eraldo Fossati in Genoa, he directed the F. Ferrara Laboratorio di Economia Politica set up by de Pietri Tonelli and transformed the Bollettino della Rivista Bancaria into a nationally important review, *Ricerche Economiche*, which he was editorial director of throughout his time in Venice[1].

An early and extremely prolific writer, in the course of his long academic career he ranged very widely over a great many themes in economic research from the most challenging theoretical questions to eminently empirical and applicative themes. Despite this intense activity, his work – for reasons which remain unexplored – never received the attention it deserved on an academic level, a fact which also holds for the other writers linked to the Pareto tradition. It is likely that he suffered the negative consequences of the sudden and rapid decline of the Pareto tradition in Italy after the Second World War (Graziani 1991).

La Volpe is a particularly important case in point because, as I will attempt to demonstrate here, his analytical contributions were first rate. There is nothing accidental about the importance attributed by Pier Carlo Nicola (2000) in his *Mainstream Mathematical Economics in the 20th Century* to La Volpe's contribution, a contribution which was more important in certain aspects than that of his teacher Luigi Amoroso, economic mathematician par excellence of the inter-war period in Italy. A posteriori, this acknowledgement would appear to be fully justified by La Volpe's first-rae contribution in the 1930s contained above all in the essay which won him his teaching post, *Studi sulla teoria dell'equilibrio*

*Dynamic equilibrium and Giulio La Volpe* 87

*economico dinamico generale* (1936). Unfortunately this was only ever published in Italian with the result that his theory was not able to spread beyond national boundaries. The importance of his academic work was only recognized much later as a result of the work of Massimo Di Matteo and Micho Morishima who pushed for its translation into English in 1993. In his introduction to the work, Morishima observes that "there is no doubt that the present volume is one of the supreme theoretical contributions made by the Italian economics in the pre-war period" (1993: xxvi). The purpose of this chapter is to provide an overview of La Volpe's main achievements in the 1930s and early 1940s, his most prolific scientific period. These achievements constitute one of the most interesting attempts made by the Pareto school to overcome the static vision of economic equilibrium, a project which Pareto merely outlined in a brief essay in 1901.

After the Second World War, La Volpe's academic energies were diluted into a multiplicity of channels and he only sporadically returned to his original attempt to found formal dynamics, abandoning, moreover, the concept of temporary equilibrium in order to move closer to a formula which was more workable but also less theoretically convincing, more in line with new econometric tendencies. For my purpose here, an analysis of La Volpe's pre-Second World War work will suffice.

## La Volpe's dynamic equilibrium as *temporary equilibrium*

Whilst Amoroso's approach to the equations of dynamic equilibrium is the culmination of a long and tortuous research process, La Volpe's most significant research and achievements, on the other hand, took place almost entirely at the outset of his long academic career with the publication of his 1936 essay. In his introduction, La Volpe explicitly declares that his objective is to develop Walras's[2] and Pareto's theories of general economic equilibrium in a dynamic direction:

> This study starts from Walras's and Pareto's equilibrium theory, perfected by Amoroso and de Pietri-Tonelli, appropriating its methods and general framework and attempting to build a theory of economic movement founded on a wider context. And this taking into account (with the guidance of Amoroso and de Stefani) not only of the *forces operating pro tempore* – the vital forces of the system – which are insufficient to explain historical continuity, but also the *forces of inertia*, representing the weight of the past, and the *guiding forces* (speculation) expressing the human capacity to anticipate and shape future events.
>
> (La Volpe 1936: 6)

Despite this reference to the forces of inertia, which more than anything else constitutes a concession to his teacher Amoroso, this passage shows the main novelty of La Volpe's framework. In order to build a theory of economic movement it is no longer sufficient to look for analogies with rational mechanics but rather to widen the timeframe to take account of the expectations of economic

## 88 *Dynamic equilibrium and Giulio La Volpe*

subjects as far as future economic choices are concerned. This is an element which differentiates economic from mechanical phenomena. This was also the new framework which was emerging on an international level (Tinbergen 1934)[3] from both the analytical and empirical points of view. In line with these new tendencies in dynamic analysis, La Volpe too attempted to set out a dynamic framework based on expectations in which the strongly original element was constituted by the application of the calculus of variations.

La Volpe further underlines in his introduction that his objective is to reach a microeconomic foundation of the theory of dynamic economic equilibrium. In his own words:

> I have thus attempted to construct a micro-dynamic theory of general equilibrium showing how market equilibrium is established in every instant as is shown by the behaviour of economic subjects, consumers and firms on the basis of forecasts and plans for the future and the way in which this equilibrium changes continually over time by means of changes in individual plans. This is the salient point of the theory. Whilst it is certainly true that it is difficult to predict the future, impossible to avoid errors in projecting present market tendencies into the future and easy to overestimate one's own perspective evaluations in one way or another, it is equally true that, in this way, economic activities are regulated at every moment.
>
> (La Volpe 1936: 7)

As is often the case in Pareto school writers, the main additions concern the theory of consumer behaviour which acts as a general paradigm which is then extended to producer behaviour. La Volpe also uses a similar framework when he touches first on consumption theory – and thus to the construction of the demand curve – and then on production theory – and thus to the supply curve – in order to reach a framework of general economic equilibrium.

Let us consider the consumption side. La Volpe's starting point is intertemporal utility – which he calls the individual's *action plan* – which demonstrates two important characteristics which were common in later literature. The first is, as Rosenstein-Rodan (1934: 79) suggests, that the period taken into account is no longer a generic time interval, as in dynamics of the first kind, but the individual's whole life and the issue thus becomes one of determining the best sharing out of consumption over the course of a lifetime. As the final date of the plan is unknown, a new analytical problem develops – known as the condition of transversality – which La Volpe resolves in an original way anticipating a solution which will later become the standard optimal growth model. The second is that the utility which the agent expects to obtain over time now depends also on expectations which take shape at a given moment. For La Volpe:

> the consumer determines his behaviour on the market in every infinitesimal interval of time on the basis of a calculation which is extended to the future and carried out in order to obtain a maximum of satisfaction over the whole

## Dynamic equilibrium and Giulio La Volpe   89

(expected) course of his life. It is a kind of plan of use of all means possessed, both real and projected, which will certainly determine his present conduct and that of the future if his forecasts and the other data in his calculations do not vary.

(La Volpe 1936: 17)

It follows that:

> The consumer's economic problem is the most complex imaginable as he must take account of movements in prices and interest rates as he forecasts them in the present time. As well as deciding how much to consume and how much to save, he must determine which part of his assets he intends to invest for profit and the part he intends to set aside for the maintenance of durable consumer goods for his own needs and, at the same time, how to share out the former between the various consumption goods, decide how much to retain in order to be able to regularly pay his daily dues, the work to cede and the distribution of expenses between the various goods: a whole series of strictly independent choices to be made simultaneously which present considerable difficulties in relation to an analysis of rigorous lines.

(La Volpe 1936: 18)

From a formal point of view La Volpe makes use of an intertemporal utility function separable over time so that the utility obtained in a specific interval is independent from its past or future values, thus making it an issue which can be evaluated analytically. It emerges as depending also on expectations formed at the time $t_0$ and valid for successive periods $\tau$ with $\tau > t_0$. For this reason he refers to an *evaluation function of future utility*. Following the utility which agent $i$ expects to obtain from a consumption flow in a specific period $(t_0, \tau)$ is worth the following integral

$$\int_{t_0}^{t} U_i(C_0(t_0, v), \dots, C_{h+m}(t_0, v)) dv \qquad [1]$$

in reference to a generic basket of goods and services $(C_0, \dots, C_{h+m})$ given the expectations established over time $t_0$. At any time, consumers must make choices to determine an optimal consumption profile taking account of intertemporal budget. For La Volpe this latter is made up of forecasts on the quantity of work and other services that the economic agent expects to have at his disposal in future, on the share of profits he will receive, his financial choices and finally his planned consumption flow. It is important to underline that, in La Volpe's framework, expected prices, which constitute a fundamentally important variable, depend both on the level of current prices and variations in them, and that the same goes for interest rates. Using his original notation the intertemporal budget, as it relates to the individual consumer, becomes the following (ommitting the time suffixes in order to avoid overburdening the notation):

# 90 *Dynamic equilibrium and Giulio La Volpe*

$$\sum_{j=0}^{h} p_j(H_j - C_j) + rF + R - \dot{F} - \sum_{j=h+1}^{h+m} p_j C_j = 0 \tag{2}$$

where the first term in [2] represents the balance of services purchased or supplied (between 0 and $h$ in number) in the time interval, including labour. The second term, $rF$, denotes the income consisting of interest on accumulated savings, while the third, $R$, is the amount of income from shareholding. There are two other terms: the variation in saving by unit of time, $\dot{F}$, and the final sum, which indicates spending on consumption (consumption goods range from $h_{t+1}$ to $h_{t+m}$). La Volpe hypothesizes that, at this stage of the analysis, both current and expected prices, as well as both the current and expected interest rate, are constant, so that the unknowns reduce to determination of current and future consumption, and of planned financing.

The maximization of [1] under the inter-temporal budget constraint [2] also leads La Volpe, following Amoroso, to use the calculus of variations, which, moreover, he relegates in the notes to the end of the volume. La Volpe was not a mathematician and to obtain these results, he enlisted the help of two talented young Neapolitan mathematicians who he thanks in the preface, Giulio Andreoli and Gianfranco Cimmino,[4] who both worked in the field of functional calculus. Instead of using the Euler equation, like La Volpe, a more direct result can be obtained by applying the optimal control theory, the technique of dynamic optimization which was developed in the engineering field only in the early 1960s and then also used extensively in economics in the second half of that decade. On the basis of the optimum principle the issue is reformulated as that of the search for the maximum of the following Hamiltonian function:

$$H = U(C_0, \ldots, C_{h+m}) + \lambda \left( \sum_{j=0}^{h} p_j(H_j - C_j) + rF + R - \dot{F} - \sum_{j=h+1}^{h+m} p_j C_j \right) \tag{3}$$

The first order conditions are the following, one for the control variable, consumption, and the other for the state variable, savings,

$$\dot{H}_{C_j} = 0 \qquad \dot{U}_{C_j} = \lambda p_j \tag{4}$$

$$\dot{\lambda} = -\dot{H}_F \qquad \dot{\lambda} = -r\lambda \tag{5}$$

The solution of the dynamic system represented by [4] and [5] is facilitated by the fact that the two differential equations are separable variables. Obtaining the value of the shadow price ($\lambda$) by direct integration from [5] and substituting it in [4], we obtain the following expression that defines the optimal consumption trajectory of the generic good or service $C_j$ in function of time,

$$\frac{\dot{U}_{C_j}}{p_j} = Ae^{-rt} \tag{6}$$

*Dynamic equilibrium and Giulio La Volpe* 91

where the parameter $A$ is a constant to be determined, but still independent of time, and $r$ is assumed, by hypothesis, to be given. Equation [6] establishes the fundamental achievement of La Volpe's approach to the determination of the consumer's dynamic equilibrium. From these he derives that which he will call the two laws of consumer equilibrium. The first states that, given $t$, expenses should be distributed in such a way as to match the marginal weighted utility rates, exactly as in the static case. The original feature is in the second law according to which the distribution of maximum satisfaction over time requires that the marginal weighted utility rate should decrease in line with interest rates, taking into account the constant $A$ which depends on the initial conditions. The smaller the value of $A$, the lower the marginal utility and therefore the more consumption is postponed from the present to the future. Equation [6] is, in actual fact, a system of equations, because it must be related to $h$ goods and services and the number $m$ of consumers who, along with budget constraints and the transversality condition make the system specific. La Volpe observed:

> This system of equations represents the dynamic equilibrium and the historical movement of consumers. In fact, given $t$, it supplies the conditions that must exist in the plans in order that they, at any given moment, set themselves for the future, and, in function of $t$, describes the movement over time of individual consumer savings, through the constant succession of economic plans.
>
> (La Volpe 1936: 24)

La Volpe's dynamic consumer equilibrium is thus, according to the definition given it by Hicks in *Value and Capital* (1939), a temporary equilibrium because it is determined on the basis of the prices which the consumer forecasts on the market in the future. If these vary then the whole optimal consumption profile will also change instantly. La Volpe adds:

> In the individual dynamic equilibrium problems are all solved simultaneously by means of a unit calculus of economic affordability which is an inseparable whole. Consumption and saving, supply and demand of goods and services and funds (forecast) and extension of personal wealth are all linked together and cannot be determined separately as they are the result of a careful search for maximum welfare which coordinates all of them. They therefore depend on all the data of the issue: on appreciation of the benefits of future consumption, on available funds and the resources the consumer expects to have at his future disposal, on price and share forecasts and, through these, on relative actual (market) values and tendencies in them. If even one of these elements takes on a certain weight in relation to another, the entire individual behaviour will be modified.
>
> (La Volpe 1936: 29)

Moving from consumption to production, La Volpe's handling of firm dynamic equilibrium is conceptually close to that of the consumer and is rather encouraged

## 92  *Dynamic equilibrium and Giulio La Volpe*

because investment is in itself a dynamic element. Furthermore, every investment project is finalized with a certain delay and this explains why marginal costs must be greater the longer the productive period. Applying the calculus of variations once again, La Volpe determines the dynamic functions of the supply of goods (La Volpe 1936: 56).

Taking the dynamic functions of demand by consumers and the dynamic functions of supply by firms, market equilibrium requires that excess of demand on the markets is nil at any time. The equation system contains $(1+h+m+1)$ unknowns, the wage, the prices of $h$ productive services, the prices of $m$ goods and lastly interest rate with a corresponding equal number of functional relations. For every $t$ value, the solutions give the equilibrium at that moment of time and, in function of $t$, the description of the historic evolution of an economy starting from a given initial instant. The final result is a great picture on the functioning of a competitive economy:

> In line with the fundamental principle of the dynamic, as stated in the preface, the market achieves a position of equilibrium at any given time. Consumers are in equilibrium because the plans by which they regulate their behaviour involve a maximum of present and future satisfaction. Firms are in equilibrium because, at any given time, they balance their financial statements and regulate investments and thus funds on the basis of long or short term plans which aim to create the greatest possible gap between revenues and production costs. The whole market is in equilibrium because prices and interest rate are fixed at levels which simultaneously equal total supply and demand of goods, services and funds.
>
> (La Volpe 1936: 93)

It is worth underlining the two main aspects characterizing the dynamic equilibrium in La Volpe's approach. In the first place, equilibrium moves from static to dynamic to the extent that it is determined by the supply and demand equations in which quantities are exogenous function of time, equations which are micro-founded because they derive directly from the process of intertemporal optimization. La Volpe considers this process to be an important step towards the creation of his plan to build a dynamic equilibrium left unfinished by Pareto. Second, whilst it is in continual movement, the economic system is always in a position of equilibrium. A notion – that of dynamic equilibrium – which may seem an oxymoron at first glance actually becomes a perfect standpoint from which to study evolution in economic systems. This equilibrium changes continually because the action of the forces of change are balanced by the action of the limitations in such a way that the condition of equilibrium – that is the equality of supply and demand on each single market – is always verified in the economic system. This very strong idea that the markets are always in equilibrium has been taken up with great success in recent times – and with the due statistical methods – by the exponents of the theory of rational expectation which has made of it one of the essential methodological canons of their approach to economic dynamics.

## An important analytical achievement: the condition of transversality

One element in the building of La Volpe's dynamic equilibrium deserves highlighting both in its analytical aspect and in terms of economic interpretation because it undoubtedly constituted an original result which might have given him considerable international prestige. This is the way in which he dealt with and resolved the problem of the condition of transversality – or final condition – in that, in his approach, the final instant is not given in an exogenous way as usually occurs in the problem of the calculus of variations but must itself be characterized in an optimal way. This mathematical problem derives from the fact that the solution to a problem in the calculus of variations leads to the the definition of a second order differential equation which requires two conditions around it to be fixed. In his 1933 article analysing the dynamic problem of the producer, Amoroso identified these two conditions in the initial stock of the available resources and the rhythm given by their use. Whilst the first condition has immediate economic significance, the second would appear difficult to interpret and is essentially akin to an *ad hoc* hypothesis, a specific assumption introduced to meet analytical needs. Faced with this same mathematical problem, La Volpe took the first condition and introduced a second one, thereby clearly anticipating what later work would consider the (necessary) condition of transversality.

In order to resolve the consumer issue, La Volpe assumes that the following final condition in relation to savings is applicable:

$$F(t,\tau) = 0 \qquad per \qquad t = \tau \qquad\qquad [7]$$

On the basis of [7], in the final instant of the period considered, savings must be nil and thus on that date the individual must have used all of his available financial resources. In this way the mathematical problem is well placed and it is possible to identify from all possible trajectories that which has optimum characteristics. La Volpe is worried by the limited probability of this hypothesis and, in order to obviate this limitation in his model, he also considered the case of inheritance (1936: 44–48).

Whatever its mathematical aspect, La Volpe does not run away from the economic contents of [7], which is even more important in that it constitutes a condition of economic rationality and enables him to widen the scope of his analysis to cover the individual's entire life cycle. Taking up [2], forward integrating it and taking account of the condition of transversality, he achieves the following expression:

$$\int_t^\tau \sum_{j=0}^{h+m} p_j C_j e^{-rt} = F(t) + \int_t^\tau (\sum_{j=0}^{h} p_j H_j + R) e^{-rt} \qquad\qquad [8]$$

where we have considered, for the sake of simplicity, a constant interest rate. In [8] the term on the left represents the present value of total consumption, calculated

## 94 *Dynamic equilibrium and Giulio La Volpe*

in the time given, while the term on the right represents the present value of the total wealth available to the individual. La Volpe's conclusion is that the present value of the expenditure for all of an individual's consumption, at a given moment, over the entire planned course of his life, must be equal to the assets he owns at that moment. In his own words:

> It is evident that if an individual saves for a certain amount of time, he will need to spend in future, and if the individual spends more than he owns, he will need to save.
>
> All this does not exclude the eventuality of individuals who choose to accumulate assets for a longer or shorter period of time in order to spend the profits but this works in any case on the assumption that sooner or later even assets will be consumed [...]. It is thus by deferring the consumption of present resources or anticipating the future consumption of resources that maximum well-being tends to be achieved. But individuals never reach this goal because they are continually forced to change direction.
>
> (La Volpe 1936: 29)

In this passage La Volpe has anticipated and grasped the deeper meaning of the necessary condition for economic consistency that must be respected in the process of intertemporal optimization. This condition was later taken up in Milton Friedman and Franco Modigliani's life-cycle theory, as well as in 1960s' literature on optimal growth but no mention has ever been made to La Volpe's pioneering work in first identifying and using it.

## Temporary equilibrium in Hicks and La Volpe

The significant analytical achievements in La Volpe's early work, his appropriate use of functional calculus and his definition of the transversality condition, passed relatively unnoticed both nationally and internationally. In Italy, the reactions of the Pareto school were mixed. De Pietri Tonelli gave it an enthusiastic review in 1936, stating that this was the way to achieve a dynamic equilibrium theory. He noted:

> But luckily there are those who are taking what seems to me a positive path, because it has always been thus: it is the way of pure analysis. Here the rational economy, making use of the other sciences, of the least imperfect of investigative methods, may avail itself of the subtleties of the functional calculus, applying it to specific cases or even better, as has as yet only rarely been done, attempting the vastness, the stature and the beauty of general constructions which are so satisfying to our Latin minds.
>
> (de Pietri Tonelli 1963: 348)

On the other hand, whilst recognizing its merits, Palomba, who at that time was working on his own version of dynamics, also emphasized the limits constituted

*Dynamic equilibrium and Giulio La Volpe* 95

by the fact that, from his point of view, it did not achieve a genuinely dynamic vision. In his own words:

> Even if we skim over many of the details of La Volpe's study, it is clear that, in its fundamental conception, it is a work of static economics. It extends static economics in many important ways, greatly broadening the content of the latter and bringing the time element into play, but dynamic economics – or rather the laws that govern general dynamics, escape the attentive reader of the volume. He states, it is true, that in an economy's historic trends forces, while subject to constraints, are at all times in equilibrium; he considers hereditary forces, inertia and speculative forces, but uses them only to hem them into a conception that remains that of the *Lausanne School.* In short, no true dynamic discovery emerges from these pages or formulas which, however, are of undeniable interest and extremely acutely analysed.
>
> (Palomba 1936: 43)

Neither was Amoroso inclined to accept the novelty of La Volpe's methods, and in his later writings (1938, 1942) he remained faithful to an approach with similarities to rational mechanics, completely neglecting the role of expectations. Internationally, only one review in the *Journal of Political Economy* is worthy of mention. In it J. Murray Thompson noted that the work:

> is based on the theory of equilibrium of Walras and Pareto as extended by Amoroso and Pietri-Tonelli. In order to bring his system a step nearer reality, Giulio La Volpe adds to the forces operating at the time under consideration, what he calls forces of inertia and directing forces. The former represent the weight of the past and the latter the human capacity of individuals to anticipate future events and to shape their activities in the light of these anticipations.
>
> (Murray Thompson 1938: 590)

Aside from this review, there was no other response at the international level, as La Volpe's work was neither translated into any other language nor did he publish articles in foreign journals as Amoroso did (1940). International recognition of the value of La Volpe's contribution came only a few decades later with the aforementioned translation in 1993 of the 1936 volume edited by M. Morishima and M. Di Matteo.

In his long introduction Morishima emphasized that one of the main merits of La Volpe's essay was that it anticipated the concept of temporary equilibrium formulated by Hicks in *Value and Capital* (1939) three years later. This is definitely an important step in any analysis of La Volpe's academic contribution from a historical perspective. In fact, the methodological intention of the two scholars was the same – the dynamic extension of the theory of general economic equilibrium – as was the theoretical instrument identified, the importance of the role of expectations. Also entirely similar is the mechanism by means of which

96 *Dynamic equilibrium and Giulio La Volpe*

expectations affect economic variables as expected prices depend essentially on current ones and variations in them. However, alongside these aspects in common there are also differences which are important to consider because they are based on a different conception of economic dynamics.

An initially distinguishing element and the most obvious, though it is not in itself fundamental, concerns the mathematical tool used. In this field, La Volpe is decidedly ahead of Hicks. While Hicks' purpose is to get to dynamics without abandoning the tools of comparative statics, for La Volpe it is a question of building a general dynamic model which requires, by definition, a significant leap forward from an analytical point of view – the determination of the appropriate equations in which the economic magnitudes depend over time and also, another essential aspect, that they are obtained through an optimization process. However, this analytical difference should not be overstated as the extension of the period chosen by Hicks, the week, can also be reduced at will as, rather than a chronological criterion, it is a logical criterion which consists in the fact that within the period expectations remain constant.

A second difference is of greater significance. We have seen that, as it is defined, La Volpe's dynamic system is in a position of equilibrium at any given moment, an equilibrium which is always changing as it depends on a multiplicity of factors which interact between themselves. Moreover, these changes must be consistent with each other and this condition of economic rationality is ensured by the intertemporal constraint constituted by the transversality condition. It follows from this framework that, in La Volpe's analysis, as indeed in the Pareto school as a whole, the issue of identifying the conditions which ensure the stability of equilibrium are almost entirely absent. This stability aspect, on the other hand, takes on a fundamentally important role in Hicks' dynamic framework. Since the latter considers dynamic equilibrium to be a succession of individual temporary equilibria, an important issue, which is very similar in comparative statics, becomes one of whether the system, after the disturbance introduced by expectations, tends to return to an equilibrium position or rather to move still further away from it. In Hicks, dynamics is intrinsically linked to the problem of the stability of equilibrium. In his essay of 1939, this stability condition is identified, following the Marshall tradition, in the elasticity of expected prices as against current prices. If the value of this elasticity is less than unity, the initial imbalance will be reabsorbed and the system will be stable, but if it is higher, the system will become unstable and the initial imbalance will widen. It follows from this that expectations play a role of greater importance in Hicks than in La Volpe. In the former they are the key factor in determining the dynamics of the economy, while in the latter they can be regarded as a subsidiary element, a component that, alongside many others, helps to determine the trajectory of the economic system.

In fact, beyond the common reference to expectations, Hicks and La Volpe have a very different approach to economic dynamics, the former more related to adjustment mechanisms of comparative statics, the latter closer to a genuinely dynamic vision in which economic growth is a continuous function of time. This confirms Weintraub's hypothesis (1991) in which he analysed Hicks' 1939 contribution and spoke of a bifurcation in the history of dynamic analysis. A first direction was the Hicks-Samuelson line which limited dynamic analysis to the study of the stability conditions of the general competitive equilibrium. This line of research found full expression in the section Samuelson devoted to dynamics in his *Foundations* (1947). The second approach, namely that of dynamic equilibrium, then came to fruition in the theory of accumulation and growth, both descriptive and optimal, which developed in the 1960s. La Volpe, especially in view of the analytical tools used, can be numbered among the forerunners of this second approach, of which, however, he did not grasp its potential and remained tied to its original Pareto school framework.

## From dynamic equilibrium to corporative dynamics

Just two years after his 1936 essay La Volpe published a book that was intended to complement his earlier work and which at the same time also contained some significant innovations that are clear from its title *Ricerche di Dinamica Economica Corporativa* (1938). In it he sets the individualistic view of economic action entirely aside in order to adhere explicitly to a state-planned economy of a corporative kind. He then further complements these thoughts by his large 1948 work, *Convenienza Economica Collettiva*, which, after his short-lived corporative phase, was his most important theoretical contribution to the field of general economic equilibrium. This latter work brought the most creative phase of La Volpe's thinking to an end at least as far as pure theory is concerned. Let us briefly consider the evolution of his thought in these two essays, starting in this section with his 1938 work.

In his 1938 essay La Volpe's intention is to position his dynamic approach within the framework of the principles of corporative economics and it is for this reason that economic dynamics is transformed in it into "corporative economic dynamics." La Volpe's shift from economic liberalism to corporatism, in common with other Pareto school thinkers such as de Pietri Tonelli or Amoroso, takes place by means of the deliberate subordination of economic thinking to sociology and political science. Linked to the principle of scarcity, the economic paradigm in these authors remains central but is more instrumental in function as compared to exogenous, collective type functions which can only be laid down by the managerial class (de Pietri Tonelli 1931). As has been pointed out (Mancini, Perillo and Zagari 1982), this shift to corporatism by top economists officially came with the publication of Amoroso and De Stefani's 1934 article *La Logica del Sistema Corporativo* ("The Logic of the Corporative System"). La Volpe's essay is an interesting example of how this happened.

The essay opens with the usual discussion on static and dynamic economics. If static theory reached its apex with Walras and Pareto, La Volpe observes that dynamic analysis has been left far behind:

> But the study of the continuous succession of the concrete positions of the system in which the movement consists has progressed little. Statics studies

98 *Dynamic equilibrium and Giulio La Volpe*

discontinuous equilibrium positions which are disconnected from each other, and we understand very little of the movements that occur to achieve these positions, nor of the oscillations that occur when the balance is disturbed and forces develop that tend to restore it.

(La Volpe 1938: 13)

And even the analytical schemes of two years earlier now seem adequate to him to represent the dynamic reality of economic phenomena. He further observes:

Research of this kind that would be necessary to encompass the fundamental aspects of economic life present the greatest difficulties. With the use of the potential offered by mathematics, it is not too difficult to formulate the equations of dynamic equilibrium, even in more general cases, but this work can help to clarify the complexity of the situation in a rigorous way. It is, however, incapable of helping us to an understanding of the dependence of the unknowns of the balance by its data. Mathematics is still not capable of solving systems of equations which are also encountered in the less general problems of dynamic equilibrium.

(La Volpe 1938: 63)

What remains for La Volpe, then, is the inductive approach representing the dynamics of the economy as a vast and complex evolutionary process that evolves over time through the implementation of the expectations of economic agents whose plans are continuously revised on the basis of the results of experience. Freed from the need for a rigorous and analytically coherent formulation, La Volpe groups the fundamental factors of his dynamic scheme into three broad categories: original, derivative and unknown. The former reflect the political, moral or demographic elements that form the backdrop to economic activity, the second elements are the result of economic choices made in the past but which influence the present and the latter are the unknown factors representing the solutions of the system of general equilibrium exactly in the same way as statics. His analysis is initially static and it then becomes dynamic because the different elements in the setting are considered in different time intervals which are linked together by heredity phenomena or by economic forecasts. If in any period which La Volpe calls elementary, everything should remain unchanged, the economy would remain constant over time and the economic process would replicate itself in a uniform way. With the data of their problems remaining unchanged, subjects would have no interest in changing their plans or behaviour, which are already adjusted to achieve maximum results. But this does not occur. With the passage of time, for exogenous and endogenous causes, all the data of the problem are modified and the equilibrium moves incessantly thus becoming a dynamic equilibrium. Just like Pareto, La Volpe would appear to be returning to the dynamics of successive equilibrium, reinterpreting them from a sociological and institutional perspective. Every single state of the economy depends on a set of conditions, both forecast and hereditary, which change over time. For La Volpe the main factors of economic dynamics are those that Pantaleoni had identified previously. First, the demographic variable. Increases or decreases in population can be interpreted as original or derivative of economic dynamics depending on the perspective in which they arise: original, if population tendencies depend on changes in moral or psychological conditions, derivative if they depend on economic variables such as the distribution of wealth. Technical progress is a second important factor that determines economic dynamism which, sooner or later, leads to changes in amounts invested, quantities produced and prices and, therefore, in those elements that La Volpe called derivatives. Extra-economic factors such as the moral underpinning of economic behaviour or the gradual replacement of the public management of firms by private management, are also of special interest. In this general perspective, La Volpe argues that it is of no importance to determine whether, after the initial impulse, the system is brought back to a new position of equilibrium or if the conditions of the system are continually redefined as a result of the changing nature of the elements and objectives pursued by the system. This type of dynamic is very similar to the dynamics of the second kind that Pantaleoni set out (La Volpe 1938: 114).

Whatever La Volpe's actual intentions – to achieve a higher degree of realism by means of a structured classification of the factors involved in the dynamics of the economy – the results he obtains are very modest. With the continual addition of causal relationships, both static and dynamic, the theory comes no closer to concrete phenomena but quite the contrary – it loses sight of the fundamental links. The final outcome of La Volpe's complex theoretical construction is a generic sociological pattern in which everything depends on everything which empties the theory of every possible interpretative value. Abandoning the solid analytical apparatus of his work of two years earlier, rather than bringing the theory to a solid realism, he has consigned it to a blind empiricism in which, from time to time, the specific causal factor requires identifying.

The major novelty is in the final section in which he clarifies what constitutes the shift from a traditional dynamic equilibrium, considered up to this point, to a corporative (while still dynamic) one. Whatever impression La Volpe's turning point may give, it does not require major changes in the economic categories used but occurs by means of the recognition of the essential role of the state in economic life. We are a very long way from the debates on corporative versus ethical man that were a feature of the first rather confusing phase of corporative economic theory. It is no longer a question of overcoming individual hedonism but rather of keeping account of the fact that the co-ordination of the economy cannot be guaranteed by chaotic market mechanisms but only by strategic planning on a public level. In the corporative system, which is dynamic in that public aims are changing, the state plays a central role.

> In the corporative system the state is at the heart of economic life, interprets the national purpose and is actively involved in bringing it about. As we have already noted, this action is carried out in two great approaches. In the former, national interests are pursued by means of the management of economic

## 100  *Dynamic equilibrium and Giulio La Volpe*

means by public or public interest companies created by the State and placed under its control. Public finance, a potent instrument of manoeuvre, enters into this branch of activity and occupies a pre-eminent position in it. Thus new service goods are added to traditional ones (assistance, defence, work improvement, etc.).

The latter consists of the issuing of norms by the central organs of the State and its corporative entities which are generally referred to as corporative which all companies must obey and which constitute links to the activities of the same.

(La Volpe 1938: 123)

As a Paretian, La Volpe can interpret the action of the state and the new judicial relationships set up by the Fascist regime in Italy as a new constraint on economic action to be added to that of resource scarcity. Having noted these constraints, economic science can continue to deal with the sharing out of scarce resources between a range of ends, that is concrete methods to achieve ends defined socially by the ruling classes.

This clear separation between the political element – the ends to be fulfilled – and the technical element – the marginalist principle of optimal choice, lead Volpe, like others in the Pareto school, to a whole hearted acceptance of the methodological organization proposed by Robbins in his celebrated 1932 *Essay on the Nature and Significance of Economic Science*. In his second chapter Robbins deals with the question of neutrality in economic science as far as ethics are concerned. In his vision, economics is a question solely of means not of ends. This authoritative methodological approach was taken up and extended by the Pareto school which took it to its extreme consequences. From neutrality as far as ends are concerned, moving on to arguing that this could be subordinated without losing its status as a science is straightforward. This ideological element was then restated by La Volpe in his *Economia e Filosofia* article the following year in which he states that "economic efficiency is an attribute not of the ultimate ends we adhere to but rather of the action taken to bring them to fruition in that they are guided by that principle" (La Volpe 1939: 460). This distinction between means and ends was the compromise solution which enabled the Pareto school scholars to preserve the scientific basis of their economic reasoning whilst remaining within the framework of murky corporative logic, reducing, moreover, the role of the economist to that of a technocrat at the service of the political system.

### Towards welfare economics

This very intense youthful phase in La Volpe's academic activity came to an end with a third monograph entitled *La Convenienza Economica Collettiva* in 1948 in which he took a completely different theme, that of the evaluation of economic choices no longer from an individual but rather from a social point of view. It is well known that the so-called first theorem of the welfare economy, according to

*Dynamic equilibrium and Giulio La Volpe* 101

which perfect competition leads to a certain optimum for the collective, was first fully formulated in the mathematics appendix to Pareto's *Manuale* (1906). It is equally well known that this principle of evaluation referred to as the Paretian optimum was then forgotten for a number of decades until it was reformulated by Kaldor and Hicks at the end of the 1930s in returning to a debate which had been started by Pigou in his 1924 *The Economics of Welfare*. Then in the 1950s the concept achieved universal fame and a second theorem was added which became one of the foundation stones of the welfare economics and one of the most important achievements of the axiomatic turning point in economics. The first theorem of the welfare economics has always provoked a number of doubts. Considered by some to be at most a mathematical achievement of modest practical value, others have considered it the rigorous foundation of the principle of the invisible hand, one of the best known economic assumptions from Adam Smith onwards.

Pareto introduced the notion of maximum welfare (ophelimity) for the collective in a first article in 1884 in reference to the optimal choice of production coefficients. He then further developed this concept in his *Corso* (1896/7) too in substantially similar terms. Pareto demonstrated that in a regime of free competition firms are prompted to choose those production coefficients which maximize total production and, consequently, collective welfare. It is only in *Manuale* (1906) and after a heated debate with young mathematician Gaetano Scorza that Pareto fully and definitively took on the theme of maximum utility for a collective in both production and consumption. The most fully developed handling of the issue is to be found in the French edition of the *Manuale* written in 1909 where almost half of the mathematics appendix is devoted to this issue. Clearly, to Pareto himself too, his approach to the issue of maximum utility for a collective is one of his most important contributions to economic science. Curiously there is no mention in Pareto of what was later to be referred to as the second theorem of the welfare economy, that is, that a condition of Paretian optimum can be replicated by the competitive economy. This was certainly neither an oversight nor a coincidence. The underlying reason is to be found in the fact that, for Pareto and his school, the maximum position for individuals and society depends on the initial allocation. It was, therefore, a relative maximum. If the initial resources of economic agents were changed, the final position would also be different in terms of utility for the individual economic agents. And this initial allocation can always be modified by means of specific public action.

These Pareto themes found limited resonance in the writings of Pareto's students and for almost two decades the first theorem of the welfare economy was forgotten. In Amoroso's 1921 text, *Lezioni di Economia Matematica*, the idea that free competition leads to the maximum welfare for society is a proposition which is seen as problematic. Whether Amoroso considered the theme fully dealt with by Pareto or whether he considered it relatively uninteresting, the fact remains that the Pareto school's most important mathematician dealt with it only marginally. Amoroso limits the validity of the achievement by highlighting three problematic issues. The first relates to the structure of the system constraints considered. To compare similar positions, Amoroso notes that the constraints, i.e. the system of

## 102 *Dynamic equilibrium and Giulio La Volpe*

equations, which refer to the resources, remain the same. But this does not necessarily occur and happens, "for example, to companies for whom general expenses are a significant part of their total costs" (Amoroso 1921: 414). Amoroso knew very well as did the other Italian economic mathematicians who dealt with the theory of general economic equilibrium, that increasing returns was incompatible with the competitive framework. The second thorny issue was time. Amoroso believed that the maximum guaranteed by competition was always a momentary maximum, but he felt that it was important to take account of the time dimension, what we would now call intertemporal of economic action. Lastly, Amoroso underlined the merely conventional character – this is the term he uses – of the Pareto definition. The fact that a configuration guarantees the maximum utility, does not, for Amoroso, mean that it is to be preferred but rather only that it does no harm to at least one individual. From a social point of view, Amoroso cites the example of a collective monopoly, that an advantage for all consumers can be preferable to lower profits for a few companies. This debate on possible compensations between subjects was restarted by Kaldor in 1939.

A similar position was expressed also by de Pietri Tonelli in his 1921 lessons. De Pietri Tonelli's approach is very similar to Amoroso's. The first theorem of the welfare economy is a mathematical result which is difficult to use as a guideline for practical action. In his own words:

> *General conclusions on exchange and production in free competition.* The previous specific considerations enable us to come to the general theoretical conclusion that if it were possible to carry out economic transactions in a regime of free competition, it would lead, in the final analysis, to points of equilibrium in which the (O) condition would be satisfied or, in other words, the maximum ophelimity for the collectivity *I* would be considered to have been achieved. But it is important to add right away that in the real world, perfect free competition is a long way from being present or even potentially present, and the maximum ophelimity for the collectivity remains, like competition, a convenient theoretical abstraction.
>
> (De Pietri Tonelli 1921: 303)

In the final analysis, then, Pareto's followers attributed limited importance to the first theorem of the welfare economy. Their methodological plan was different from that of their teacher. It was no longer a question of freeing the economic theory from what remained of the utilitarian philosophy – this had already been achieved – but rather of developing new analytical tools capable of interpreting the new economic situation.

It was a debate which was returned to only in the 1940s. For the centenary of Pareto's birth, the *Giornale degli Economisti* hosted a series of articles about Pareto of which many were merely commemorative but others analysed hitherto unexplored or little considered aspects of Pareto's work. Some of these dealt with precisely the issue of the collective maximum. Dominedò in his *Le Condizioni del Massimo Collettivo di Ofelimità di Pareto* (1948) provided a first analysis of some of these open questions. Bordin, in his *Di Taluni Massimi di Utilità Collettiva* (1950) dealt with the question from an analytical point of view. Lastly Zaccagnini in *Nuovi Problemi della Polemica Scorza-Pareto* (1950) returned to this neglected issue in the Pareto literature. In general terms these Pareto economists were decidedly critical of the total absence of realism in the first theorem of the welfare economics. In particular, they underlined the fact that the individual maximum was always effectively a relative maximum, dependent, that is, on the political choices of the initial distribution.

This was the context of La Volpe's contribution in a long monograph devoted precisely to the conditions that must be respected if the society is to achieve an optimal allocation of resources. La Volpe concentrates principally on three aspects of the issue. The first relates to the nexus between optimum conditions and the initial distribution of resources. He takes up the position of the other Paretians according to whom it is entirely arbitrary to define society's optimum production without taking into account the initial distribution of resources and thus the maximum identified is never an absolute maximum but only a relative one. In his own words:

> All this brings us to the conclusion that earnings, or dividends, national currency, responding to these conditions are not an absolute maximum but rather a conditional maximum depending precisely not only on individual utility assessments but also on individual distribution factors (particularly the economic quantities relative to each individual's initial position such as quantities of goods owned, credit ratios, etc.) and, in general, on the existing distribution system.
>
> (La Volpe 1948: 23)

The second aspect that La Volpe was interested in was the temporal dimension of the economic process and thus of optimal allocation too. The issue of collective economic convenience cannot, in his opinion, be separated from the moment in time these choices take place. The general problem, the optimum use of goods over time, or the temporal distribution of investments, production and consumption, and the issue of the sharing out of available resources in each period of time dealt with. In his opinion, this issue cannot be resolved analytically but requires precise consideration of the issues at stake, some hereditary in nature, others forecasts, just as in the framework of his 1938 essay. La Volpe's realism prevents him from adhering to the idea proposed in the subsequent literature of perfect knowledge of all futures markets.

Lastly, the third aspect to be considered is the one that La Volpe defines as teleological and thus relative to the end to be achieved. He notes:

> As in the case of the particular problem of collective convenience which implies a choice between different consumption, or different and alternative needs, interests and objectives, the solution to a general problem of collective convenience requires forming a scale of collective importance or preference

## 104  *Dynamic equilibrium and Giulio La Volpe*

> relative to the various forms of consumption possible in the various fields of private and public economy in the country.
>
> (La Volpe 1948: 157)

La Volpe's position is fully in accordance with the theme of the function of social welfare developed by Tinbergen (1952). In this perspective, the welfare economics is capable of proving an evaluation tool of the optimality of economic orders beginning with an aggregate function which sets out the preferences of those responsible for economic policy decisions. It follows that the analysis itself does not lead to an absolute maximum for the collectivity but rather a relative maximum. Thus the function of social welfare, including among its variables also public preferences relating to the distributive framework, completes a concept which would otherwise remain incomplete. This scholar of economics limits himself to recognizing the existence of this function without confronting the complex issue of building it on the basis of individual preferences. The task thus became one of evaluating the coherence between the ends that policy makers put forward and the suitability of the means set aside to fulfil them. Problems linked to aggregation are overcome by means of the full recognition of their political nature which belong, that is, to public ends, economic policy measures, avoiding falling in this way into the trap of the false distinction between positive economy and normative economy. This position was later taken up authoritatively in the Italian context by Federico Caffè in 1966. For La Volpe the entirety of optimal conditions for society can only be fulfilled by chance and it is for this reason that he devotes the final part of his work to the various types of economic manoeuvre and public actions in order to obtain the optimum position for the society. He does not miss the chance, either, to underline his closeness to Pareto in his *Trattato di Sociologia* in which, having abandoned the attempt to determine the collective optimum, Pareto discusses the potential for determining the optimal conditions for the society as an autonomous subject.

La Volpe's considerations are a good summary of the approach of the Pareto school to the issue of the welfare economy both in terms of depth and breadth. They are not, as we will also see in the next paragraph with Eraldo Fossati, attracted by the new formalisms of convex analysis which later dominate the 1950s thanks to the work of Arrow and Debreu inevitably losing contact with the international debate. The fundamental reason for this consists of the fact that the importance of the economic role of the state is now considered an established fact in terms both of its economic and institutional aspects. Because the shift from individual preferences to coherent social choices came up against serious difficulties, the function of social welfare was identified in the preferences of those responsible for political decisions. The Pareto school, then, motivated by a critique of the first theorem of the welfare economy moved in the direction of the full recognition of the second theorem in which optimum choice was explicitly linked to the ends of public action whether it be combating inflation or unemployment or strengthening foreign trade.

## Concluding observations

After the Second World War, La Volpe intensified his academic activities but was unable to reach the achievements of his 1936 essay. He published a considerable amount of work on a great variety of themes ranging from banking theory and comparative cost to the theory of the market forms. Furthermore, as head of study services he directed a number of enquiries of an applicative type, the results of which were published in *Ricerche Economiche*, which he transformed from a straightforward statistical bulletin to a front rank economic theory review. He returned frequently to the theme which was dearest to him of the economic dynamics of general economic equilibrium putting forward a new methodology which he called variational dynamics (La Volpe 1967, 1977). These were mostly input-output models with delayed variables which were designed to fill the gap between abstract theories and the needs of empirical research.

This project of la Volpe to build a new economic dynamics did not achieve its objectives. La Volpe, unlike Amoroso, was not an economic mathematician. He thus did not possess the analytical baggage required to deal with such advanced analytical issues. Rather than going into greater depth on the application of the functional calculus, as was occurring in the 1960s with the theory of optimal growth, he tried to follow a different but unproductive approach of dynamizing the input-output models. As has been observed (Di Matteo 1998), La Volpe's reserved nature – a characteristic, for that matter, of many in the Pareto school – led him to a certain isolation which meant that he never achieved the academic recognition that he undoubtedly deserved. This arrived only much later when the 1936 essay was finally published in English and the ground-breaking nature of his theoretical perspective emerged.

## Notes

1 For further biographical information see M. Di Matteo (1998).
2 In La Volpe's work, in fact, references to Walras are always linked to Pareto and have no importance in their own right. Walras is considered to have been the great founder of the static theory of general economic equilibrium (as for example, in de Pietri Tonelli in 1936) but then effective references are always to Pareto's writings.
3 As Tinbergen observes in his article *Annual Survey of Significant Developments in General Economic Theory* published in Econometrica in 1934 : "Among the variables appearing in dynamic utility functions there are many relating to the future. Of these some may, indeed, be known with certainty. Most of them, however, will not be known, and it is only the *expectance* of a certain amount that can be considered by the subject or that, unconsciously, influences his acts. Such expectances–as well as quantity expectances–play an important role in real phenomena, as was long since recognized. In the last few years, however, remarkable analyses have taken place in this respect" (Tinbergen 1934: 28).
4 Andreoli (1892–1969), a Neapolitan Mathematician who was very close to the fascist party, made a number of contributions to the field of differential equations. Cimmino (1908–1989), student of Mauro Picone and Renato Caccioppoli, worked mainly on linear differential equations (ordinary and partial differential), the calculus of variations and numerical computation.

# 6 Eraldo Fossati and the role of uncertainty

## Introduction

Eraldo Fossati (1902–1962) was a versatile economist with numerous interests. This is testified to by the broad compass of his inquiries, which ranged from the pure theory of general economic equilibrium, through empirical analyses (such as his detailed study on the New Deal of 1937), to studies on the history of economic thought (in particular the monetary theories of Hungarian and Italian economists of the nineteenth century).[1] Fossati can be considered as one of the leading exponents of the Paretian tradition in Italy. A frequent participant in the international debate, he made a major contribution to the renewal of economics in Italy during the post-war period, through the creation, in 1948, of the journal *Metroeconomica*, which he edited until his untimely death in 1962.

Two distinct phases can be identified in Fossati's theoretical work, although they both belonged within a unitary thematic framework consisting of the dynamization of economic theory. The first is characterized by the dominant influence of the Paretian theory of general economic equilibrium, which still in his last works Fossati considered a fundamentally important stage in the development of economic theory. Indeed, he would become one of the foremost members of the Paretian school in Italy, together with other prominent economists of the period between the two wars, such as Alfonso de Pietri-Tonelli, Luigi Amoroso, Guido Sensini and Giulio La Volpe. As we shall see, Fossati's specific contribution to this tradition of inquiry was his attempt to overcome the schemes of statics by drawing directly on the thought of the Austrian school.

The second phase, that of Fossati's maturity, is marked by his encounter with Keynes' *General Theory*, a crucial event which determined the evolution of economic thought (not only Italian) in the post-war period, and by recognition of the importance of empirical research in economics. Unlike the other economists belonging to the Paretian school, who were hostile to the new notions propounded by Keynesian theory,[2] Fossati made an original proposal for integration between the two perspectives, considering Keynes not as a revolutionary economist but rather as an innovator who furnished new tools with which to understand the real workings of contemporary economic systems with their chronic unemployment

*Eraldo Fossati and the role of uncertainty*   107

(Fusco 1997: 92). Because of his constant intellectual endeavour to identify elements of contact and continuity between what at first sight were different positions, Fossati can be considered a transition economist who adhered to the Paretian tradition but sought to make it compatible with the new ideas advanced by Keynes in the *General Theory*. Pareto and Keynes were the two central referents in his intellectual development, also chronologically, and in his search for a dynamic theory: the former in the juvenile phase of Fossati's thought in the 1930s, the latter in its mature phase of the post-war period.

The aim of this chapter is to reconstruct, albeit in a preliminary manner, some of the salient stages in Fossati's inquiry and, in particular, his theoretical contributions. The purpose is to show how their importance and originality place Fossati among the most outstanding Italian economists of the central period of the last century. This work of critical reconstruction is all the more necessary because Fossati, perhaps also because of his bashful and reserved character, has been "more appreciated as a scholar abroad than in Italy" (Papi 1962: 16).

## Fossati's research programme

Fossati graduated in law at Pavia in 1926, and also in political science. After his graduation he spent some time abroad to further his studies, in particular in Vienna where he came into contact with Hans Mayer, at that time an influential representative of the second generation of the Austrian School. In fact, a period spent in Germany or Austria was then regarded as an essential part of an economist's training. Mayer, and especially his particular contribution to general equilibrium, left his mark on the young Italian scholar. As an economist, Fossati took an active part in the international debate; in 1957 he became fellow of the *Ecometric Society* (the next Italian economist was to be Pasinetti in 1987) and contributed in the post-war period to the renewal of economic theory in Italy via the establishment of *Metroeconomica*, a new journal that he edited until his unexpected death in 1962. A neoclassical economist, he believed in the neoclassical approach and particularly the Paretian theory of general equilibrium. After the Second World War he recognized the importance of the aggregate approach and turned his attention to Keynesian theory. He regarded the Keynesian underemployment equilibrium as a great conquest of economic science which transformed its nature from revolutionary to evolutionary. A strong supporter of the formal rigour of economic reasoning, in the last part of his career he also criticized the use of sophisticated mathematics in economics, maintaining that conditions which are perfect from the mathematical point of view are quite artificial from the viewpoint of economic research and cannot serve the creative life of economic science.

Fossati's thought on dynamic economic theory can be divided into two different phases although these derive from a single design. In the first period he presented a formal model of the Austrian approach in which subjective uncertainty played a key role. This was illustrated in two essays published in the

108  *Eraldo Fossati and the role of uncertainty*

middle years of the 1930s: *Osservazioni sulla legge di Wieser* (1935) and *Ricerca sulle relazioni tra il tempo e l'utilità* (1937). In these essays Fossati sought to go beyond the static Paretian scheme by adopting Mayer's causal-genetic approach. The second phase coincided with the diffusion of Keynesian theory also in Italy. After showing the limitations of the quantitative theory of money in the real economy, Fossati argued in favour of accepting the main conclusions contained in the *General Theory*. In 1955 he published *La politica economica razionale,* a book in which he tried to show how Pareto and Keynes could be reconciled. He argued that the main problem lay in the gaps among the temporal horizons of agents: Pareto's theory was entirely static, that of Keynes was partially dynamic (Fossati 1955: 235).

Fossati's interest in dynamic theory was precocious, and it came to constitute the focal point of his research programme in the field of pure theory, developed in different periods from different standpoints. As Papi noted, "in the course of his studies Fossati never ceased dealing with the antithesis between statics and dynamics" (Papi 1962: 6). Fossati's preference for analysis of dynamic phenomena was already present in his first theoretical article, published in 1930, *Osservazioni sulla statica e sulla dinamica con particolare riguardo al tasso di sconto*. In the article's long first part, which provided a detailed description of the state of economic theory at the time, Fossati put forward his main argument, namely that the static part of economic theory had been fully explored, mainly via the contributions of Walras and Pareto. The task was now to develop the dynamic part in order to study economic reality in its historical context. For the young economist, analysis of the stationary state, the core of neoclassical economics, was no longer a satisfactory instrument with which to study monetary phenomena. Money and time: this was the fundamental relationship characterizing his inquiries from their beginning to later reflections on Keynesian theory and the relevance of econometric practice.

## Equilibrium versus dynamics: the Wieser-Mayer line

The Austrian school was an important channel for the entry of marginalist theory into Italy. The works of Austrian economists, Menger, von Wieser and Böhm-Bawerk were well known in Italy because Italian authors had considerable familiarity with the German language. The Austrian theory was viewed as a version, interesting but with some shortcomings, of the newly-developed subjectivist approach. The Italian economists, on the other hand, preferred the classical view based not so much on deductive argument as on inductive reasoning (Gioia 2003). The Austrian approach probably exerted its greatest impact during the 1930s in the field of business cycle analysis. The decade opened with Hayek's influential work, *Prices and Production*, which dominated the discussion on money and the cycle for the next few years. Hayek's key argument was that the trade cycle arose because the organization of the banking system made it difficult to avoid a period of excessive monetary expansion. Hayek's connection among

*Eraldo Fossati and the role of uncertainty* 109

monetary expansion, change in the production structure, and economic fluctuations was extensively discussed in Italy, most notably by L. Einaudi, A. Cabiati, C. Bresciani-Turroni and M. Fanno (Pavanelli 2000; Realfonzo 2000).

Fossati's interest in the Austrian School was rooted in the early phase of the movement, in von Wieser's work and in that of Hans Mayer, his successor to the chair of Political Economy at Vienna University. Fossati was interested neither in the theory of imputation presented in *Natural Value* (1889), the only aspect to which Wieser gave a formal presentation, nor in in the general theory of social evolution based on power conflicts between various agents contained in *Das Gesetz der Macht* (1924). Rather he was attracted by a minor aspect, namely the way in which Wieser sought to incorporate the time dimension into his neoclassical theory. In *Natural Value*, time is introduced indirectly using the concept of "plan," because planning involves a time horizon. In Wieser's perspective, utility depends not only on the quantity of a good, but also on the moment when it becomes available to the economic agent. Time is a second dimension of individual choice which is difficult to incorporate in the static marginalist approach.

The tensions that derive from the Walrasian theory and time-dependent, dynamic economic phenomena were developed further by Mayer. He issued a warning in regard to the success of Walrasian theory. In his *Il concetto di equilibrio nella teoria economica* (1934), he examined the thought of advocates of the general economic equilibrium, paying particular attention to Walras and Pareto. Mayer distinguished two types of theoretical approach to the question of how economic prices are formed: *causal-genetic theories* which pay attention to the formation of prices and seek to explain price correlations via knowledge of the laws of their genesis; and *functional theories* which, by precisely determining the conditions of equilibrium, seek to describe the relation of correspondence among prices in the equilibrium situation. His conclusion was that the "functional prices theory," i.e. general equilibrium theory, was unable to explain how prices were formed in the real market. According to Mayer, these theories did not increase understanding of the economic system because formal relationships depicted a particular situation – a state of equilibrium – in which the price formation process had already taken place. Mayer criticized the formalist approach thus:

> What is the result of our long and laborious peregrination through the systems represented by the theory of equilibrium? The hypothesis of equilibrium has proved to be inauspicious for this purpose. [...] it has *de-dynamized* the economic process which is, in its most profound essence, dynamic; it has deprived it of its driving force.
>
> (Mayer 1934: 799)

In the causal-genetic approach proposed by Mayer the scope of inquiry is quite different. The price theory is not a theory of equilibrium prices but a theory of the price formation process. The real price level depends on the way in which a specific trading process occurs, and in particular on the subjective expectations according to which human action takes place over time. The causal-genetic

110 *Eraldo Fossati and the role of uncertainty*

approach can be summarized as follows: it seeks to provide an explanation for economic phenomena viewed as resulting from the interaction among individual plans of action characterized by subjective uncertainty. This conclusion opens the way to the subjectivist paradigm as a research programme in which the subjective dimension of expectations prevents them from being treated as mere variables within stable functional relationships. Inasmuch as they are creations of the individual mind, expectations are unpredictable and cannot be formalized.

## Fossati's escape from Paretian theory: the subjectivist approach

Fossati tackled the problem of building dynamic analysis using the Wieser-Mayer subjective approach in the two essays mentioned above. In the first, *Osservazioni sulla legge di Wieser*, he elaborated on the essential methodological component of Wieser's theory in the dynamic context: planning activity. He used the idea of a planning period to build a dynamic conception of time. Fossati accepted the idea that the crucial distinction between the static and dynamic case is that, in the latter, marginal utility depends not only on the quantity of an economic good, but also on the time in which the good is available. In dynamic analysis, the economic calculus must be extended to encompass the entire planning horizon:

> The economic calculation involves the simultaneous choice of the best uses of all the possible intervals, said uses determining the utility of the individual doses of a good. The purpose of the economic calculation is to achieve the maximum satisfaction possible, not limited to a period of need but to an economic period, for which the principle of the equilibrium of satisfaction over time must apply.
>
> (Fossati 1935: 26)

Basically, Fossati's argument in the 1935 essay was that it is possible to see the same physical commodity as two different commodities, of today and tomorrow, because they are available in different periods of time. It was by using the same idea that K. Arrow and G. Debreu were able to construct their famous model of intertemporal equilibrium 20 years later. However, this formalist way of solving the problem was not coherent with the Austrian approach, and it was abandoned in Fossati's later article, *Ricerca sulle relazioni tra il tempo e l'utilità* (1937), where Fossati analyses the problem of the functional approach of building a dynamic conception of economy by focusing, from the causal-genetic point of view, on the interrelations among phenomena, searching for the influence of disequilibrium forces in the economy. Fossati is persuaded that the differences between these two approaches are not as wide as might be imagined at first glance, because the functional equilibrium is a particular case, the static one, of the general case, which is the dynamic one. If a difference exists, it is an ontological one concerning the nature of the objects under investigation.

*Eraldo Fossati and the role of uncertainty* 111

The functional theory is static insofar as it stresses the fact that the concept of equilibrium is indispensable for analysis of the intertemporal system of prices, while the causal approach is truly dynamic insofar as its starting point is the limited extension of forward markets in the real world:

> The two types of investigation are thus performed on two different terrains, the first has its rigidly *static* nature, the second is essentially *dynamic*. The functional theory can disregard the time factor as an element operating within it, since the equilibrium is achieved *instantaneously*, whereas the genetic-causal theory is not able to disregard time because it is concrete. This concept of the new school of Vienna can be interpreted, in this respect, as an attempt to make the static concept as dynamic as possible, so that it becomes a particular case of dynamics.
>
> (Fossati 1937: 36)

The genetic approach represented a direct criticism of the scientific endeavour to base economic theory on models of theoretical physics. The equations that describe motion in the Newtonian static universe are unaffected by either the past or the future. In analysis of the dynamic process, however, the economic system can no longer be regarded as the pure activity of interrelated markets; it must be viewed as a process in time. The temporary equilibrium depends crucially on expectations concerning the future values of the price variables that contribute in each market to determining the agent's current economic behaviour. What is distinctive about Fossati's approach is its emphasis on what can be called "structural uncertainty," that is, a lack of complete knowledge on the part of the economic agent about the structure itself of the economic problem faced. Economic inquiry becomes dynamic not because time elapses but rather as an inevitable consequence of our ignorance. The causal-genetic approach requires the principle of perfect foresight, the cornerstone of the traditional theory, to be abandoned. In Fossati's words:

> The process of continuous variations, which represents the normal dynamism of economic life, torments the individual in his action due to his inability to interpret the future. *Imperfect* knowledge therefore, and not the variations, forms the basis of economic dynamics since, if the law of the latter were known, we would be capable of perfect prediction. From the said partial imperfect knowledge derives the configuration of the world as a world of *uncertainty* and *risk*, factors which in the said manner form basic elements for economic research.
>
> (Fossati 1937: 66)

Fossati seeks to formulate a particular vision of dynamics by introducing the notion of uncertainty, a route completely different from that followed by other Italian economists, such as Amoroso, who on the contrary pointed out mechanical

## 112 *Eraldo Fossati and the role of uncertainty*

analogies. In the historical realm, where time is not a logical fiction, economic agents are not omniscient beings able to formulate perfect plans of action with regard to the future; they make mistakes and are forced to revise their plans. Over time, circumstances change and plans must be revised and adapted to such change. Unexpected obstacles may impede the planned course of action. The revision of plans occurs as experience is gained over time; but in attempting to understand human action we must take account of the subjectivism of interpretation. Fossati shares the view that all human action takes place in a world of uncertainty and insists that our ignorance of the future invalidates any theory that attributes knowledge of the future to the economic actors engaged in providing for it.

Fossati developed this central dynamic theory based upon the subjective dimension of expectations by moving in two different but complementary directions. The first was an attempt to formalize subjective uncertainty in the intertemporal equilibrium within the Austrian setting. The second was based on the role of money in the economic system. Among other aspects, Fossati considered also the possibility of integrating the Paretian equilibrium with the approach of *General Theory*, according to his personal predilection for emphasizing the contact points between different theories.

## The formalization of dynamic general equilibrium

Fossati was a Paretian economist who argued for a formalist turn in economic theory and maintained that mathematics was the true language of economics. The main purpose of his 1937 essay was to attempt to build a formal intertemporal model of general equilibrium, to which he was to return many times. Fossati viewed the future as fundamentally unknowable and criticized the probability theory as applied to decision-making for failing to take account of this fundamental ignorance. The construction of the probability calculus relies on certain knowledge about the structure of the world, whereas in reality agents do not have such knowledge on the states of the world. According to Fossati, any action that we begin in the present may have any one of a large number of possible outcomes which, if they occur, may affect the conditions of our future action, our future means, thus leaving little room for the constancy of variables.

Fossati conducts formal analysis of the dynamic model in Chapter 4, *Tentativo di soluzione dinamica del probema*. As a first stage, he assumes that the consumer's problem is that of maximizing utility over the entire period of time. In this intertemporal setting, at every step the consumer has to choose the optimal demand for goods. The second stage of Fossati's analysis addresses the problem of introducing uncertainty. Fossati's contention is that radical uncertainty takes the distinctive form of a loss $L_n$ which, by definition, cannot be known in advance. Using this hypothesis, if $x_n$ are all the parts of a total supply $P$ that has to be split among $n$ periods, we obtain the following sequence:

$$P_1 = P - x_1$$
$$P_2 = (P - x_1)(1 - c_1) - x_2$$
$$P_3 = (P - x_1)(1 - c_1)(1 - c_2) - x_2(1 - c_2) - x_3 \qquad [1]$$

$$\cdots\cdots\cdots\cdots\cdots\cdots\cdots\cdots\cdots\cdots\cdots\cdots\cdots\cdots\cdots$$

$$P_n = (P - x_1)(1 - c_1)\ldots(1 - c_{n-1}) - x_2(1 - c_2)\ldots(1 - c_{n-1}) - \ldots - x_n = 0$$

where consumption in every period depends on the past choice and the present measure of loss.

As sequence [1] shows, in every period consumption depends on the past choice and the present measure of loss, representing the effect of the lack of knowledge about the future. The economic meaning of this complex intertemporal relation becomes more evident if the residual supplies are transformed into a single intertemporal constraint, as follows:

$$P = x_1 + \frac{x_2}{1 - c_1} + \frac{x_3}{(1 - c_1)(1 - c_2)} + \ldots + \frac{x_n}{(1 - c)\ldots(1 - c_{n-1})} \qquad [2]$$

We can see that equation [2] is the usual consumer's budget constraint, where the true prices are now represented by the compound loss factor.

The consumer's problem in this intertemporal context is that of maximizing the separable utility function, $U = U_1(x_1) + U_2(x_2) + \ldots + U_2(x_n)$, under the constraint [2]. The solution is obtained, as in the static case, by using the Lagrange method. The consumer maximizes lifetime utility by equating the marginal utilities at the different periods of time. The fundamental relation is the following:

$$U'(x_1) = U'(x_2)\frac{1}{1 - c_1} = U'(x_3)\frac{1}{(1 - c_1)(1 - c_2)}$$
$$= \ldots U'(x_n)\frac{1}{(1 - c)\ldots(1 - c_{n-1})} \qquad [3]$$

According to Fossati, in light of [3] the consumer maximizes his wellbeing when the weighted marginal utilities referred to the goods in different times are equalized; maximum satisfaction in time requires the rate of the weighted marginal utility to be a function of the loss.

Fossati thought that his model could be considered a first step towards a true dynamic analysis in two respects. First, according to equation [3], there is no single demand function, but there are as many demand functions as the periods considered. The general form of this relation is $x_n = f(p_n, L_n, t_n)$. Second, the marginal utility, the key variable in the choice problem, now depends, through the loss function, on the period of time in which the various quantities of good are employed. The consumer's model becomes dynamic from the formal point of view because the choice is related to time, and from the substantive one point of view because it is based on expectations about the future. Fossati sums up the conclusion in this way:

## 114 *Eraldo Fossati and the role of uncertainty*

> The result that characterizes the present inquiry consists in having made marginal utility a function not only of the quantities of the doses of the good, but also of their uses over time. This is delimited in the economic period, which represents an interval that is not abstract but real, defined by subjective and objective elements, an interval within which the individual must systematically provide for the satisfaction of needs .... The static concept of marginal utility, the one that established a direct dependence on the quantity of good consumed in the unit of time, is therefore superseded.
>
> (Fossati 1937: 80)

Fossati's aim was all the more ambitious because he was convinced that in this way the differences between the functional and the causal approach of general equilibrium could be overcome. The functionalist element of his approach must be related to the fact that each agent is involved in an intertemporal maximization process about future choices. This method makes it possible to study ideal phenomena by defining the general conditions of general equilibrium. Nevertheless, because the loss expected is continually reconsidered according to the subjective dimension, there is room for the causal dimension of human action.

> Instead of one single plan we can therefore conceive a number of successive minor plans stemming from the trunk of the original one and corresponding to the number of periods of need, plans that represent the subsequent transformations determined by the flow of time. This process of revision thus combines a functional treatment and a causal treatment of economic development which, instead of opposing each other, integrate each other in the dynamic investigation.
>
> (Fossati 1937: 79)

In the light of Fossati's main theoretical contributions on economic dynamics published in the 1930s, we may ask whether he succeeded in giving the Paretian theory a dynamic development. Looking at purely analytical aspects, Fossati was less innovative than the other exponents of the Paretian school. While the systematic use of the functional calculus instead of differential calculus put Amoroso and La Volpe at the frontier of research into dynamic economics, Fossati ignored these new mathematical tools. From the mathematical point of view, his model is only superficially dynamic; it is in fact wholly static because time acts as a completely exogenous variable. Moreover, epistemological limits derive from the difficulty of building economic dynamics on the categories drawn from subjective uncertainty as an *ad hoc* exogenous variable. In Fossati's work there is no effort to obtain a microeconomic foundation for decisions in a context of uncertainty. It is no coincidence that this approach based on a radical subjectivism was largely undeveloped at international level, if we exclude Shackle's contribution, to which Fossati gave considerable credit as editor of *Metroeconomica*.

Summarizing, the dynamic model proposed by Fossati in 1937, albeit original and interesting, has some serious limitations. Even though the dynamic aspect was tackled with a particular analytical expedient, the final result is very far from the demands of realism which constituted Fossati's starting point. Theoretical elegance, as often happens in economics, led to even more fragile results in empirical terms. To obtain more useful theorizing on uncertainty in the general equilibrium, the disaggregate approach and the quantitative theory of money had to be abandoned. This was the new perspective adopted by Fossati in the following decades, when he turned towards Keynes. It is not surprising that Fossati did not develop the Austrian line of inquiry in the post-war period and that he never wrote his planned book on dynamics.

## Beyond the quantitative theory of money

The mature phase of Fossati's inquiry was characterized by his gradual adoption of Keynesian theory. In 1955 this conversion gave rise to *Elementi di Politica Ecomomica Rationale*, the core arguments of which constitute one of the most interesting attempts to merge the Paretian and Keynesian theories together. As one reads in the introduction, "the treatment is of an evident Keynesian inspiration due not only to pure theoretical interest but also to my experience of participating in a foreign organization of international economic cooperation" (1955: viii). Here Fossati is referring to his work as an economic adviser to the *Special Mission* for Trieste of the *Economic Cooperation Administration*, the agency created to administer the funds of the Marshall Plan.

Fossati's encounter with Keynesian theory came about at the level of the pure theory of money. He had especially in mind the ideas set out in Chapter 13 of the *General Theory* on money demand and liquidity preference. To understand this decisive phase in Fossati's thought – which was unique in the Paretian tradition – one must consider the results of his reflections of those years on the role of money in the theory of general economic equilibrium. It was dissatisfaction with the traditional theory and criticism of the quantitative theory which induced Fossati's fully-acknowledged shift from Pareto to Keynes. This was the perspective adopted by Fossati in his 1946 essay, *Nota sull'Utilità della Moneta*, which prepared the way for his Keynesian turn, and also in Chapter 10 of *Elementi di Economia Razionale* published in the same year.

In the two texts of 1946 Fossati resumed his early reflections on money framed within the theory first formulated in Italy by G. del Vecchio (1917). As early as 1930 Fossati had observed that "the value of money, like that of every other good, must be determined according to the dictates of marginal utility, which must naturally be applied to the specific case with particular criteria" (1930: 89). But it was well known that this approach was trapped in a vicious circle, given that it was impossible to distinguish the utility of money from the utility of the goods that could be purchased with it. The issue of the micro-foundation of money could not be left unresolved in the ambitious endeavour to construct general economic equilibrium. As Fossati wrote in 1960:

## 116 *Eraldo Fossati and the role of uncertainty*

The fundamental problem facing our discipline, therefore, is that of determining whether it is possible to integrate general equilibrium theory with monetary theory; a problem which presupposes that it is possible to construct a theory of money using the same process of analysis as employed by equilibrium theory.

(Fossati 1960: 239)

For Fossati, this would not be possible if economists continued to adhere to the quantitative principle which considered money as only a means to facilitate transactions. Achieving a pure theory of money demand would require explicit reference to Keynes' theory of liquidity preference (Fossati 1948: 105). His thesis was clear: the quantitative principle cannot be taken as the basis for the theory of money. For the neoclassical Fossati, the demand for money, like that for any other good, could only derive from its utility at the margin; only this element could explain the fact that individuals hold a part of their wealth in liquid form, according to a rational calculation. But in what did the marginal utility of money consist? It could only have the nature of an indirect utility. Fossati wrote:

In order to understand the meaning of such demand it is necessary to introduce the uncertainty factor into our examination and accordingly turn our attention to the time element. We must therefore examine the presuppositions of the dynamic approach, which the problem of money adduces as almost a point of passage from statics.

(Fossati 1946: 204)

An individual's money demand is therefore manifest as a demand for liquidity with which to make future payments. These latter, however, are characterized by uncertainty and risk. In a static context in which there is no uncertainty, money demand is nil, so that it makes no sense to speak of money's value as the reciprocal of the price level. It is only in a dynamic context that money demand is admissible, and it will be evaluated by the individual with reference to the marginal utility of all goods available, in both the present and the future (Fossati 1946: 207).

In conclusion, for Fossati money thus becomes – in its distinctive form as a store of value – the product of an insurance process undergone by the individual as soon as the static state, in which all variables are constant and there is perfect foresight, is left behind. In the static theory, every surplus of income over consumption takes the form of a saving which market mechanisms automatically transform into an investment decision. In the dynamic theory this surplus can take the form of idle liquidity. For this reason it is therefore impossible to integrate monetary theory into the equations of the general economic equilibrium. In Fossati's words:

The obstacle which has prevented consideration of money theory from this standpoint is the failure of utility theory to distinguish between *the desire for saving and the desire for reserve liquidity.* In the static theory, as said, every surplus of production on consumption is summed by the term 'saving'; in the dynamic theory, instead, this surplus, in monetary form, may represent not only saving but also reserve liquidity.

(1960: 258)

This criticism of quantitative theory brought Fossati closer to Keynes' thought as expressed in the *General Theory*. As he wrote in 1948,

one cannot deny, in light of Keynes' work, that dynamic problems can be summed in the word 'money'. The invalidation of Say's, in which consists the thrust of Keynes' work, is the vital expression of the monetary essence of the dynamic problem.

(Fossati 1948: 101)

The monetary character of the economic system became the new theoretical horizon within which to conjugate the static theoretical tradition with the essentially dynamic Keynesian formulation. Hence Keynesian theory became, for Fossati, a special case of a general dynamic theory still to be constructed (Fossati 1948: 105).

## From general economic equilibrium to rational economic policy

The endeavour to integrate Pareto and Keynes was the distinctive feature of the mature phase of Fossati's thought. This project was already present in Fossati's essay of 1949, *Vilfredo Pareto and J. M. Keynes: One or Two Economic Systems?*, and it was expounded in his 1955 book *Elementi di Politica Economica Razionale*.

The latter text, which consisted partly of university lectures and partly of previously published articles, had several purposes; but its central intent is to show that the Keynesian approach was a turning point in the development of economic research because it opened new horizons and resolved old problems, such as the inclusion of money in the schemes of general economic equilibrium theory. It was divided into three parts: an introductory part devoted to the customary exposition of Pareto's theory on general economic equilibrium; a central part containing a detailed presentation of the Keynesian theory, mainly as regards monetary aspects; and a third, empirical, part devoted to discussion of the problems raised by application of the econometric method. The fact that Fossati used the expression "rational economic policy" in the title is unsurprising because the book was a further attempt to demonstrate continuity with the "rational economics" espoused by the Paretians. The rational aspect of economic policy derived, as in the case of individual choices, from the fact that the state must resolve the problem of the optimal allocation of resources.

The first part is interesting because, besides the usual exposition of the blocks of equations of the general economic equilibrium, Fossati addresses the complex

## 118 *Eraldo Fossati and the role of uncertainty*

problem of aggregation, whose solution allows one to pass from the microeconomic analysis to aggregate analysis. Nevertheless, for our purposes here the most signifcant passage in the book is the second part of Chapter 6, entitled *Significato dell'opera Keynesiana alla luce della teoria dell'equilibrio economico generale*. Here Fossati addresses the problem of the relationship between the two theoretical systems. After noting that despite almost 20 years of discussion, the dispute in Italy over the value of the Keynesian theory had not yet subsided, he describes its overall argument, seeking elements of compatibility between the two systems of thought:

> For some years I have asked myself why we must continue to divide ourselves between Keynesians and anti-Keynesians, without realizing that, in truth, if we assert a contrast of this kind, we affirm only an apparent contrast, because an equilibrium with full employment cannot be opposed to an equilibrium without full employment. And this is for the obvious reason that no contrast can exist between two terms that are not comparable. Which prompts the question of whether we should not instead address the problem of how to integrate these two systems. To tell the truth, we need to recognize that if we reject the scientific contribution that Keynes has left us in order to defend the tradition, this will impoverish our thought to the same extent as would happen if we rejected the heritage that the tradition has bequeathed us.
>
> (Fossati 1955: 90)

For Fossati, the Paretian and Keynesian systems are – to use the terminology of the philosopher of science T. Kuhn – two incommensurable scientific paradigms because they are based on different presuppositions and methodologies. But, paradoxically, precisely for this reason they may be two complementary paradigms, equally essential for understanding of the workings of economic systems. The Paretian theory, because of its static nature, hypothesizes that the system is able to achieve full employment automatically thanks to the perfect flexibility of prices; by contrast, the Keynesian theory, as the first step towards a dynamic account, assumes that there can be equilibrium with unemployment, because a part of income remains idle in the form of a liquid reserve. From this point of view, if economic science is not to be deprived of the most significant contributions, it must entertain the idea "that Keynes' theory can be considered a natural integration of general equilibrium theory" (Fossati 1955: 90). On addressing the crucial issue of the saving/investment nexus, Fossati writes:

> One thus sees the full *inversion* of the Keynesian conception and the absolute absence of possible conflict between the two conceptions, the Keynesian and the traditional ones, that have provoked so many disputes on applicative grounds in these years. For if one posits the problems of the static account, the dominant role of saving ensues; if the same problems are posited by the dynamic account, there naturally ensues the dominant role of investment.
>
> (Fossati 1955: 103)

Hence also the prevalence of saving over investment, or vice versa, one of the crucial issues in the theoretical dispute, must not be considered in absolute terms, but rather evaluated according to the point of view that interests the analyst: static the former, dynamic the latter.

In his essay of 1955 Fossati further clarifies that the bridge between Pareto and Keynes lies in monetary analysis, the logical basis for a critique of the law of markets. The Mill-Say Law, which Fossati described as a cornerstone of the traditional theory, assumes an elementary economy based on barter, but it is entirely inadequate in the case of modern economies, in which money performs functions other than that of a means to facilitate transactions. This reprises the issue of the complex relationship between statics and dynamics. Fossati writes:

> The Mill-Say Law is too static to hold for dynamic analysis because it annuls the essence of money, and it is too dynamic to hold for static analysis because it wants to insert therein the monetary fact.
>
> This apparently paradoxical statement derives from the proof, which I have provided elsewhere, that it is impossible to integrate the static theory with the dynamic theory. The Mill-Say Law starts from the dynamic field, in that it assumes a monetary economy, and it finds the dynamic principle which it seeks in the static field. But it fails to realize that a static system is the limiting case of a dynamic system, and, as such, omits the monetary fact that the law claims to interpret.
>
> (Fossati 1955: 260)

Fossati's criticism of the law of markets, based on the theory of liquidity demand determined by uncertainty concerning future events, induces him to maintain that the traditional view and the Keynesian one are not opposed to each other but are instead complementary, once the roles of time and monetary variables in the workings of the economic system have been clarified. Of course, also the Keynesian edifice is not entirely satisfactory as a dynamic theory, but "it is easy to judge it more dynamic than every other system that assumes the absolute lack of the time factor in the relationships among its variables" (Fossati 1955: 90). The new perspectives furnished by Keynes fill another gap in the traditional theory: that of a consistent account of the state as an essential component of the economic system. In a dynamic context, the state can no longer be considered as merely interfering in economic life, but "recognition should be made of its activity as an integrator, as a corrective to individual action in view of the goals set by the state for the national economic system" (Fossati 1955: 115).

Finally, it should be pointed out that Fossati's adherence to Keynesian theory was not induced by theoretical considerations alone. It also stemmed from his civic commitment to resolving Italy's economic difficulties of the time. He frequently intervened in the columns of daily newspapers to debate current economic issues. This correspondence was collected in *Problemi dei Nostri Giorni* (Fossati 1959), which he considered, not a minor work, but rather

120  *Eraldo Fossati and the role of uncertainty*

an application of the theoretical principles set out in *Elementi di Politica Economica Razionale*. In this regard, it completes the said *Elementi* as a deliberate response to the current claim that theorists are unconcerned with concrete facts, which is a wholly contradictory assertion, given that theory is born from concrete facts and must be tested against them.

(1959: 5)

To be cited, for instance, is a newspaper column of April 1946, *Con Keynes o Contro Keynes*, in which he criticised C. Bresciani-Turroni's thesis that the cause of Italy's economic problems was, according to the neoclassical orthodoxy, the insufficiency of private saving. Fossati observed that this traditional idea might be valid in a context of full employment, but the Italian economic situation of the time was very distant from that ideal and it required large-scale public initiatives backed with funds from the Marshall Plan. It was not a matter of being with Keynes or against Keynes, but rather of acknowledging that, *à la* Keynes, it is not possible to deal with economic stagnation by relying on market forces alone; required instead is decisive action by the state in the field of public investments.

To summarize, Fossati's adherence to Keynesian theory developed linearly, and theoretically it marked a shift from a static vision to a dynamic one hinging on the role of money in an advanced economy. The variations of economic magnitudes over time derive from uncertainty and from expectations, assuming the concrete form of a liquid money reserve. One of the clearest manifestations of this dynamic aspect is involuntary unemployment, excluded by the traditional theory, which can only be reduced with public investment to support private enterprise.

## Criticism of Fossati's axiomatic theory of general equilibrium

Fossati returned to issues related to general economic equilibrium in the second half of the 1950s, after the Keynesian turn. His occasion to do so was provided by the translation into English, edited by his friend G. L. S. Shackle with the title *The Theory of General Static Equilibrium*, of his 1946 book *Elementi di economia razionale: La statica*. The translation contained a preface by Shackle which stated that the aim of the book was to provide English-speaking scholars with an account of the Paretian theory of general economic equilibrium.

Publication of Fossati's book did not go unnoticed, and it was promptly reviewed by L. R. Klein, a leading exponent of mathematical and econometric research. Klein expressed reservations concerning the analytical part of the book relative to general economic equilibrium. He observed:

Its blend of all the relationships into a coherent whole through the methods of the celebrated Lausanne School [...] One of the great new developments in general equilibrium theory does not find its way into the book, unfortunately. This has to do with the solvability of the system. If one expresses all the intricate interrelationships of the entire economy in the form of a set of simultaneous equations, as did Walras and Pareto in what has become one of the most significant theoretical developments in economic theory, under what conditions is it possible to determine a meaningful economic solution? Professor Fossati looks at this system from the point of view of counting equations and unknowns.

(Klein 1958: 336)

The criticism was explicit and apposite. The old method of the Lausanne school was mathematically entirely unable to deal with the new issues concerning the existence and uniqueness of equilibrium. The traditional criterion of logical consistency, which only required that the number of unknowns be equal to that of the equations, had to be replaced with more sophisticated analytical tools drawn from topology if deficiencies or ambiguities were to be prevented.

Klein's criticism elicited a brief rejoinder from Fossati, which was published just before his death, *The Criterion of Determinacy of General Equilibrium* (1962), and bearing a significant subtitle which smacked of self-defence, *Why Post-Paretian Treatments were not Discussed by E. Fossati in The Theory of General Static Equilibrium*. Fossati developed two kinds of thought in regard to the new axiomatic approach in the field of general economic equilibrium. First, he recapitulated the mathematical advances that had been achieved, above all by Wald and von Neumann, and he fully acknowledged their heuristic value. If these advances had not been mentioned in the 1957 book, this had been out of deliberate choice and certainly not due to underestimation of the results achieved.

For Fossati, it was precisely the success of the new approach in mathematical terms, based on the notion of the set and its properties (for example that of convexity), which raised new and even more fundamental problems for the relationship between mathematical analysis and economic theory. Whilst the axiomatic vision carried forward by Debreu and his supporters gave full rigour and great generality to the theory, there was nevertheless the risk that analytical tools would come entirely to prevail over economic intuition. This was the case, according Fossati, of the notion of convexity, which had been introduced with the sole purpose of guaranteeing the mathematical result, that of the uniqueness of the solution. As he put it:

Whilst it is true that the notion of convexity of the indifference surfaces is a fundamental element of mathematical economics, doubts are raised by the introduction of certain sets and certain functions; an introduction required in order to use certain general theorems which, in fact, restrict the range of the economic results. Hence a convexity of sets is required from Arrow to Debreu in their integrated model for equilibrium to exist (the convexity of the set of possible production plans implies non-increasing returns).

(Fossati 1962: 223)

## 122   *Eraldo Fossati and the role of uncertainty*

Another decisive, but debatable, hypothesis, was that when there is excess supply, the price of a resource is nil. And yet, Fossati pointed out, this does not happen in the labour market, where there is always a surplus of supply, and therefore unemployment, but wages do not for this reason diminish to zero. To reconcile the theory with reality, Arrow and Debreu assumed that the rule of free goods applied to all goods, but not to labour. According to the Paretian Fossati, in this way too many serious problems were simply resolved by hypothesis, thereby almost nullifying the model's heuristic value. He wrote:

> Here is our question: down to our own day, the attempt to find the conditions under which the systems of equations expressing the economic process would have a unique solution has followed certain lines: can these lines satisfy our sense of economic reality? The conditions we have in mind are those sufficient conditions which, not being in strictness necessary, are yet deemed indispensable for uniqueness of the solutions.
>
> To tell the truth, one would to be tempted to say no. The search for conditions which are perfect from the viewpoint of mathematical analysis, but artificial from the point of view of economic research, cannot serve the creative life of economic science.
>
> (Fossati 1962: 22)

This did not mean that mathematics should not be widely applied in economics, for only in this way could the discipline acquire scientific structure. It simply meant that mathematics also had limits in its application – like every investigative device, for that matter – which should be borne firmly in mind as its application intensified. This applied all the more in a highly abstract field of research like general economic equilibrium. Fossati warned that, in the name of a misunderstood formal rigour, economic analysis might become subordinate to mathematics, so that economics was reduced to some sort of applied mathematics with scant relevance to economic reality. Moreover, these difficulties did not concern the economist alone but also, in entirely symmetrical manner, the mathematician as well:

> This conflict between the need for mathematical analysis and the need for economic consistency tends also to arise in the mathematician, who seems increasingly concerned to seek analytical developments derived from the specific nature of economic inquiry, and thus to move beyond the phase of the pure formal virtuosity that characterizes large part of current studies.
>
> (Fossati 1957: 225)

This warning that economic theory might lose its nature as an empirical science and become a branch of mathematics was also expressed by other members of the Paretian school. In effect, apart from Amoroso's important study of 1928, the Paretian school produced no significant results in this area of inquiry – the problem of existence and uniqueness of equilibrium – which they considered more mathematical than economic in nature. On the one hand, the Paretians viewed the new techniques derived from topology as vacuous formal exercises with little to do with the interpretation of reality; on the other, these techniques were still confined to the static case and were unable to say anything about the issue that most interested the Italian scholars, that of economic dynamics. Whilst the axiomatic approach to general equilibrium theory constituted, for Fossati, a deviation from the high road of economic research, the Paretians had a very different attitude towards the empirical and statistical approach then spreading in Italy as well. In the 1950s Fossati showed great interest in econometric research, which he sought to develop in Italy, amongst other things by creating the first course of econometrics at the University of Genoa.

In Italy, it was not only the Paretians (Sensini, La Volpe, Fossati, Amoroso, Palomba) who set little importance on axiomatization *à la* Debreu. In effect, during the 1960s animated debate on the theory of general economic equilibrium was generated in Italy by publication of P. Garegnani's book, *Il capitale nelle teorie della distribuzione* (1960), with its critique of the Walrasian theory of the formation of new capital goods. The discussion that ensued (Napoleoni 1965; Graziani 1965) highlighted the difficulties of the traditional theory of general economic equilibrium in the field of dynamic analysis.

## Conclusions

In this chapter we have tried to identify the major feature of Fossati's work in the first part of his intellectual career during the 1930s. The focus has been on pure economics, even though Fossati was also very interested in the institutional aspects of economy. He was a convinced follower of Pareto and was, indeed, quite certain that the model of general equilibrium was the main conquest of the entire history of economic thought. However, Fossati was not dogmatic in his adoption of neoclassical views. He stressed the impossibility of mechanically applying economic theories to reality, which is, in itself, historical and dynamic. What is more, even though he believed that the static part of economic theory was now established, he tried to build the other part which, in his view, was very much more important, namely dynamics. He explained that in constructing the theory of dynamics it was necessary to abandon the typical logic of choice, in favor of a method of analysis which assigned a central role to true uncertainty following the Austrian tradition. Fossati argued that it is inappropriate to analyse uncertainty in terms of probabilities, since the distinguishing feature of uncertainty, as opposed to risk, is that we have no information on which to base such calculations. As a mathematical economist he sought to construct a formal model but this attempt was not successful. The mathematical apparatus was modest, based on the traditional differential calculus together with a loss function assumed *ad hoc.* It is worth noting that the undoubtedly more important contribution of Shackle also suffered the same fate. In the 1950s Shackle's decision theory was mostly discussed with reference to its technical content, but in the 1960s his influence diminished considerably and his readers are now to be found

124  *Eraldo Fossati and the role of uncertainty*

among economists working on heterodox traditions rather than among mainstream economists. The formalization of the Austrian approach to uncertainty remains an open question.

In the period following the Second World War Fossati's inquiry took a very different path. On the one hand, he stressed the need to strengthen the international scope of Italian economists by founding a new journal, *Metroeconomica*. From its inception *Metroeconomica* provided an international forum for the dissemination of new developments in economic theory which attracted leading economists. On the other hand, in contrast with the majority of Italian economists, Fossati found a new basis for framing dynamic analysis in Keynes' *General Theory*. He participated in the small group of Italian economists who recognized the relevance, not only in analytical terms, of the Keynesian revolution. Although the Paretian equilibrium was a major conquest at the theoretical level, the economic reality facing the economist was nevertheless very far from these ideal conditions and had to be analysed with instruments which were perhaps less sophisticated but more useful in explaining economic phenomena. There is no doubt that Fossati contributed significantly to the renewal of economic inquiry in Italy, supporting the passage from a static and abstract vision to a dynamic and empirical one.

## Notes

1  A list of Fossati's main publications is provided by Shackle in the profile written for *Econometrica* (1965).
2  For an overview of the problematic reception of Keynes' *General Theory* in Italy see Bini and Magliulo (1999) and Magliulo (2003).

# 7 Dynamic equilibrium and the economic cycle

## Introduction

Economic cycle theory has constituted one of the most important research fields in the period between the two World Wars. Nearly all the economists of that period contributed to the discussion on the causes and the characteristics of economic cycles (Kyun 1988). They advocated for the need both to find an answer to the consequences of the *Great Depression* of 1929, as well as to construct a theory of economic dynamics that would be as rigorous and complete as static theory. In a long and detailed review that appeared in *Econometrica* in 1935, titled "Annual Survey: Suggestions on Quantitative Business Cycle Theory," J. Tinbergen found a distinction between non-mathematical theories of the business cycle, primarily represented by the positions of Hayek and Keynes, and theories of a mathematical character that in the early 1930s had received a big boost from a small group of mathematical economists, such as Frisch, Evans, Roos, Kalecki and Tinbergen himself, to name a few. Within the broad debate on the causes of the economic cycle these economists intended to develop mathematical models that were able to represent the cyclical trend of macroeconomic variables through the introduction of temporal delays, differential equations or integral equations (Boumans 2005). The most important contributions in this direction were those by Frisch (1933, 1936) and Tinbergen (1933, 1934, 1935). Frisch's research was designed to transform economic dynamics into a scientific discipline through the extensive application of statistical methods, as demonstrated by the Yale lectures of September 1930 (Bjerkholt and Qin 2011). In Tinbergen, the empirical element is even more dominant. His research in the 1930s on economic dynamics was focused on two aspects: the development of adequate analytical models and their empirical verification through statistical analysis (Weintraub 1991).

Within this vast scope of research on constructing economic dynamics it is possible to identify one original direction started in the 1920s by G. Evans and his student Roos. This research was taken up again and developed in the next decade in Italy by Paretian economists. As noted by R. Dimand (1988) in a review of the mathematical theories on the economic cycle between the two World Wars, it is possible to identify an Italian element in the international

126 *Dynamic equilibrium and the economic cycle*

debate, composed primarily of contributions from Amoroso (1932, 1935, 1940), Vinci (1934, 1937), Bordin (1935) and Palomba (1939). In the 1930s these leaders of the Italian Pareto school sought to develop a non-monetary theory of the economic cycle that was highly analytical in style, in keeping with their view of general economic equilibrium. This current also had some international visibility as there were some contributions (Vinci 1934; Amoroso 1935, 1940) that were published in the newly founded *Econometrica*, the journal of the *Econometric Society* and some of the best-known Italian economists contributed to its creation. These works have so far not received the attention they probably deserved, as a great deal of Italian economic thinking between the two World Wars was wrongly assimilated to confusing corporatism (Faucci 1990). In fact we will see how it is possible to observe in the writings of the Italian mathematical economists of that period some important analytical contributions that were on the frontline of international research.

The purpose of this chapter is two-fold. First, it is starting to fill a historic gap by systematically presenting the research which the Pareto school continued in the field of the mathematical theory of the economic cycle, to highlight the vitality of Italian economic research in the international context. Second, retrospectively analysing what can be defined as the first formulation of a real theory of the economic cycle can be useful to understand the theoretical roots of subsequent developments of economic cycle theory in this direction. In particular, to understand the fact that to integrate the theory of the cycle with the theory of economic equilibrium, the public had to wait until the 1980s with the research of Lucas and other exponents of the real business cycle theory.

## Economic cycle theory in the Italian context: a comprehensive glance

With the crisis of 1929 the debate in Italy among economists was also focusing on economic cycle theory. The great interest of scholars in the cyclical phenomenon, and in particular in crises, depended not only on the size of the cycle itself but also on the difference between the data and the restrictions of traditional models, according to which a spontaneous tendency to equilibrium prevailed in the economic system. Thus was born the need to revisit the existing economic theory and there were several attempts to give a more comprehensive explanation of the phenomena taking place in the economic systems of the time: from the contributions more clearly attributed to neo-classical tradition, which found their ultimate expression in the Austrian school, to the works that were further away from tradition, which slowly paved the road, even in Italy, for the innovative Keynesian movement.

The debate over the cycle in the 1920s and 1930s included a wide variety of positions in the field. However, it is well known that the most important contributions came from Hayek and Keynes. The comparison of the Austrian school and the Keynesian approach broadly characterized the debate in those years. These two approaches develop the Wicksellian model starting from very different methodological assumptions and reaching opposite conclusions. The Austrian school applied the postulates of the neoclassical model (the merchandise-like nature of currency, the logical precedence of savings on investments) to the theory of the cycles, integrating the model with the theory of the flexible multiplier of bank deposits, and with the analysis of the relationship between natural interest rate and monetary interest rate proposed by Wicksell. In other words, it was proposed that the banking system not act like a financial intermediary in the strictest sense, but rather multiply banking deposits and, therefore, result in an increase in the amount of money in circulation, up to the limit imposed by the mandatory reserve ratio. And it is precisely to the phenomenon of the multiplication of bank deposits, which is considered an abnormal expansion of credit by the banks, that the Austrian school attributed the cause of the cycle. According to the Austrian school, banks and currency can therefore be considered the origin of the pathological dynamics of the capitalist economy.

The Keynesian approach is completely different. Based on the analysis conducted by Keynes in his *Treatise* (1930) the amount of currency in circulation would be *demand-driven*: the demand of credit determines the credit given and the Central Bank assumes a role as a lender of last resort. According to this viewpoint, the neoclassical idea, that deposits make loans, is flipped on its head, stating in fact the opposite: it is loans that generate deposits. From this point of view there cannot be a credit expansion that is considered excessive. The cycle is triggered not by monetary variables, but the movement of real variables, by an internal not external shock to the system: the disparity between the distribution of production supply in consumer goods and those of investment and the allocation of monetary income in consumption and savings. This social conflict between the categories of consumers and producers may occur due to, for example, business owners incorrectly estimating the future composition of the demand, or to changes in taste or propensity to consumption/consumer savings, not properly planned and anticipated by the producers.

The Austrian approach was shared in Italy by the majority of economists for several reasons, primarily their neoclassical lineage. In addition, at that time knowledge of German and Germanic literature was somewhat widespread, which greatly contributed to the spread of Austrian ideas. Among the supporters of the Austrian school one of the most authoritative voices was Gustavo Del Vecchio. In his writings he asserts, in the wake of the Austrian school of thought, that banks can act both as pure financial intermediaries as well as by multiplying deposits. In the first case, they merely serve to ensure equality between the deposits (savings) collected and credits (loans) granted. In the latter case, the loans may exceed the savings, resulting in an excess of money in circulation, which triggers the ascending phase of the cycle. He accepts the idea of the multiplier of bank deposits and Wicksellian circuit theory. In line with the Austrian approach, with regard to the Wiksellian theory, he welcomes the idea of the circuit and the distinction between the two interest rates, but maintains, in line with the neoclassical approach, the idea of bank-created currency: such currency is not to be considered a bank liability. In addition to Del Vecchio, other proponents of the

## 128 Dynamic equilibrium and the economic cycle

Austrian school in Italy were certainly Einaudi, who attempted to explain the depression of the 1930s in a Hayekian way, and Papi, Vito, Gangemi and Mortara.

Among those who had a critical position towards the Austrian approach were primarily Costantino Bresciani Turroni and Marco Fanno. For the former, the causes that trigger the cycle are to be found in the technical innovations that improve production processes and encourage the creation of new firms. It is under the pressure of these innovations that the banking system, pressed by a strong demand for loans, eventually expands credit. Therefore the currency plays an important though not decisive role in the occurrence of the economic cycle. Also, the decisions of savings and investment are taken from different subjects and the variations of savings, rather than depending on the interest rate, are dependent on the income.

Along with Bresciani Turroni there were other contributions critical of the Austrian approach that suggested new interpretations of overinvestment and that opened the way for theories of underinvestment. Here, Fanno's contributions were a key factor. The imbalance that characterizes the economic cycle according to Fanno is not caused by the action of the banking system, which has the possibility, at least in theory, to expand credit limitlessly, but rather from a discrepancy between the decisions of firms and households and the production decisions and income use decisions, in the absence of a spontaneous market balancing mechanism. Marco Fanno highlights the possibility that the cycle originates in the errors of business owners, who fail, given the existence of fiction lags, to correctly predict qualitative changes in demand or changes in the propensity to consume. Variations of the present and expected profits, are thus considered the prime cause of the cycle. The balance between savings and investments is thereby altered very easily because of a number of factors. Fanno identifies several different ones, both internal and external to the economy, from a change in the propensity to consume or household savings, to the introduction of innovations to the productive system, from the outbreak of wars to variations in harvests. Among these Fanno focuses in particular on the imbalance resulting from an increase in the share of income that families devote to savings. The imbalance between savings and investment can result not merely in a fluctuation from the line of secular expansion, but in a real cyclical phenomenon, referring in particular to the context of a progressive economy.

The factors most responsible for economic fluctuations are, therefore, according to the non-Austrian position, internal to the economic system, such as variations in the propensity to consumption, the production of new goods, or early replacement of the worn-out ones. These are the main causes of the cycle, which are then enhanced, according to Fanno, by the action of the multiplier and the different lags. Especially important are errors of time by the producers who fail to anticipate – given the amount of time that elapses between the moment when the decision is made of how much and what to produce and the moment when the final product is available – the upcoming changes in tastes or consumer preferences. The writings first of de Viti de Marco, and later on of Fanno and Bresciani

*Dynamic equilibrium and the economic cycle* 129

Turroni move toward what Keynes will define as the monetary theory of production. In fact, the theory of the bank as the creator of currency, the idea that loans precede deposits, the socio-historical method of analysis, as well as the triangular structure of the agents are much more consistent with the Keynesian approach than with the neoclassical approach. In the following paragraphs we will see the cycle theory of the Paretians that leaned more toward Keynes than toward Hayek.

## The analytical core of the Paretians' theory

The authors that we will consider wanted primarily to provide a mathematical theory of the economic cycle. The road was opened by three key figures from Harvard barometer that had highlighted how some economic quantities follow an oscillatory trend, with phases of expansion followed by phases of contraction. It was now necessary to identify the underlying analytical mechanism, to use the expression of Tinbergen (Tinbergen 1935), i.e. the set of quantitative relationships between variables that could explain these movements of economic quantities.

The search for an adequate analytical model would be an essential element in the mathematical theories of the economic cycle in the 1930s. It was a process that proceeded by trial and error (Boumans 2005: 42), starting with the simple introduction of temporal delays between variables by Aftalion (1927). Then it went on to increasingly complex analytic forms that contained integral or differential expressions (Tinbergen 1933). It was discovered this way that there was a multitude of mathematical models potentially able to reproduce the typical mechanisms of the economic cycle.

What was the analytical core of the economic cycle theory developed by Amoroso and other Paretians in the 1930s? The analytical framework used by this group of economists was that of harmonic oscillations. It is interesting to note how this analytical characterization was one of the main directions of research internationally as well. At the annual meeting of the *Econometric Society* held in Leiden (the Netherlands) in 1933 Tinbergen addressed the issue of whether the theory of harmonic oscillations could be useful in the study of the economic cycle (Marshack 1934). For these mathematician-economists, including Amoroso, who came from the field of physics, it was rather natural to arrive at the theory of harmonic oscillations, also because of the close similarity between the cyclical movement of the economic variables and the movement of the simple pendulum. The comparison of the economic cycle with the movement of the simple pendulum is a heuristic element that is often repeated in the literature on the economic cycle of the 1930s (for example in Frisch 1933), confirming the importance of mechanical analogies in economics. Until the formalist shift in the 1950s, it had a central role in economic theory both in terms of the similarity of the mathematical tools used and in the similarity of the results obtained (Grattan-Guiness 2010: 538).

The core of the Paretians' analytical model consisted of a linear differential equation of the second order with constant coefficients, of the generic type,

$$a\ddot{y}(t) + by(t) = 0 \qquad\qquad [1]$$

## 130 *Dynamic equilibrium and the economic cycle*

The general integral of the equation [1] is of the periodic type and leads to an oscillating motion of the quantity itself with respect to time, even if this motion is not generated by a periodic cause. [4] is a well-known equation in physics as it represents the equation of a simple pendulum. It is now clear why it could be one of the avenues explored in the 1930s to construct the economic cycle theory. First of all, the variables of interest were found to have an oscillatory character, as required by the economic cycle theory. The mathematician-economists in those years tried to emphasize the empirical character of the solutions found, trying to derive the length and breadth of the cycle phase directly from the preliminary study of the time series. Second, [4] was entirely consistent with an internal economic cycle theory. Once the economic system had been set in motion, for example by technical progress or changes in consumer preferences, it tended to follow a cyclical trajectory determined by economic forces that acted automatically. Third, the solution found explicitly depended on time, and from an economic point of view, this meant that the dynamic was a phenomenon of equilibrium, in the sense given to this term by the literature of the 1930s. Therefore even the economic cycle could be considered a form of dynamic equilibrium, a situation in which the quantities changed slowly over time according to a specific law (Masci 1934b).

The [1] equation was not the only mathematical model available to generate oscillations. An isolated attempt to use a different model, namely that of the Lotka-Volterra equations, will be proposed by Palomba in 1939 in his *Introduzione all'economia dinamica*, about the relationship between spending on consumption and spending on capital goods (Gandolfo 2008). This remarkable analytic starting point will not be further developed within the Pareto environment, and after the war, Palomba himself chose to follow the theoretical approach of his teacher Amoroso (such as *Fisica economica*, 1959).

## Amoroso's model of 1932

Amoroso, as we have seen, began to deal with dynamics in a strict sense towards the end of the 1920s with the 1929 article, "Differential equations of economic dynamics," about the dynamic determination of the demand and supply curves. His main purpose in this article was to extend Evans' analysis of the case of the monopoly to the more general one of market equilibrium. Three years later, a group of studies of dynamics were collected and systematized in the essay *Contributo alla teoria matematica della dinamica economica* (1932), which was one of four contributions published in the *Fifth Volume of the New Series of Economists* (1932) dedicated to economic dynamics. The other three contributions comprised one written by Pantaleoni on the trade union, the volume on the theory of economic development by Schumpeter, and an essay on the theory of costs by Clark, also containing the writings of the leading authors in Italy in the field of dynamic analysis. Amoroso offered a very limited mathematical contribution to these vast theories.

Amoroso develops his mathematical theory of cyclic movement taking into account an economy divided into two sectors: a productive sector and a commercial sector. There are also two variables to determine: the trend of the general level of

*Dynamic equilibrium and the economic cycle* 131

prices and that of the volume of production. Following the path opened by Evans and Roos, Amoroso makes the model dynamic by explicitly introducing the changes in prices and production. In analytical terms, the equations to consider become first order differential equations with constant coefficients. The first equation establishes a direct relationship between industrial production $Q$ and the variation of the level of prices ($\dot{P}$). This equation is called by Amoroso the *indus- try equation*. In symbols,

$$Q(t+\omega_1) = a + m^2 \dot{P}(t) \qquad [2]$$

The equation [2] has two characteristic elements. The first is that the production is not dependent on the absolute level of prices but on its variation. So production is not guided by the current level of prices but by the forecast of its variation. In Amoroso's case, these are expectations that are always fulfilled, which we might call, in current terms , rational expectations. Second, although it is minor, the reaction of production occurs with a certain lag, represented by the parameter $\omega_1$, and which is comparable to the phase delay in harmonic motion.

The second equation of the model is introduced directly and justified by Amoroso based on common sense observations. This equation, which Amoroso calls the *equation of business*, connects the price level and the expected produc- tion variation. This time there is a reverse reaction: commercial speculation anticipates the fact that an increase in supply will lead to a decrease in the level of prices, and this has a stabilizing effect on the price itself. In symbols,

$$P(t) = b - n^2 \dot{Q}(t+\omega_2) \qquad [3]$$

Also in equation [3] the relationship between the two variables, the variation of production and the level of prices, is not instantaneous but takes place with a lag as prices take into account, in advance, the fluctuations of production. Amoroso defines [2] as the dynamic equation of supply and [3] as the dynamic equation of demand. If the temporal phase shift in the two equations is the same, which Amoroso calculates as seven months, the system is reduced to a single second order differential equation,

$$\ddot{P} + \lambda^2 P = \lambda^2 b \qquad [4]$$

with $\lambda = 1/mn$. Notice how this last equation fully satisfies the criterion that will be formulated by Frisch at this time according to which a relationship becomes dynamic when it contains the variable and its first derivative, i.e. the direction of the variation. In Amoroso's case, what he finds is the second derivative because he wants to give the variables an oscillatory pattern that is possible only by considering difference equations or differential equations of the second order.

The general integral of [4] in price levels is as follows,

$$P(t) = A \cos (\lambda t) + B \sin (\lambda t) + b \qquad [5]$$

## 132  *Dynamic equilibrium and the economic cycle*

The equation [5] represents the correct result, that is a periodic function that describes the cyclical path of prices as a function of time. An analogous equation also applies to the production volume index. As one can see, it is not the nature of the cause, but the shape of the solution that generates the cyclical nature of the effects. Because one of the two correlations between the two sectors is direct while the other is inverse, Amoroso will talk about a principle of action and reaction, similar to the third law of Newtonian mechanics, governing cyclical dynamics as a whole. In his words: "in short, the economic movement is cyclical because there is, overall, a principle similar to what in mechanics is called the principle of action and reaction" (Amoroso 1932: 433). With this model, Amoroso believes to have generalized the cyclical model of Roos of 1930 which was limited to the case of a single good, highlighting its further potential. Amoroso, like Pareto, also denies that the economic cycle is attributed to monetary causes. He observes: "These opposing trends cause price fluctuations which cannot be traced to monetary factors. No currency corrections, no changing the price of gold, no currency manipulations could ever eliminate them" (Amoroso 1932: 433).

Amoroso's model is undoubtedly an ingenious analytic construction certainly in line with the most advanced analytical standards offered by mathematical economists of the early 1930s. Beyond the strictly mechanistic interpretation proposed by Amoroso, the most interesting element is the introduction of expectations, or speculative intent to use the term used then, in the most basic form of the first derivative of a variable. It is no coincidence that Amoroso also tied cyclic dynamics to expectations. This was a very common approach and will be used again by other Italian economists, although in another form, such as Fanno (1931) and Papi (1934a). The importance of expectations for the construction of economic dynamics will be most clear at the end of the decade in Hicks's definition of temporary equilibrium in *Value and Capital* of 1939.

Beyond its analytic success, Amoroso's model introduces the problematic aspect of how expectations are formed. They are simply taken as exogenous trends without being derived from a rigorous theory of rational behaviour. The issue of the formation of expectations, a theme that will be central to the post-war macroeconomic debate, is completely ignored in Amoroso's model. This methodological limitation can be traced back to the approach that mathematical economists of this period took toward economic dynamics. Their primary research purpose was to offer an analytic representation of cyclic phenomena, without any concern for their rigorous theoretical foundation. We could say that if the insertion of expectations is a strong point of the model, its naive but useful way of helping construct the analytical model is a fundamental limitation. In a sense, the reasons for the mathematical success of the model opened the gate to critical observations in economic intuition.

We saw how Amoroso excluded the effect of monetary factors. Nevertheless, the role of money and monetary policy was too important to be ignored, and indeed was one of the central points in the debate over the economic cycle of the early 1930s, and it is in this research direction that Amoroso will also move. In

*Dynamic equilibrium and the economic cycle* 133

fact, the following year he would dedicate a significant part of his university course to monetary theory and an examination of the main propositions contained in Keynes' *Treatise* (1930). These lectures contain an original attempt, barely outlined, to make Keynes' equations dynamic. This would have passed completely unnoticed if his pupil, Felice Vinci, had not added it with a slight modification in an article published in *Econometrica* in 1934 titled "Significant Developments in Business Cycles." For this reason, we can speak of a Vinci-Amoroso model.

## The Vinci-Amoroso model of 1934

Felice Vinci (1890–1962), statistician and economist, took part in the debate on the mathematical theory of the economic cycle with an article in 1934 which in part referenced a long piece that was already published in the *Italian Journal of Statistics*, which he founded. The article was then referred to again the next year in Tinbergen's review published in *Econometrica*, an essay which tried to take stock of the main mathematical contributions in the field of economic cycle theory. Vinci's article constituted one of the few attempts at the international level to extend the equations in Keynes' *Treatise* in a dynamic way through appropriate formalization. The article is divided into three parts. In the first, Vinci presents a mathematical model for the determination of stock prices.In the middle section, he takes part in the Cambridge school discussion about the currency equation, and he proposes a generalization. This element is interesting because it shows us the international opening experienced by the Italian economists and in particular the importance given to the discussion of Keynes' monetary theory even in Italy. Only in the final section does Vinci attempt to dynamize Keynes' equations. In essence Vinci uses a model discussed by Amoroso in his university lessons in 1933, a model that went unnoticed as it was only published in the form of materials for a university class (Amoroso 1933).

The underlying framework of the Amoroso-Vinci model is the same found in Keynes' *Treatise* in which the economy was divided in two sectors: one produces consumer goods and the other investment goods. Another distinction, used before by Amoroso, is between the industrial system and the commercial one. The industrial system is defined by four quantities: the volume of investment goods, the volume of consumer goods, the total production volume, and the profit volume. The commercial system is characterized by four other quantities, the price of consumer goods and investment goods, the proportion of income saved and the proportion invested. These eight variables are defined in the same exact terms proposed by Keynes in his *Treatise*.

For each of these quantities, Vinci makes an equation to highlight the links that exist among them. They are differential equations with delayed or anticipated variables, so the analytical framework is the same as Amoroso's from 1932, expanded and enriched by including the Keynesian perspective. Though it is beyond our scope to analyse the model in detail (Palomba 1959: 410–418), we do wish to highlight its essential aspects, so we will limit our consideration to the

## 134 *Dynamic equilibrium and the economic cycle*

first two equations of the industrial system that deal with consumer spending and investment spending.

$$C(t+\omega) = a_1 + m_1 \dot{\Pi}(t) + n_1 [(\dot{Y}(t) - \dot{S}(t)] \tag{6}$$

$$I(t+\omega) = a_2 + m_2 \dot{\Pi}(t) + n_2 \dot{D}(t) \tag{7}$$

Equation [6] references Keynes' first equation and interprets it in differential terms. The level of consumption increases, with a lag, when the profit tends to increase and the variation of income is higher than that of savings. Equation [7] is related to the second equation of the *Treatise*, so the production of new investments goods tends to grow along with the variation of profits and the rise in savings invested, and is thus used for the production of instrumental goods. These two equations clearly highlight how the dynamic key of the model consists, as Keynes indicated, in the role exercised by profits, and in the relationship between investments and savings. The dynamic system is completed by six more equations which define the actions and reactions of the remaining variables, some direct and others inverse.

Because of the high number of equations and variables in the system, Vinci gives up on the ambitious project of explicitly determining the set of solutions and analysing their characteristics. Vinci did understand, as Amoroso had found out the year before, that in general the system was not stable because there were more direct relationships than inverse ones. Left on its own, the system did not tend toward a stationary state of equilibrium. It still remained to be determined whether the instability could be corrected through action from banks and monetary policy.

Therefore, Vinci's model, despite illuminating some crucial causal relationships, such as the role of profit in macroeconomic dynamics, was sorely lacking on the mathematical level. It was this lack of analytical rigour that Tinbergen criticized the following year. But Vinci himself pointed out in the article that what interested him was not so much mathematical perfection but rather richness on an interpretive level. In his eyes, this model was to be considered the first step towards a more detailed and articulated understanding of cyclical dynamics. In his words: "In concluding I would like to say that in my opinion it is only by basing the analysis on systems of dynamic equations such as (I)–(VIII), or similar equations, that a really scientific theory of business cycles can be developed" (Vinci 1934: 176).

In any case, neither Amoroso nor Vinci returned to this draft of a Keynesian dynamic model in the following years in order to correct its analytical defects. Both followed a different route that led to a drastic reduction in the number of variables considered. It became clear that even though increasing the number of factors considered could in theory make the analytical framework more flexible and effective on the interpretive level, in reality the mathematical difficulties were too hard to overcome. As we shall see in the next paragraph, the next year Amoroso arrived at a new economic cycle model, the definitive one.

Vinci dedicated himself to his statistical studies and only returned to the issue of formulating an economic cycle model only once, in an article entitled "Recent Tendencies of Economic Studies" in 1937. Meanwhile the international situation of Italy had deteriorated because of international political tensions, and Vinci could not participate in the *Cowles Commission* seminar to which he had been invited in 1937. Vinci's article is interesting because it shows how the publication in 1936 of the *General Theory* became the new point of reference for reflection on the economic cycle also in the Italian context.

In 1937 Vinci returned to the Keynesian concept of the two sectors but this time the number of functional relations and variables is drastically reduced and also the interpretation goes back to a more traditional one, abandoning the role of profits and imbalances between savings and investment. The model consists of three equations that are as follows,

$$I(t) = aC(t) + b\dot{C}(t) \tag{8}$$

$$C(t) = cP(t-\theta) + d\dot{P}(t-\theta) \tag{9}$$

$$\dot{P}(t-\theta) = hC(t) + kI(t) \tag{10}$$

As is evident, in the three equations there is no longer any trace of the suggestions of the *Treatise*, in particular the role of profit. Especially interesting is the equation [8] that shows the direct influence of *General Theory* (1936). In fact, this can be considered a dynamic form of the accelerator principle: spending on investment is put in relation to the level of consumption and its dynamics.

However, instead of taking the model to its Keynesian conclusion, considering income as the crucial variable, as in the later version of Hicks (1950) for example, Vinci proceeds to a neoclassical conclusion by making the level of consumption depend on prices, in this case, delayed, and on their variation [9]. Finally we have the equation [10], which we can call feedback, as Amoroso does, according to which the change in the general price index depends on the expectations of spending on consumption and spending on investment. Together, the three equations give rise to a linear differential equation of the second order, whose complex solutions will determine the cyclical path of prices of consumer goods. The 1937 model can be thought of as a hybrid model that shows the attempt to integrate, in the typically Italian approach with derivatives and delays, the new suggestions coming from the *General Theory* published only the previous year. This theoretical compromise is reinforced by the fact that the accelerator principle is placed in relation to the dynamics of prices, confirming in this way the neoclassical approach of these authors, who could not abandon the idea of the relevance of the role of prices, even at the macroeconomic level. Later on Vinci will abandon any attempt to reach a formalization of the economic cycle and in the final phase of his career will focus mostly on the theoretical foundations of welfare economics of (Vinci 1953).

## 136 *Dynamic equilibrium and the economic cycle*

### Amoroso's second model of 1935

One of the main conclusions Amoroso reached in the first economic cycle model of 1932 was the fact that currency did not have an essential role in the determination of its causes. In his university lectures of 1933 he had hypothesized a possible controlling function by the banking system, following Keynes' *Treatise*. In 1935 Amoroso reached the definitive version of his mathematical theory of the economic cycle, proposed in the article published in *Econometrica* titled "The dynamics of circulation." Meanwhile, he had taken steps toward becoming a corporatist economist and we find traces of that in this article. For Amoroso, the real achievement of the corporatist economy was precisely in its new developments in the field of economic dynamics, beginning with those on the economic cycle.

In the model of 1935, the cyclical dynamics of the economy also stem from the reciprocal relations between the various sectors of the economic system. It is therefore a multi-sector model. The main development is that beside the industrial and commercial sectors we now find a third sector, banking. As a result, the new model is composed of three equations, one for each sector, and three variables, the volume of production, the level of prices and finally the interest rate. The analytical approach is the one from 1932 whereby each quantity also depends on the variation of the other two. To make the system more complete and to overcome the mathematical difficulties from the 1933 lectures, Amoroso speculates that each equation contains three endogenous variables: the reaction of each variable to itself, which is always in the opposite direction as a force of resistance that opposes change, and then a feedback effect of the other two variables, which sometimes moves in the same direction and sometimes in the opposite direction. With these simplifying hypotheses Amoroso obtains a dynamic system with three equations in three unknowns, which can be solved explicitly. Let us consider the three equations separately.

The first equation is the *industry equation* that now becomes the following,

$$T(t) = a_{11}\dot{P}(t - \omega_3) - a_{12}\dot{r}(t - \omega_2) - a_{13}\dot{T}(t) \tag{11}$$

where the volume of production is influenced positively by the anticipated variations of the prices and negatively by variation of the interest rate. Rising prices cause a higher level of future production, while an increase of the interest rate discourages it. The last term of the equation represents the fact that moment to moment each quantity is influenced by its own trend in an inverse way, the reaction of inertia, in Amoroso's language.

The second equation, the *business equation*, becomes the following,

$$P(t) = -a_{21}\dot{P}(t) - a_{22}\dot{r}(t + \omega_1) - a_{23}\dot{T}(t + \omega_3) \tag{12}$$

Equation [12] expresses for Amoroso the dynamic law of demand and supply, that is, as a differential equation that connects prices, the amounts and their

*Dynamic equilibrium and the economic cycle* 137

derivatives. On the one hand, the market tends to determine prices in relation to the expected production trend in the opposite direction to the industrial system. On the other hand, the interest rate also exerts a negative influence on the basis of the principle of capitalization of revenue whereby the value of capital goods (prices of real estate or the course of actions and obligations) is levelled off on the value of the corresponding revenue, capitalized at market interest rate which is predicted for the near future.

Finally there is the new equation that represents the dynamic contribution of the banking sector,

$$r(t) = a_{31}\dot{P}(t - \omega_3) - a_{32}\dot{r}(t) + a_{33}\dot{T}(t + \omega_2) \qquad [13]$$

and thus the interest rate tends to move in the same direction as the expected production and depends negatively on past price variation. For Amoroso the two trends are convergent in the sense that through them the banking system slows down the momentum of the market when it is too strong and stimulates it when it manifests an excessive downward trend. This is one of the essential aspects of interest rate control that is the normal tool through which the banking system tends to affect the economic trend.

The movements of the three sectors are therefore mutually determined in a series of actions and reactions described by the equations of the model. Integrating the system of equations, Amoroso, for a particular combination of parameters, finds a real root and two complex roots such that each of the three variables takes the following expression:

$$Ae^{rt} + B\exp(st)\cos\left[\frac{2\pi t}{\sigma} + h\right] \qquad [14]$$

where various constants depend on combinations of the parameters of the original system. According to [14] the movement of three indices is then characterized by two elements: a cyclical component, as in the model of 1932, and a second component that is evolutive or long term. Amoroso does not stop to further examine this point, which he considers more of a mathematical result derived from the nature of the model than an economic result to examine. The economic system, because of the actions and reactions among the three sectors, moves with a wave-like pattern but along a path which evolves over time. And this idea that there is a strong connection between economic cycle theory and growth theory is a typical feature of Italian authors that we find, for example, even in Fanno (1947).

The 1935 model represented the most complete effort in the context of the Pareto tradition to arrive at a mathematical theory of the economic cycle that was consistent with the approach of general economic equilibrium and captured its general characteristics. Its importance was reaffirmed by Arrigo Bordin who placed it at the centre of his detailed 1935 review of this model, "The Significance of Several Modern Theories on Economic Dynamics," where he critically reviewed the main international contributions, from those farthest away by Evans

## 138 *Dynamic equilibrium and the economic cycle*

and Roos, to those that were closest by Frisch, Kalecki and Tinbergen, testifying to the fact that international literature was very well known in the Italian context as well.

If we now compare the 1935 model to the one from three years before, we can see that despite the broadening of perspective, the original limitations were not overcome, and in fact others were added. From an analytic viewpoint, there was now a new problem due to the fact that the roots of the equation system assumed values only desired for a very particular combination, and thus *ad hoc*, of the original parameters. Otherwise, the system was not stable and indeed tended to have increasingly large fluctuations over time (Palomba 1959). Amoroso does not discuss in detail this aspect of the stability conditions of the model, although it is crucial, and he simply points out that it is a matter to be resolved by empirical means. This will not be resolved either by Amoroso or by his pupils, and remains an open question.

Second, adding a new relationship of interdependence, relating to banking, made all the more acute the problem of the simplistic relative assumption concerning the formation of expectations. As Bordin observes in his discussion of Amoroso's model, the coincidence between expectations and their fulfillment was, from the viewpoint of economic theory, the most problematic aspect of Amoroso's ingenious construction. In his words:

> On the other hand one wonders if the laws of dynamics were known for their future development, would they remain as such, or would they be modified because their knowledge impacts the activities of men. It is a fact that the supposed psychological uniformities that they contain are affected by at least partial ignorance of those laws; uniformities which would necessarily be altered by the certainty of an exact forecast and, in this sense, reveal their completely contingent nature.
>
> (Bordin 1935: 130)

In other words, Bordin seems to anticipate the criticism that will be carried out in the 1970s by followers of the school of rational expectations: when making choices, the individual takes into account all the information available from the model and thus also future expectations. But if this happens no dynamics are possible since the choices are immediately advanced in the present.

In subsequent years Amoroso would abandon his studies on the mathematical theory of the economic cycle and return to his ambitious project of developing a dynamic theory of general economic equilibrium. This project would be accomplished in *Meccanica Economica*, which collected the lectures from Rome in 1940–1941 at the Regio Istituto di Alta Matematica di Roma.

## The role of investment and the Palomba model of 1939

The publication of *General Theory* (1936), which even contained a chapter dedicated to the economic cycle, would overshadow the previous *Treatise* even in the

*Dynamic equilibrium and the economic cycle* 139

Italian context. We have already seen this change of perspective in Vinci's 1937 model, where besides its bisectoral structure, which was preserved, there was a new element which was the Keynesian accelerator principle. A second attempt to integrate elements of *General Theory* in a Paretian dynamic model will be undertaken by Amoroso's main student, Giuseppe Palomba. In 1939 Palomba published a very comprehensive volume from an analytical standpoint, *Introduzione allo studio della dinamica economica*, which can be considered the last major contribution in the Pareto tradition to the mathematical theory of the economic cycle.

Regarding aspects of the economic cycle, the innovation of Palomba's model is the fact that he refers directly to *General Theory* and in particular to Keynes' investment theory (Palomba 1939: 100). In fact, Palomba's perspective was very broad as he aimed to develop a probabilistic concept of economic development under which the economic system as a whole had a wave-like and non-stationary structure. To prove this he introduced, for the first time in economics, the Lotka–Volterra equations in relation to the choice between investment expenditures and expenditures for consumer goods.

Capitalist development is characterized, according to Palomba, by an increase in the degree of complexity of the economic system due to the continuous increase of the variety of investment goods. There is here an echo of Hayek's position in the sense that the duration of the production cycle tends to increase in the course of economic development. And on this point he adds his reference to the theses of *General Theory*. Although spending on investments depends on many factors, including psychological and non-economic ones, Palomba explicitly incorporates Keynes' idea that the interest rate is the key variable to watch, given the marginal efficiency of capital. Just as his teacher, Amoroso, had sought to dynamize the equations of the *Treatise*, Palomba aims to give a dynamic aspect to the relationship between interest rate and investment spending, using differential equations with delayed variables. The model is particularly simple in that there are only two equations and two unknowns. The first equation is the following,

$$I(t+\omega) = m_1 - a_1 I(t+\omega) - b_1 \dot{r}(t) \tag{15}$$

Based on [15] the expected production of investment goods depends on the variation of the interest rate in the previous period (the mechanical reaction) and on variable itself (the reaction of inertia). With the equation [15] Palomba intended to dynamize the Keynesian investment function. The second equation describes the evolution of interest rates,

$$r(t) = a_2 I(t+\omega) - b_2 \dot{r}(t) \tag{16}$$

From [16] the level of the interest rate is determined positively precisely by investments' tendency to increase. So the higher the expected investment, the greater the tension on the interest rate.

140 *Dynamic equilibrium and the economic cycle*

Given the structure of the model, which is quite similar from a mathematical point of view to Amoroso's first one, the system's solution leads to the identification of two complex roots. As a result both the interest rate and the investment level fluctuate around the stationary state value, giving these two variables an oscillatory pattern. Palomba also reiterates the irrelevance of monetary variables: "in the connection in our reasoning the material amount of currency and credit has little importance: it is a completely supplementary and passive element." (Palomba 1939: 107). At the end of *Introduzione allo studio della dinamica economica* Palomba abandons these Keynesian suggestions and returns to looking at the economic cycle in a more traditional, but not more formalized, way, i.e. as a process determined by the different trends in revenues and costs, with the consequent formation of extra profits.

## A methodological interpretation

One of the most important developments in economics in the period between the two world wars has been the trend toward economic quantification, i.e. the growing use of mathematical and statistical methods to analyse economic relations. In the field of dynamics theory this led to the construction of mathematical models to analyse the evolution of economic variables over time. Even though the internationally recognized pioneers in this effort to provide an analytical basis for dynamic economics were Frisch and Tinbergen, we saw in the previous paragraphs that there were also other directions of research that were significantly developed in the Pareto tradition in Italy.

The process of formalization of the analysis of the economic cycle started by Evans and Roos, and carried on in Italy by Amoroso and other followers of Pareto school, was mostly characterized by two elements. The first is a formal aspect concerning the type of math used by these economists. It was a mathematical approach typical of the natural sciences, and in particular of rational mechanics, where the focus was more on the calculation and identification of functional operational forms, not on the search for more general and rigorous results. A typical example of this engineer-like approach to economic mathematics is found in *Mathematical Introduction to Economics* by Evans in 1930. This rigorous but not formalistic approach, as pointed out by Weintraub (2002), did not have much luck because it was considered a sort of applied economics, far from the pure theory that was moving towards axiomatization, a direction that led to significant results in the field of economic statics.

This brings us to a second aspect, also a methodological one. As noted by Boumans (2005) it is precisely in these years that economists began to formulate economic theory in terms of models, taking this methodology from the physical sciences. A model, in the sense of the mathematical economists that we considered, consisted of a system of equations governing the motion of a limited number of variables. For economists of the 1930s it was enough that these models were correct, i.e. able to represent the cyclical phenomenon, and simple, in the sense of including the fewest possible relationships. It was not required however

*Dynamic equilibrium and the economic cycle*  141

that they be derived from a logic of rational behaviour. For this reason Amoroso had no problem, like Evans and Roos before him, assuming that the expectations might be considered primarily as an exogenous trend. Such an argument will be completely abandoned after the Second World War and consequently the theory of the economic cycle of equilibrium enters into a period of decline.

To find another economic cycle theory as a manifestation of equilibrium the public had to wait for the 1980s with the real economic cycle theory of Lucas and Barro (Dore 1993). These economists also intended to demonstrate how economic cycle theory could emerge from the theory of economic equilibrium, so as to interpret economic fluctuations such as changes in the positions of equilibrium. In this case the logic of economic reasoning is reversed compared to that of the 1930s economists. The starting point for Lucas and the other economists of the real economic cycle is the necessity of a rational microfoundation of dynamic macroeconomics. In this context the concept of equilibrium assumes a normative connotation that was completely absent in the previous literature. What remains however is the centrality of the analytical tool identified, which in the models from the 1980s was the auto-regressive trends of technological shocks. In the real economic cycle models, the cyclical component exists only to the extent that technological shocks have a particular shape (Dore 1993). So we can say, with Lucas, that the real economic cycle models represented a step forward compared to previous models, both in terms of the statistical techniques used as well as the internal consistency of their economic logic.

Lastly we have seen how, at least until the second half of the 1930s, the community of Italian economists was not isolated from the international debate, as is sometimes believed. The areas of research pursued by Italian economists, as well as the theoretical reference models, were those that leading international theoretical economists also pursued. Especially strong was the influence of Keynes, well before *General Theory*. And there were also many accomplishments, both in the field of economic dynamics and also in statics, although their appreciation at the international level was certainly hampered by language barriers.

## Concluding remarks

Economic cycle theory was a very active field of research between the two World Wars, a period characterized by an accentuated theoretical pluralism. Economic cycle theory also saw the formulation of a wide range of approaches, each of which tended to emphasize a characteristic aspect of economic fluctuations. Building on and innovating the mathematical models of Evans and Roos in the second half of the 1920s, Paretian economists proposed models in which the economic cycle could be considered as an endogenous equilibrium phenomenon. The main exponent of this approach in Italy was Luigi Amoroso, the most prominent mathematician and economist in the first half of the twentieth century in the Italian context.

This type of modelling, and any related to the economic cycle in general, did not have much luck in the aftermath of the Second World War.

## 142  *Dynamic equilibrium and the economic cycle*

One reason can be found in the very particular analytical apparatus which basically was a revival of some dynamic approaches derived by analogy from rational mechanics. Second, expectations also proved to not be a very useful perspective in order to construct formal models able to represent the economic cycle. Third, there was less interest in these issues. In the 1950s, economic dynamics would go in an entirely different direction, that of growth theory, and as a result studies on the economic cycle would rapidly lose importance. The influence of Keynes is also of significant interest. Keynes' work was well known and appreciated in Italy well before *General Theory*. For many years afterward, Keynes as a student of money would be much more appreciated than Keynes the author proposing public intervention as a remedy to cope with the evils of capitalism.

To see an approach similar to that of the Paretian economists emerge again, it is necessary to wait until the 1980s, with the real business cycle theory. Even for economists of new classical macroeconomics, the economic cycle is a phenomenon of equilibrium, determined by non-monetary factors, as in the Paretian philosophy of the 1930s. However, the underlying methodological framework is completely different. The Paretians would not have agreed that the economic cycle could be considered the result of optimal choices on the part of the representative agent. They regarded the field of economic phenomena too complex to be analysed through the lens of the optimizing agent, and relied on a kind of analysis that was closer to the natural sciences, rigorous but empirical and descriptive.

# 8 From dynamic equilibrium to the theory of optimal growth

The previous chapters highlighted how, between the two World Wars, a theoretical approach emerged which attempted to build economic dynamics on the concept of equilibrium as a balancing of forces. The marginalist revolution had put into evidence the great potentialities of the new approach in the construction of economic statics. The greatest result obtained by the first generation of marginalist economists was the theory of general economic equilibrium which explained the variety of economic factors in an complete synthesis. The events that occurred between the two World Wars, with the initial phase of the expansion and then of the advent of the *Great Depression*, not only had put into evidence the instability of capitalist economies, but also had upset the idea of equilibrium as the optimal position of rest of the economic system, reached spontaneously. As already observed by Pareto, the economy was in continuous movement according to laws which were up to the economists to mark out. The difficult task attending scholars, and in particular mathematical economists, was to construct a theory of economic dynamics with the same formal rigour of the statics theory.

In the period taken into consideration, different approaches emerged highlighting different characteristics of the dynamic process, also in the mathematical ambit. Among these, the prevailing line of research was carried out by Frisch (1936), subsequently consolidated by Samuelson (1947). Their approach was mainly directed towards the traditional idea, drawn on statics, of equilibrium as a position of rest. Consequently, a definition of dynamics emerged consistent with this approach according to which analysis becomes dynamic when the economic system is studied outside of the position of equilibrium or of the motions taking place when approaching it. First of all, this definition of Frisch's is important because it calls attention to the fact that the dynamic theory must first produce mathematical models. Therefore, dynamics leaves the ground of historical, sociological or institutional analysis, and is reduced to a few quantitative variables. Second, for a theoretical model to be dynamic, it must not contain any reference to the temporal dimension, but rather meet a very precise formal requirement: it must contain the value of a variable and the direction it is following, that is, its first derivative. This immediately produces the operational aspect of the definition: a variable is in equilibrium when its derivative is annulled (Frisch 1933); this enables the temporal element to be provided implicitly. This aspect was

144  *Dynamic equilibrium and optimal growth*

highlighted clearly by Samuelson who carried out an in-depth discussion on the matter. In such theoretical context, the position of equilibrium of the economic system can be nothing else but a position of rest or stationary, that is a position which does not change in time. This kind of dynamics can be defined as ergodic since the state of a system in a specific instant depends only on the initial conditions and on the well-known law of motion.

The economists taken into consideration in the previous chapters contrasted this view of dynamics as disequilibrium or as an approaching motion with a different view based directly on the notion of equilibrium. In Pareto's terms, in a condition of dynamic equilibrium the system is always in equilibrium, in other words this is due to the fact that in every instant hindrances precisely compensate the forces involved. However, the final result is not a position of rest, but rather a trajectory – and in particular an optimal trajectory – which depends on the value of the initial or final conditions. In other words, the value of equilibrium is no longer constant but it varies in time. The first case was well evidenced by the role carried out by the expectations in la Volpe's model; the second case is the theory of economic planning exposed by Amoroso. The difference is that in this theoretical approach the economic reality is no longer ergodic since the position of equilibrium changes in time. It is not a coincidence that Samuelson established a link between compared statics and dynamics, a comparison which in the theory of economic dynamics is no longer possible because the latter changes in time.

These two research programmes, at least as regards the aspect which we are taking into consideration – that is long-term dynamics of the economic system – were synthesised in the 1960s in the theory of optimal growth, with the resumption of Ramsey's model on behalf of Cass and other young mathematical economists. The new approach returned to the techniques of functional calculus – typical of the economists taken into consideration in the previous chapters – which were re-proposed without mentioning the authors who had developed them first between the two World Wars. On the other hand, as in the approach carried out by Frisch and Samuelson, the system converged towards a point of equilibrium which did not change in time. Therefore, growth in the long-term period resulted as determined by factors greatly exogenous, such as growth in population or technical progress. The resumption of the approach of dynamic equilibrium, even if in the simplified form of the optimizing growth model, leads us to question why it was marginalized for several decades and was considered a not very promising research approach, to then return to the frontier of research. The previous chapters have highlighted two main factors which are the case to mention directly now. The first critical factor is represented by the kind of approach chosen, that is, general economic equilibrium. The second factor is to be found in the mathematical tool utilized, that is, functional calculus, way too advanced for the economists of those years.

## General economic equilibrium and dynamics

The economists taken into consideration up to now considered broad dynamics, that is dynamics of the economic system considered in its whole. Their ambition

*Dynamic equilibrium and optimal growth* 145

was to describe the evolutive path of the economic system throughout time. Economy registers variations continually within its basic parameters which in turn determine changes in the productive trajectories. In order to understand this overall dynamics or broad dynamics, the main path to pursue seemed that of dynamizing the equations of general economic equilibrium. However, we have seen how this project was greatly utopian and difficult to realize within the ambit of a scheme which on one hand was very elementary – based on the counting of the quantity of equations and unknowns – and on the other hand was characterized by an insuperable difficulty in the calculus. The scenario imagined by Pareto's followers was that of an economics in which all variables moved at the same time. This was intriguing from an intellectual viewpoint, but impossible to carry out on their favourite ground of research, that is formal models. Economic dynamics seemed to put into crisis the fundamental assumption of Pareto's followers, that is the centrality of the concept of interdependence among variables. In the case of dynamics, variables not only depend on each other, but this dependence has a sequential character, that is the successive variable is determined according to a law which must be determined on the basis of the previous one. This approach is the only one capable of producing the representation of an economic process as an ensemble of elements which take place in time. Basically, dynamic analysis recalled the idea of casualness, a concept which had been banned by Pareto's followers.

In order to reach a dynamic theory of the general economic equilibrium it was necessary to pursue different paths, as demonstrated by von Neumann's growth model (1945): the most original attempt to confer a dynamic lay-out to the model of general economic equilibrium. In Von Neumann's model successive periods of time are linked among each other in the sense that the resources available at the beginning of each period are those produced in the previous one. Considering all the periods as a whole, the productive process takes on the form of a circular process. The equilibrium of von Neumann's model consists of the fact that prices remain constant in time and every sector grows at a constant and exogenous rate. However, this causes the loss of the characteristic aspect, that is the typical disaggregation of the models of general economic equilibrium: an ensemble of goods whose prices and relevant quantities remain constant in time corresponds to a single composite good. Therefore, in the end, von Neumann's model, even if formally containing various sectors, can be considered an aggregate model due to the hypotheses it entails, thus transforming itself into a macroeconomic model.

This result is very interesting and contributes to explaining why the dynamic theory after the Second World War was developed almost exclusively through the use of aggregated models. The path of static analysis of general economic equilibrium had been basically completed by Pareto. The path of dynamic analysis presented many difficulties from the viewpoint of disaggregated analysis, whereas in the case of an aggregated approach these difficulties disappeared. Therefore, we can conclude that the turning point which marked the passing from static analysis to dynamic analysis coincided with the passing from disaggregated analysis to macroeconomic analysis. However, Pareto's followers never reached

146 *Dynamic equilibrium and optimal growth*

this kind of approach, and this can explain why the Italian school lost the relevance it had had between the two World Wars (Graziani 1965).

## Economics and mathematics

The debate concerning the theory of dynamic equilibrium highlights how complex the relationship is between the mathematical tool and the theoretical aspects in economics. From this viewpoint, the period between the two World Wars was characterized by great progress in the formalization of the economic debate and in the quantitative verification of the economic phenomena. As Pareto had sensed, the economic dynamic construction required new mathematical tools capable of analysing phenomena that change in time. Roos and Evans first, as mathematicians, had demonstrated the relevance of functional calculus in the field of dynamics. On this basis, it was possible to determine the optimal trajectory of the behaviour of the enterprise. This intuition was resumed and studied more in depth by the Italian Pareto school with remarkable improvements.

However, after that period, this analytical orientation was completely abandoned to then be resumed suddenly in the 1960s by the theory of optimal growth. The question is why a calculus tool which became the basis of the mathematics of economic decisions in dynamics was in its initial phase almost ignored by the community of economists. The answer can be for in a two-fold direction. The first is that at least until the Second World War the economists did not fully recognize the importance of mathematics in economics. Those involved in more analytical matters, in actual fact, were more physicists or mathematicians, rather than economists. The mathematical knowledge of the economists of the time was rather modest and the main interest was directed towards the description and interpretation of the phenomena, rather than on the construction of mathematical models. It is only in the 1950s with the formalist revolution that the economists' education was enriched with the fundamental ingredient of mastering these formal tools, thus enabling economics to take on a fully mathematical form. From this viewpoint, the economists taken into consideration were way ahead of time and their debate ended up being considered more as an abstruse mathematical analysis without an actual content which could interest the average economist.

There is also a second aspect which deserves to be considered. In order for the functional calculus to become a common tool for economic dynamics, it was necessary for it to become simpler even in its implementation. This is what happened in the 1960s with the transformation of the theory of functional calculus into that of optimal control. The theory of optimal control which had been elaborated so as to calculate engineering ballistic trajectories suggested several simple formulas with which it was possible to obtain equilibrium solutions in a more immediate manner. The first order conditions of the traditional static problem became the first order conditions of a Hamilton function to be maximized. In this way, the economist was on his favourite grounds, that of a substantially restricted problem, the interpretation of the solutions remaining the same.

*Dynamic equilibrium and optimal growth* 147

Therefore, the late success of functional calculus in economic dynamics was established owing to a new concept of economic science as a rigorous and formal discipline, as well as to new calculus methodologies made available by natural science. The fact remains that the young economists approaching these problems did not realise that they were following a path which had already been traced.

# Bibliography

Aftalion, A. (1927) The theory of economic cycles based on the capitalistic technique of production, *Review of Economic Statistic*, 9: 165–170.

Almodovar, A. and Cardoso, J. L. (2005) 'Corporatism and the Economic Role of Government', *History of Political Economy*, 37: 333–354.

Amoroso, L. (1909) 'La Teoria dell' Equilibrio Economico Secondo il Prof. Vilfredo Pareto, *Giornale Degli Economisti*, 19: 353–367.

—— (1910) 'L'applicazione Della Matematica all'economia Politica', *Giornale Degli Economisti*, 20: 57–63.

—— (1911) 'L'applicazione Della Matematica allo Studio Dei Fenomeni Economici e Sociali', *Giornale Degli Economisti*, 21: 349–370.

—— (1921) *Lezioni di Economia Matematica*, Bologna: Zanichelli.

—— (1928) 'Discussione del Sistema di Equazioni che Definiscono L'equilibrio del Consumatore', *Annali di Economia*, 4: 30–41.

—— (1929) 'Le Equazioni Differenziali Della Dinamica Economica', *Giornale Degli Economisti e Rivista di Statistica*, 28: 67–79.

—— (1930a) 'La Curva Statica di Offerta', *Giornale degli Economisti e Rivista di Statistica*, 1:1–26.

—— (1930b) *'La Visione Economica del Fascismo'*, *Economia Politica Contemporanea*, Cedam: Padua.

—— (1932) 'Contributo alla Teoria Matematica Della Dinamica Economica', *Nuova Collana degli Economisti*, Torino: UTET.

—— (1933) 'La dinamica dell'impresa', *Rivista Italiana di Statistica Economia e Finanza*, 4: 442–451.

—— (1935) La dinamique de la circulation, *Econometrica*, 3: 400–410.

—— (1938) *Principi di Economia Corporativa*, Bologna: Zanichelli.

—— (1939) 'La Teoria Matematica del Programma Economico', A.A.V.V. *Cournot nell'Economia e nella Filosofia*, Padua: Cedam.

—— (1940) 'The Transformation Value in the Productive Process', *Econometrica*, 8: 1–11.

—— (1942) *Meccanica Economica*, Città di Castello: Macrì.

—— (1957) 'Modelli Meccanici e Modelli Economici', *Studi Economici*, 12: 271–282.

Amoroso, L. and De Stefani, A. (1934) 'La Logica del Sistema Corporativo', *Annali di Economia*, 9: 247–262.

Arfken, G. and Weber, H. (2001) *Mathematical Methods for Physicists*, New York: Harcourt Academic Press.

Arias, G. (1934) *Corso di Diritto Corporativo*, Firenze: Edizioni Poligrafiche Universitarie.

Bartoli, H. (2003) *Histoire de la Pensée Économique en Italie*, Paris: La Sorbonne.

## Bibliography 149

Bellanca, N. and Giocoli, N. (1998) *Maffeo Pantaleoni: il Principe Degli Economsiti Italiani*, Firenze: Polistampa.

Bini, P. and Magliulo, A. (1999) 'Keynesianism in Italy. Before and After the General Theory', in *The Impact of Keynes on Economics in the 20th century*, edited by L. Pasinetti and B. Schefold, Cheltenham: Edward Elgar.

Birner, J. (2002) *The Cambridge Controversies in Capital Theory: A Study in the Logic of Theory Development*, London: Routledge.

Bjerkholt, O. and Qin, D. (2011) (eds.) *A Dynamic Approach to Economic Theory. The Yale lectures of Ragnar Frisch*, London: Routledge.

Boianowky, M. and Tarascio, V. (1998) 'Mechanical Inertia and Economic Dynamics: Pareto on Business Cycles', *Journal of the History of Economic Thought*, 20: 5–21.

Boninsegni, P. (1910) *Précis d'Economie Politique*, Paris: F. Rouge.

—— (1930) *Manuel Élèmentaire d'Economie Politique*, Paris: F. Rouge.

Bordin, A. (1935) 'Il Significato di Alcune Moderne Teorie della Dinamica Economica', *Giornale degli Economisti*, 70: 161–210.

—— (1936) 'Alcune Generalizzazioni di un Caso di Monopolio Bilaterale', *Giornale degli Economisti*, 76: 672–694.

—— (1938) *Un Caso di Monopolio Bilaterale*, Bologna: Zanichelli.

—— (1939) 'Le Teorie Economiche di Cournot e L'ordinamento Corporativo', in *Cournot nell'Economia e nella Filosofia*, A.A.V.V., Padua: Cedam.

—— (1948) 'Di Taluni Massimi di Utilità Collettiva', *Giornale degli Economisti e Annali di Economia*, 7: 174–189.

—— (1950) 'Equilibrio e Indeterminazione', *Giornale degli Economisti e Annali di Economia*, 9: 565–577.

Boumans, M. (2005) *How Economists Model the World into Numbers*, London: Routledge.

Brandolini, A. and Gobbi, G. (1990) 'Il Contributo Italiano alla Fondazione della Econometric Society', *Quaderni di Storia dell'Economia Politica*, 5: 39–78.

Bruguier Pacini, G. (1936) *Il Corporativismo e Gli Economisti Italiani*, Firenze: Sansoni.

Busino, G. (1989) *L'Italia di Vilfredo Pareto: Economia e Società in un Carteggio del 1873–1923*, Milano: Banca Commerciale Italiana.

Carli, F. (1938) *Le Basi Dottrinali dell'Economia Corporativa*, Padua: Cedam.

Ciocca, P. and Toniolo, G. (1976) *L'economia Italiana nel Periodo Fascista*, Bologna: Il Mulino.

de Pietri Tonelli, A. (1921) *Lezioni di Scienza Economica Razionale e Sperimentale*, Rovigo: Istituto Arti Grafiche.

—— (1931) *Corso di Politica Economica: Introduzione*, Padova: Cedam.

—— (1961) (ed.), *Scritti Paretiani*, Padova: Cedam.

—— (1963) *Economia e Politica. Scritti Vari*, Padova: Cedam.

Debreu, G. (1959) *Theory of Value: An Axiomatic Analysis of Economic Equilibrium*, New Haven, CT: Yale University Press.

Del Vecchio, G. (1917) *Questioni Fondamentali sul Valore della Moneta*, Roma: Ateneum.

—— (1934) *I Principi della Carta del Lavoro*, Padua: Cedam.

Demaria, G. (1930) 'Saggio Sugli Studi di Dinamica Economica', *Rivista Internazionale di Scienze Sociali*, 38: 107–130.

Dimand, R. (1988) 'Early Mathematical Theories of Business Cycles', in *Keynes, Macroeconomics and Method*, D. E. Moggridge (ed.), London: Edward Elgar.

Dimand, R. and Veloce, W. (2007) 'C. F. Roos, H. T. Davis and the Quantitative Approach to Business Cycle Analysis and the Cowles Commission in the 1930s and the early 1940s', *The European Journal of the History of Economic Thought*, 14: 519–542.

## 150 *Bibliography*

Di Matteo, M. (1998) 'Giulio La Volpe', *Rivista Italiana degli Economisti*, 3: 157–160.

—— (1993) 'Foreword Part I', in G. La Volpe, *Studies on the Theory of General Dynamic Economic Equilibrium*, M. Morishima and M. Di Matteo (eds.), Basingstoke: MacMillan.

Dominedò, V. (1950) 'Le Condizioni di Massimo Collettivo di Ofelimità di Pareto', in *Vilfredo Pareto*, G. Demaria (ed.), Milano: Rodolfo Malfasi.

—— (1966) 'Mondo Fisico e Mondo Economico nel Pensiero di Luigi Amoroso', *L'Industria*, 10: 25–41.

Donzelli, F. (1997) 'Pareto's Mechanical Dream', *History of Economic Ideas*, 5: 127–178.

—— (1991) 'Il Metodo degli Equilibri Successivi di Pareto e il Metodo della Dinamica Economica', in *Pareto Oggi*, G. Busino (ed.), Bologna: Il Mulino.

Dore, M. (1993) *The Macroeconomics of Business Cycle*, Cambridge: Blackwell.

Duarte, P. (2009) 'The Growing of Ramsey's Growth Models', *History of Political Economy*, 41: 161–181.

Edgeworth, F. (1922) 'The Mathematical Economics of Professor Amoroso', *Economic Journal*, 32: 400–407.

Evans, G.C. (1922) 'A Simple Theory of Competition', *American Mathematical Monthly*, 29: 371–380.

—— (1924) 'The Dynamics of Monopoly', *American Mathematical Monthly*, 31: 91–117.

—— (1925) 'The Mathematical Theory of Economics', *American Mathematical Monthly*, 32: 104–110.

—— (1930) Mathematical Introduction to Economics, New York: McGraw-Hill.

Fanno, M. (1931) 'Cicli di Produzione, Cicli del Credito e Fluttuazioni Industriali', *Giornale degli Economisti*, 71: 329–370.

—— (1936) *Introduzione alla Teoria Economica del Corporativismo*, Padua: Cedam.

—— (1947) *Teoria delle Fluttuazioni Economiche*, Torino: UTET.

Faucci, R. (1990) 'Materiali e Ipotesi Sulla Cultura Economica Italiana fra le Due Guerre Mondiali', in *Il Pensiero Economico: Temi, Problemi e Scuole*, G. Becattini (ed.), Torino: UTET.

—— (2004) 'Il Dopoguerra e la Fine dell'Isolamento', in *La Formazione degli Economisti in Italia*, G. Garofalo and A. Graziani (eds.), Bologna: Il Mulino.

—— (2000) *L'economia Politica in Italia: dal Cinquecento ai nostri Giorni* Torino: UTET: Libreria.

Finoia, M. (1980) *Il Pensiero Economico Italiano*, Bologna: Cappelli.

—— (1983) 'Il Pensiero Economico Italiano degli Anni Trenta', *Rassegna Economica*, 3, 565–591.

Fossati, E. (1930) 'Osservazioni Sulla Statica e la Dinamica con Particolare Riguardo alla Teoria dello Sconto', in A.A.V.V., *Economia e Politica Contemporanea*, Padova: Cedam.

—— (1935) 'Osservazioni sulla Legge di Wieser per la Determinazione del Valore di una Provvista di Beni Omogenei', in *Frammenti di Teoria Dinamica*, E. Fossati 1953, Bologna: Cappelli Editore.

—— (1937a) 'Ricerca Sulle Relazioni tra il Tempo e l'utilità', in *Frammenti di Teoria Dinamica*, E. Fossat (ed.), Bologna: Cappelli Editore.

—— (1937b) *New Deal: il Nuovo Ordine Economico di F. D. Roosevelt*, Padova: Cedam.

—— (1937c) *Linee di Economia Corporativa*, Firenze: Casa Editrice Poligrafica Universitaria.

—— (1946) *Elementi di Economia Razionale*, Padova: Cedam.

—— (1948) 'Vilfredo Pareto nel suo e nel nostro Tempo', in *Frammenti di Teoria Dinamica*, E. Fossat (ed.), Bologna: Cappelli Editore.

—— (1953) *Frammenti di Teoria Dinamica*, Bologna: Cappelli Editore.

## Bibliography   151

— (1955) *Elementi di Politica Economica Razionale*, Milano: Giuffrè.

— (1957) *The Theory of General Static Equilibrium*, Oxford, Basil Blackwell.

— (1959) *Problemi dei nostri giorni: note economiche del periodo 1946–1957*, Milano, Giuffrè.

— (1960) *Oeconomica Varia: Excepta*, Milano: Giuffrè.

— (1962) 'The Criterion of Determinacy of General Equilibrium', *Metroeconomica*, 14: 18–23.

Frisch, R. (1933) 'Propagation Problems and Impulses Problems in Dynamics Economics', in *Economic Essays in Honour of Gustav Cassel*, London: Allen & Unwin.

— (1936) 'On the Notion of Equilibrium and Disequilibrium', *Econometrica*, 3: 100–105.

Fuà, G. (1980) 'L'economia Politica in Italia dalle Origini alla Prima Metà del 900', in *Il Pensiero Economico Italiano*, M. Finoia (ed.), Bologna: Cappelli.

Fusco, A. M. (1997) 'Gli Studi di Economia in Italia: Momenti di Riflessione Teorica (1946–1966)', in *Storia, Economia e Società in Italia 1947–1997*, M. Arcelli (ed.), Roma: Laterza.

Gallegati, M. (1984) Analisi Parziale e Teoria Pura: l'economia Politica Marshalliana in italia 1885–1925, *Annali della Fondazione Luigi Einaudi*, 16: 355–409.

Gandolfo, G. (2008) 'Giuseppe Palomba and the Lotka-Volterra equations', *Rendiconti Lincei*, 347–357.

Garegnani, P. (1960) *Il Capitale nelle Teorie della Distribuzione*, Milano: Giuffrè.

Garofalo, G. (2005) 'Gli Economisti in Italia negli Anni 1950–1975', *Economia Politica*, 12: 381–3293.

Gioia, V. (2003) 'Gli Economisti Italiani e la "Scuola Austriaca": dalla Teoria del Valore alla Scienza delle Finanze', in *Le Frontiere dell'economia Politica*, P. Brucci (ed.), Edizioni Polistampa: Firenze.

Giva, D. (1996) 'Luigi Amoroso e la Meccanica Economica', *Il Pensiero Economico Italiano*, 4: 95–112.

Grattan-Guinnes, I. (2010) 'How Influential was Mechanics in the Development of Neoclassical Economics? A Small Example of a Large Question', *Journal of the History of Economic Thought*, 32: 531–581.

Graziani, A. (1904) *Istituzioni di Economia Politica*, Torino: Bocca.

— (1965) *Equilibrio Generale ed Equilibrio Macroeconomico*, Napoli: Edizioni Scientifiche Italiane.

— (1991) 'The Italian Economic Journals and Some Major Turning-Points in Economic Theory' *Economic Notes*, 21: 121–133.

Guccione, A. and Minelli, E. (1999) 'Consumer Theory and Axiomatics: A Note on an Early Contribution by Luigi Amoroso', *History of Political Economy*, 31: 587–589.

Guerraggio, A. (1990) 'L'economia Matematica in Italia tra le Due Guerre: Luigi Amoroso', *Quaderni di Storia dell'Economia Politica*, 8: 23–37.

Guidi, M. L. (2000) 'Corporative Economics and the Italian Tradition of Economic Thought. A Survey, *Storia del Pensiero Economico*, 40: 27–45.

Hicks, J. (1932) *The Theory of Wages*, London: Macmillan.

— (1939) *Value and Capital*, Oxford: Clarendon Press.

— (1950) *A contribution to the theory of the trade cycle*, Oxford, Clarendon Press.

Ingrao, B. and Israel, G. (1990) *The Invisible Hand*, Cambridge, MA: MIT Press.

Jannaccone, P. (1912) "Il Paretaio." La Riforma sociale XXIII: 337–368.

Kaldor, N. (1939) 'Welfare propositions in Economics and Interpersonal Camparisons of Utility', *The Economic Journal*, 49: 549–552.

## 152 Bibliography

Keppler, J. H. (1994) 'Luigi Amoroso (1886–1965): Mathematical Economist, Italian Corporatist', *History of Political Economy*, 26: 589–611.

Keynes, J. M. (1930) *A Treatise on Money*, London: Macmillan.

Keynes, J. M. (1936) *The General Theory of Employment, Interest and Money*, London: McMillan.

Klein, L. R. (1958) 'Review of Fossati's the Theory of General Static Equilibrium', in *L'alfabeto dell'economia razionale*, E. Fossati (ed.), Giuffrè: Milano. 1964: 183–184.

Kyun, K. (1988) *Equilibrium Business Cycle Theory in Historical Perspective*, Cambridge: Cambridge University Press.

La Volpe, G. (1935a) 'Elements of a Mathematical Theory of Dynamic Economic Equilibrium', in *Italian Economic Papers*, L. Pasinetti (ed.), Bologna: Il Mulino, 1988.

—— (1935b) 'A Theory of Dynamic Economic Equilibrium and Historical Motion', in *Italian Economic Papers*, L. Pasinetti (ed.), Bologna, Il Mulino, 1988.

—— (1936) *Studi Sulla Teoria dell'equilibrio Economico Dinamico Generale*, Napoli: Jovene.

—— (1938) *Ricerche di Dinamica Economica Corporativa*, Padova: Cedam.

—— (1939) 'Economia e Filosofia', *Rivista Italiana di Scienze Economiche*, 9: 456–472.

—— (1948) *Convenienza Economica Collettiva*, Padova: Cedam.

—— (1965) 'La Ricerca Strutturale come Fondamento dei Modelli Econometrici di Programmazione', *Ricerche Economiche*, 19: 311–319.

—— (1967) 'L'analisi Variazionale come Fondamento dei Modelli Econometrici', *Ricerche Economiche*, 21: 231–252.

—— (1977) 'La Dinamica Eso-Endogena e i Problemi Diretti e Inversi nella Ricerca Economica', *Rivista di Politica Economica*, 67: 111–152.

—— (1993) *Studies on the Theory of General Dynamic Economic Equilibrium*, London: Macmillan Press.

Lombardini, S. (1956) '*Storia delle Dottrine Economiche*', in *Dizionario di Economia Politica*, C. Napoleoni (a cura di), Milano: Edizioni Comunità.

McLure, M. (2001) *Pareto, Economics and Society: The Mechanical Analogy*, London: Routledge.

—— (2007) *The Paretian School and Italian Fiscal Sociology*, New York: Palgrave Macmillan.

Magliulo, A. (1992) 'The Debate over the Business Cycle in the 1930s. An Explanation of Italian anti-Keynesianism', *Storia del Pensiero Economico*, 23: 24–51.

—— (2003) 'Il Keynesismo in Italia (1913–1963). Le Ragioni di una rivoluzione Mancata', in *Le Frontiere dell'economia Politica*, p. Barucci (ed.), Firenze: Edizioni Polistampa.

Magnani, I. (2005) 'Il Paretaio', *Economia Politica*, 22: 69–100.

Mancini, A., Perillo, F. and Zagari, E. (1982) *La Teoria Economica del Corporativismo*, Napoli: Edizioni Scientifiche Italiane.

Marshack, J. (1934) 'The Meeting of Econometric Society in Leiden', *Econometrica*, 2: 87–91.

Masci, G. (1933) *Lezioni di Statistica*, Napoli: GUF.

—— (1934a) 'Crisi Economica ed Economica Corporativa', *Rivista Internazionale di Scienze Sociali*, 32: 222–256.

—— (1934b) *Saggi Critici di Teoria e Metodologia Economica*, Catania: Studio Editoriale Moderno.

—— (1941–1942) *Corso di Economia Politica Corporativa*, Roma: Società Editrice del Foro Italiano.

Mayer, H. (1934) 'Il Concetto di Equilibrio nella Teoria Economica, in *Economia Pura*, G. Del Vecchio (ed.), *Nuova Collana degli Economisti Italiani e Stranieri*, Torino: UTET.

## Bibliography   153

Meacci, F. (1998) (ed.) *Italian Economists in the 20th Century*, Cheltenham: Edward Elgar.

Mirowski, P. (1989) *More Heat than Light*, Cambridge: Cambridge University Press.

Montesano, A. (1972) 'La Nozione di Economia Dinamica', *Giornale degli Economisti e Annali di Economia*, 3: 185–228.

Moore, H. L. (1929) *Synthetic Economics*, New York: Macmillan.

Morishima, M. (1993) 'Foreword' in *Studies on the Theory of General Dynamic Economic Equilibrium*, La Volpe G., London: Macmillan Press.

Mornati, F. (1999) *Pasquale Boninsegni e la Scuola di Losanna*, Torino: UTET.

Murray, R. (1911) *Sommarii di Lezioni di Economia Politica*, Firenze: Sansoni.

Napoleoni, C. (1965) *L'equilibrio Economico Generale*, Torino: Boringhieri.

Nicola, P. C. (2000) *Mainstream Mathematical Economics in the 20th Century*, Berlin: Springer.

Nuccio, O. (1985) 'Edificio Economico ed Edificio Politico-Economico. Economia e Ideologia nell'opera di L. Amoroso', *Rivista di Politica Economica*, 75: 883–939.

Palomba, G. (1936) 'Aspetti e tendenze della teoria dell'equilibrio economico generale', *Politica economica*, XXVI: 12–56.

—— (1939) *Introduzione allo Studio della Dinamica Economica*, Napoli: Jovene.

—— (1956) *Morfologia Economica*, Napoli: Giannini.

—— (1959) *Meccanica Economica*, Napoli: Giannini.

—— (1961) *L'espansione Capitalistica*, Napoli: Giannini.

Pantaleoni, M. (1889) *Principi di Economia Pura*, Milano: Treves.

—— (1909) 'Di Alcuni Fenomeni di Economica', in *Scritti Vari di Economia*, Vol. II, *Erotemi*, Bari: Laterza.

Papi, G. U. (1934a) *Teoria delle Fluttuazioni Economiche: l'ordinamento Corporativo Italiano*, Padua: Cedam.

—— (1934b) *Lezioni di Economia Generale e Corporativa*, Padua: Cedam.

—— (1962) 'Eraldo Fossati', *Metroeconomica*, 14: 5–17.

Pareto, V. (1971 [1896–97]) *Corso di Economia Politica*, Torino UTET.

—— (1901) 'Le Nuove Teorie Economiche con Annessa Appendice. Le Equazioni dell'equilibrio Dinamico', *Giornale degli Economisti*, 23: 235–59.

—— (1965 [1906]) *Manuale di Economia Politica*, Torino: UTET.

—— (1982 [1906]) 'Applicazioni della Matematica all'economia Politica', reprinted in *Ouvres Complètes* 26, Giovanni Busino (ed.), Genéve: Librairie Droz.

—— (1973) *Epistolario 1890–1923*, G. Busino (ed.), Accademia Nazionale dei Lincei, Roma.

Pavanelli, G. (2000) 'Note sulla Teoria Austriaca del Ciclo e le Sue Implicazioni di Politica Economica nel Dibattito Italiano degli Anni Trenta', in *Science, Institutions and Economic Development*, V. Gioia and H. Kurz (eds.), Milano: Giuffrè Editore.

Pigou, A. C. (1920) *The Economics of Welfare*, London: Macmillan.

—— (1927) *Industrial Fluctuations*, London: Macmillan.

Pomini, M. (2008) 'Abitudini, Aspettative e Incertezza. L'equilibrio Dinamico nella Scuola Paretiana', *Economia Politica*, 25: 95–138.

—— (2009) 'The Paretian Tradition of Dynamic General Equilibrium in Italy's Interwar Period', *History of Economic Ideas*, 20: 57–83.

Pomini, M. and Tusset, G. (2009) 'Habits and Expectations: Dynamic General Equilibrium in the Italian Pareto School', *History of Political Economy*, 41: 311–42.

Porta, P. L. (2004) 'Tradizione e Innovazione negli Studi Economici nell'Italia del Novecento', in *La Formazione degli Economisti in Italia*, G. Garofalo and A. Graziani (eds.), Bologna: Il Mulino.

## 154   *Bibliography*

Rabbeno, U. (1891) 'The Present Condition of Political Economy in Italy', *Political Science Quarterly*, 6: 439–496.

Ramsey, F. (1928) 'A Mathematical Theory of Saving', *Economic Journal*, 38: 543–559.

Realfonzo, R. (2000) 'Note Sulla Teoria Austriaca del Ciclo e Gli Economisti Italiani nel Periodo tra le Due Guerre, in *Science, Institutions and Economic Development*, V. Gioa and H. Kurz (eds.), Milano: Giuffrè Editore.

Ricci, U. (1939) *Tre Economisti Italiani: Pantaloni, Pareto, Loria*, Bari: Laterza.

Roos, C. F. (1925) 'A Mathematical Theory of Competition', *American Journal of Mathematics*, 47: 163–165.

—— (1927) 'A Dynamical Theory of Economics', *Journal of Political Economy*, 35: 632–656.

—— (1930) 'A Mathematical Theory of Price and Production Fluctuations and Economic Crisis', *Journal of Political Economy*, 38: 501–522.

—— (1934) *Dynamic Economics*, Bloomington, IN: The Principia Press.

Rosenstein-Rodan, P. N. (1934) 'The Role of Time in Economic Theory', *Economica*, 1: 77–97.

Samuelson, P. (1941) 'The Stability of Equilibrium: Comparative Statics and Dynamics', *Econometrica*, 9: 97–120.

—— (1947) *Foundations of Economic Analysis*, Cambridge: Cambridge University press.

Schumpeter, J. A. (1954) *History of Economic Analysis*, New York: Cambridge University Press.

Screpanti, S. and Zamagni, E. (2005) *An Outline of the History of Economic Thought*, Oxford: Oxford University Press.

Sensini, G. (1912) *La Teoria della Rendita*, Roma: Loesher.

—— (1955) *Corso di Economia Pura*, Roma: Maglione.

Shackle, G. (1965) 'Eraldo Fossati, 1902–1962', *Econometrica*, 33: 641–643.

—— (1967) *The Years of High Theory*, Cambridge: Cambridge University Press.

Shell, K. (1969) 'Application of Pontryagin's Maximun Principle to Economics', in *Mathematical System Theory and Economics, vol. 1*, H. W. Kuhn and G.P. Szego (eds.), Berlin: Springer-Verlag.

Sraffa, P. (1926) 'The Laws of Returns under Competitive Conditions', *Economic Journal*, 36: 535–550.

Thompson, M. (1938) 'Review of Studi Sulla Teoria dell'equilibrio Economico Dinamico Generale', *Journal of Political Economy*, 46: 590–591.

Tinbergen, J. (1933) 'L'utilisation de équations functionelles et de nombres complexes dans la reserche économique', *Eonometrica*, 1: 36–51.

—— (1934) 'Annual Survey Developments in General Economic Theory', *Econometrica*, 2: 13–36.

—— (1935) 'Annual Survey: Suggestions on Quantitative Business Cycle Theory', *Econometrica*, 3: 241–308.

—— (1952) *On the Theory of Economic Policy*, Amsterdam: North-Holland.

Toniolo, G. (1980) *L'economia dell'Italia Fascista*, Bari: Laterza.

Tusset, G. (2004) *La Teoria Dinamica nel Pensiero Economico Italiano (1890–1940)*, Firenze: Edizioni Polistampa.

—— (2009) 'The Italian Contribution to Early Economic Dynamics', *The European Journal of the History of Economic Thought*, 16: 267–300.

von Neumann, J. (1945) 'A model of general economic equilibrium', *The Review of Economic Studies*, 3: 1–9.

Vinci, F. (1934) 'Significant Developments in Business Cycles Theory', *Econometrica*, 2: 125–139.

*Bibliography* 155

—— (1956 [1937]) 'Recenti Tendenze degli Studi Economici', *Analisi Economiche*, Bologna: Zanichelli.

—— (1953) *I Fondamenti dell'economica*, Milano: Istituto Editoriale Cisalpino.

Walras, L. (1974 [1874–1877]) *Elementi di Economia Politica Pura*, Torino: UTET.

Weintraub, E. (1983) 'On the Existence of a Competitive Equilibrium 1930–1950', *Journal of Economic Literature*, 21: 1–39.

—— (1991) *Stabilizing Dynamics*, New York: Cambridge University Press.

Weintraub, R. (1998) 'From Rigor to Axiomatics: The Marginalization of Grif.th C. Evans', *History of Political Economy*, 30: 227–259.

Weintraub, S. (2002) 'How Economics became a Mathematical Science', Durham, NC: Duke University Press.

Wicksell, K. (1958 [1907]) 'Selected Papers on Economic Theory', E. Lindahl (ed.), London: George Allen.

Wieser, F. von (1893) *Natural Value*, London: Macmillan.

—— (1926) *Das Gesetz der Mact*, Vienna: Springer.

Zaccagnini, E. (1947) 'Massimi Simultanei in Economia Pura', *Giornale degli Economisti e Annali di Economia*, 6: 258–292.

—— (1950) 'Nuovi Problemi della Polemica Scorza-Pareto', in *Vilfredo Pareto*, G. Demaria (ed.), Milano: Rodolfo Malfasi, 37–46.

—— (1958) 'Sulle condizioni sufficienti di massimo simultaneo', *Giornale degli Economisti e Annali di economia*, 18: 15–57.

Zagari, E., Perillo, F. and Mancini, O. (1982) *Teoria Economica e Pensiero Corporativo*, Napoli: Edizioni Scientifiche Italiane.

# Index

d'Alembert's principle 30, 32–4, 39, 69
Allen, R.G.D. 20, 59
Amoroso, Luigi: action and reaction
principle 132; *L'applicazione della
Matematica all'Economia Politica* 66;
business equation 131, 136; calculus
of variations 73–4, 76–8, 84; consumer
theory 68–71, 74–8; *Contributo alla
teoria matematica della dinamica
economica* 65–6, 73, 130; corporative
economics 23, 26, 63, 80, 81–3, 85,
136; correspondence with Pareto 64,
67–8; *La curva statica di offerta* 24,
65, 72–4; *La discussione sul sistema
di equazioni...* 65, 67–72; *La dinamica
dell'impresa* 73–4; dynamic equilibrium
29, 32, 47, 58–9, 63, 65–74, 83–5, 87,
97, 111–12, 126, 144; "The Dynamics
of Circulation" 136; dynamization of
offer curve 3, 24, 65; economic cycle
3, 4, 66, 73, 129, 130–8, 139, 140, 141;
energy viewpoint of productive process
78–81; *Le equazioni differenziali
nella dinamica economica* 70, 72,
130; Eulero's equation 77, 79, 85n;
fascist regime 81–2, 85; from statics to
dynamics 65–7, 68–9, 74–8; functional
calculus 63, 75–6, 114; general
dynamic equilibrium of consumption
74–8; general dynamic equilibrium of
production 76, 78–81; generally 14,
64–5, 123; industry equation 131, 136;
intertemporal theory of consumption
3, 101–2; Lagrange's marginal utility
77; Lagrange's ophelimity 76–7, 84;
Lagrange's production equation 79;
*Lezioni di Economia Matematica* 9,
22, 24, 65, 66–9, 70, 76–7, 78, 80,
101; *La logica del sistema corporativo*

(with De Stefani) 26, 82, 83, 97;
mathematical theory of economic cycle
4, 9, 83; *Meccanica Economica* 14, 66,
70–1, 74–5, 138; *Modelli meccanici e
modelli economici* 85n; neoclassical
economics 83; Pareto school 1, 3, 8–9,
12; principle of heredity 74; rational
mechanics 67, 69; stable/unstable
equilibrium 68–9; *La teoria matematica
del programma economico* 66, 74, 83;
*The Transformation of Value in the
Productive Process* 3, 74; *La visione
economica fascismo* 81
Andreoli, Giulio 90
applied economic theory 21–2
Arias, Gino 25
Arrow, Kenneth 121–2; intertemporal
equilibrium 104, 110
Austrian school 3, 5; and Fossati 106,
107–10, 112; economic cycle theory
126–8; Paretian criticism 19, 21

Barone 7, 12
Barro 141
Böhm-Bawerk, Eugen von 108
Boninsegni, Pasquale 10; Pareto school 8;
*Precis del'economie politique* 12
Bordin, Arrigo: *Alcune generalizzazioni
di un caso di monopolio bilaterale*
26; dynamic equilibrium 15–16, 41,
126; *Equilibrio ed indeterminazione*
15; generally 15–16, 17; mathematical
theory of economic cycle 4; Pareto
school 1, 9, 14, 15; *Il significato di
alcune moderne teorie matematiche
della dinamica* 15–16, 40; *Di Taluni
Massimi di Utilità Collettiva* 103;
welfare economics 16
Borgatta, Gino: Pareto school 8

Breglia, A. 25
Bresciani-Turroni, Costantino 109, 120, 128–9

Cabiati, A. 109
calculus of variations 60, 62; Amoroso 73–4, 76–8, 84; La Volpe 90, 92, 93
Carli, Filippo 25
Cass, David: optimal growth theory 60, 144
Castelnuovo, Giulio 64
causal-genetic theories 109, 110, 111, 114
Cimmino, Gianfranco 90
Clark 130
classical tradition 6; Paretian criticism 19; rent theory 20
competition: general economic equilibrium 18–19, 23; Lerner index 24; perfect and imperfect 24, 42
condition of transversality 3, 60, 88–9, 93–4
consumer theory: Amoroso 68–71, 74–8
convex analysis 104, 121
corporative economists 23, 25–7, 63; Amoroso 23, 26, 63, 80, 81–3, 85, 136; corporative turning point 26; corporative wages 25–6; La Volpe 97–100
Cossa, Luigi 7
Cournot solution 55, 61, 67
creative destruction 46
crisis theory: dynamic theory 34–7, 46

Dalla Volta 7
Darwin, Charles: theory of evolution 29–30, 47
Debreu, Gérard 121–2, 123; intertemporal equilibrium 104, 110
Del Vecchio, Gustavo 1, 27, 49, 50; economic cycle 127–8; monetary theory 23
demand curve 20, 39, 51–2, 57
demand function 17, 51, 52, 54–62
Demaria, Giovanni 46, 50, 53, 66
De Stefani, Alberto: *La logica del sistema corporativo* (with Amoroso) 26, 82, 83, 97
De Viti 7
De Viti De Marco, Antonio 128–9
differential calculus 20, 114, 123
Dimand, R. 125
Di Matteo, Massimo 87, 95
Dominedò, Valentino: *Le Condizioni del Massimo Collettivo di Ofelimità di Pareto* 102–3

Donzelli, F. 34
duopolistic market: Cournot solution 55, 67; simultaneous maximums 17
dynamic equilibrium: d'Alembert's principle 30, 32–4, 39, 69; Amoroso 29, 32, 47, 58–9, 60, 63, 65–74, 83, 126, 144; and economic cycle theory 125–42; and marginalism 23–4; Bordin 15–16, 41, 126; calculus of variations 60, 62, 76, 84, 92, 93; causality, principle of 41; condition of transversality 3, 60, 88–9, 93–4; contribution to dynamic theory 4; crisis theory 34–7, 46; decline of theory 4, 86, 146; dynamization of offer curve 3; economic cycle 3, 125–42; economic quantification 140; evaluation function of future utility 89–90; Evans and Roos 2, 53–7, 58–9, 72–3, 125; exchange and production 38; first order (successive equilibriums) 2, 29–32, 37–41, 43–6, 47, 98–9; Fossati 3–4, 60, 63, 76, 84, 106–24; functional calculus 2–3, 47, 50, 53–7, 60, 61–3, 75–6, 144, 146–7; general dynamic equilibrium of consumption 74–8; general dynamic equilibrium of production 76, 78–81; general economic equilibrium 3, 29–34, 49–50, 55–7, 87–8, 112–15, 144–6; generally 1–2, 23–4, 47, 49–50, 143–7; historical equilibrium 58; inertia 34–5, 60, 69, 76–7, 79, 84, 87; international context 48–63; intertemporal equilibrium 104, 110; intertemporal of economic action 3, 101–2; intertemporal utility 60, 88, 89–90; La Volpe 3, 29, 76, 84, 86–105, 144; laws of consumer equilibrium 90; mathematical aspects 23–4, 72–3, 76, 83, 143–4; *mobile equilibrium* 42, 50–3; money demand 116–17; monopolies 29–30; Moore 49–53, 58, 63; non-logical actions 29, 30; optimal control theory 90, 144; origin 23; Palomba 32, 58, 126; Pantaleoni 23–4, 31, 43–6, 47; Pareto 28–47; Pareto tradition 1–2, 23–4, 47, 57–63, 96, 144; de Pietri Tonelli 61–3; principle of heredity 74; rational mechanics 29–34, 47, 67, 69; role of expectations 84, 86–105, 132, 144; role of uncertainty 4, 106–24; second order (continuous variation in function of time) 2, 29–37, 43–6, 47, 76, 78, 79, 83–4; Sensini 29, 38–40, 43; sociological approach 30, 97;

158  *Index*

subjectivist approach 110–12; synthetic economics 49–50; *tatonnement* 41–2; temporary equilibrium 3, 42, 60, 87–97; time element 20, 30–9, 41–6, 50–1, 59, 60, 75–6, 144; trend ratios 51; Vinci 32, 58–9, 126; Walras 2, 31, 41–3, 47, 56, 57, 61

eclectic approach 5
*Econometrica* journal 4, 126
*Econometric Institute* 55
*Econometric Society* 9, 55, 63, 64, 107
economic cycle: Amoroso 3, 4, 66, 73, 129, 130–8, 139, 140, 141; Austrian school 126–8; Del Vecchio 127–8; dynamic equilibrium 3, 125–42; Evans and Roos 131, 132, 140, 141; expectations (speculative intent) 132; growth theory 137; harmonic oscillations 129–30; Hayek 125, 126–7, 139; investment theory 138–40; Keynes 125, 126–7, 133–5, 138–40, 141, 142; Keynesian accelerator principle 139; mathematical theories 4, 125, 129–42; money and monetary policy 132–3; non-mathematical theories 125; Palomba 130, 138–40; Pareto 28, 35–7, 132; Pareto school 126, 129–42; rational mechanics 140; real business cycle 141, 142; Tinbergen 129–30; Vinci-Amoroso model 133–5, 139
Edgeworth, Francis 21, 67, 70
Einaudi, L. 7, 109, 128
Einstein, Albert: theory of relativity 14
empirical research 21–2
Euler equation 90
Eulero equation 77, 79, 85n
Evans, Griffith: dynamic equilibrium 2–3, 23, 53–7, 58–9, 73, 125; "The Dynamics of Monopoly" 54, 55; economic cycle 131, 132, 140, 141; functional calculus 2–3, 47, 50, 53–7, 75, 146; *Mathematical Introduction to Economics* 55, 62, 140; "A Simple Theory of Competition" 54
evolutionism 29, 47
expectations: dynamic equilibrium 84, 86–105, 132, 144; economic cycle 132

Fanno, Marco 7, 109; dynamic equilibrium 58; economic cycle 128–9, 133, 137; *Introduzione allo studio della teoria economica del corporativismo* 27; monetary theory 23

fascist regime: Amoroso 81–2, 85; labour market 25–6; La Volpe 100
Fossati, Eraldo: and Keynesian theory 106–7, 108, 112, 115–20, 124; and the Austrian school 106, 107–10, 112, 123–4; causal-genetic theories 109, 111, 114; *Il concetto di equilibrio nella teoria economica* 109; *Con Keynes o Contro Keynes* 120; *The Criterion of Determinacy of General Equilibrium* 121; dynamic theory 3–4, 32, 58–9, 60, 63, 76, 84, 106–24; *La politica economica razionale* 108; *Elementi di Ecomomica Razionale* 115, 120; *Elementi di Politica Ecomomica Razionale* 115, 117–18, 120; empirical research 22; formalization of dynamic general equilibrium 112–15; functional theories 109, 114; general economic equilibrium 106, 107, 109, 120–3; mathematical analysis 112, 122; neoclassical economics 107, 108, 109, 116, 120, 123, 127; *Nota sull'Utilità della Moneta* 115; *Osservazioni sulla legge di Wieser* 108, 110; *Osservazioni sulla statica e sulla dinamica...* 108; Pareto school 1, 9, 14; *Problemi dei Nostri Giorni* 119–20; *Ricerca sulle relazioni tra il tempo e l'utilità* 108, 110; role of money in general economic equilibrium theory 115–17; role of uncertainty 4, 106–24; subjectivist approach to dynamic analysis 110–12; *Vilfredo Pareto and J. M. Keynes* 117
Fovel, Massimo 25
Friedman, Milton: life-cycle theory 94
Frisch, Ragnar 2, 4, 16, 23, 24, 47, 125; economic dynamics 58, 84, 140, 143, 144
Fuà, Giorgio 8
functional calculus 144, 146–7; Amoroso 63, 75–6, 114; Evans and Roos 2–3, 47, 50, 53–7, 62, 75, 146; La Volpe 63, 94, 114; Pareto school 60, 61–3; Volterra 3
functional theories 109, 114

game theory 17
Gangemi 128
Garegnani, P.: *Il capitale nelle teorie della distribuzione* 123
general economic equilibrium: Amoroso 49, 74–81; and social equilibrium 30; criticism by Jannacone 12; criticism of previous theories 19–20; dynamization 3, 29–34, 49–50, 55–7, 87–8, 112–15,

144–6; economic cycle 126; Fanno 7; Fossati 106, 107, 109, 120–3; generally 1, 6; joint costs and substitute goods 7; mathematical analysis 20–1, 48–9, 146–7 maximum profit 57; *mobile equilibrium* 42, 50–3; money demand 116–17; Moore 49–53; non-competitive markets 18–19, 23; optimistic representation of reality 23; Pareto school 1, 2, 18–20, 60; Pareto's economic cycle theory 35–7; partial equilibrium and 7–8, 11–12, 13, 20–1; de Pietri Tonelli 31–2, 49; problems with 19–20, 48–9; role of money 115–17; Roos 55–7; Sensini 19–20, 32, 72; simultaneous maximums 17; stable/unstable equilibrium 68–9; static theory 49–53, 74–8, 87, 145; tastes and obstacles 6; time element 50–1; trend ratios 51; Vienna Circle 48

*Giornale degli Economisti* 7

Graziani, Augusto 5–6; *Equilibrio Generale ed Equilibrio Macroeconomico* 85n; *Istituzioni di economia politica* 6; *Principi di economia* 68

*Great Depression* 49, 66, 125, 143

growth theory 58, 137, 142

Guccione, A. 70

harmonic oscillations 129–30

Hayek, Friedrich 108–9; economic cycle 125, 126–7, 139; *Prices and Production* 108

Hicks, John 2, 20, 101; temporary equilibrium 3, 42, 91, 94–7, 132; *The Theory of Wages* 25; *Value and Capital* 3, 91, 95–6, 132

historical equilibrium 58

historicist approach 5

inertia: dynamic theory 34–5, 60, 69, 76–7, 79, 84, 87

intertemporal utility 59, 60, 88, 89–90; Amoroso 3, 101–2

invisible hand principle 101

Jacob, Carl Gustav 17

Jannaccone 7; *Il Paretaio* 12

Kaldor, N. 101, 102

Kalecki, Michal 16, 125

Keynes, John Maynard: accelerator principle 139; economic cycle 125, 126–7, 133–5, 138–40, 141, 142; Fossati and Keynesian theory 106–7, 108, 112, 115–20, 124;

*General Theory* 4, 106–7, 108, 112, 115, 117, 135, 138–9; investment theory 139–40; liquidity preference theory 116; macroeconomic theory 4, 9, 19; *Treatise* 4, 127, 133–4, 136, 138–9; underemployment equilibrium 107

Klein, L.R. 120–1

Knight 15

Kuhn, T. 118

labour market: as bilateral monopoly 24–6; corporative economists 25–6; fascist regime 25–6; Pigou 25

Lagrange's equation 39, 68, 113

Lagrange's marginal utility 77

Lagrange's ophelimity 76–7, 84

Lagrange's production equation 79

La Volpe, Giulio: calculus of variations 90, 92, 93; condition of transversality 3, 60, 88–9, 93–4; *La Convenienza Economica Collettiva* 97, 100–1; corporatism 97–100; dynamic equilibrium 3, 26–7, 29, 32, 46, 58–9, 63, 76, 84, 86–105, 144; *Economia e Filosofia* 100; evaluation function of future utility 89–90; factors of dynamic scheme 98–9; functional calculus 63, 94, 114; generally 86–7, 123; intertemporal utility (action plan) 59, 60, 88, 89–90; Keynesian theory 4; laws of consumer equilibrium 90; optimal control theory 90; Pareto school 1, 9, 14; *Ricerche di Dinamica Economica Corporativa* 97–8, 105; role of expectations 86–105, 144; *Studi sulla teoria dell'equilibrio dinamico generale* 3, 63, 86–7, 95; temporary equilibrium 3, 60, 87–97; transversality related to final wealth 60; welfare economics 100–4

Lerner index 24, 72

life-cycle theory 3, 94

literary economics 21

Lotka-Volterra equations 14, 130, 139

Lucas 141

McLure, M. 1

macroeconomic theory 9

Magnani, I. 12

marginalism 1, 143; introduction to Italy 5, 6–7, 108; labour market 24–5; Marshall's *Principles of Economics* 7; Moore 50; optimal choice principle 100; static aspects 23–4, 28

Marshall, Alfred 1, 21, 58; marginalism 23, 28; monetary theory 23; partial

160 *Index*

equilibriums 6–8, 11–12, 13; *Principles of Economics* 7
Marshall Plan 115, 120
Marx, Karl 19
Masci, Guglielmo 25–6, 50, 52–3; criticism of Moore's statistical approach 52–3; fixed and variable capital 44; *Lezioni di Economia corporativa* 27; *Lezioni di statistica* 50
mathematical analysis 122–3, 143–4, 146–7; dynamic equilibrium 60, 72–3, 76, 83; economic quantification 140; Fossati 112, 122; general economic equilibrium 20–1, 48–9; Pareto school 1, 13, 20–1, 47, 58, 60; Sensini 11–12, 21; theory of economic cycle 4; virtual velocities 34
maximum profit 57
Mayer, Hans 107, 108–10
Mazzola 7
Menger, Carl 50, 108
*Metroeconomica* journal 106, 107, 124
Mill-Say Law 119
Minelli, E. 70
*mobile equilibrium* 42, 50–3
models, economic 140–1
Modigliani, Franco: life-cycle theory 94
monetary theory 23
monopolies: dynamic equilibrium 29–30, 54, 55, 57
Moore, Henry Ludwell 2–3, 47; dynamic equilibrium 49–53, 58, 63; marginalism 50; *mobile equilibrium* 50–3; *Synthetic Economics* 49–50; trend ratios 51
Morishima, Micho 87, 95
Mortara 128
Murray, Roberto: Pareto school 8, 10, 12; *Sommarii* 12

Napoleoni, Claudio: *Storia delle dottrine economiche* of *Dizionario di Economia Politica* 85n
natural selection, theory of 30
*n* enterprises 17
neoclassical economics 46, 83, 107, 108, 109, 116, 120, 123, 127, 135
Neumann, John von 121, 145
Newtonian mechanics 111, 132
Nicola, Pier Carlo: *Mainstream Mathematical Economics in the 20th Century* 86
*n* monopolists 17, 24

non-competitive market: general economic equilibrium 18–19; perfect and imperfect competition 24; simultaneous maximums 17

offer curve: dynamization 3
oligopolistic market: Amoroso 65; Evans 54; perfect competition 24; pricing 24; Roos 55; simultaneous maximums 17
ophelimity 66, 76, 101
optimal control theory 90, 144
optimal growth theory 60, 144

Palomba, Giuseppe 94–5; dynamic equilibrium 32, 58, 126; economic cycle 130, 138–40; *L'espansione capitalistica* 15; generally 14–15; *Introduzione all'economia dinamica* 130; *Introduzione allo studio della dinamica economica* 14, 139, 140; mathematical theory of economic cycle 4; *Morfologia Economica* 15; Pareto school 1, 9, 14; rational mechanics 22; sociological approach 14–15
Pantaleoni, Maffeo 5, 6, 7, 11–12, 64, 130; *Di alcuni fenomeni di dinamica economica* 43; dynamic theory 23–4, 31, 43–6, 47; economic equilibrium 43; first and second order dynamics 43–6; neoclassical economics 46; Pareto's dynamic theory compared 43–6; *Principi di economia pura* 5; time in dynamic theory 46
Papi, Giuseppe 108; economic cycle 128, 133; *Lezioni di economia generale e corporativa* 27
*Paretaio* 12
Pareto school: common scientific and methodological grounds 18–22; criticism by Jannacone 12; decline 1, 9, 86, 146; development 8–9; dynamic equilibrium 1–2, 23–4, 47, 57–63, 96; dynamic theory 23–4, 28–9, 47; economic cycle theory 126, 129–42; economic/political-collective dichotomy 27; empirical research 21–2; general economic equilibrium 1, 2, 18–20, 32; generally 1; mathematical approach 1, 13, 20–1, 47, 58, 112; mature phase 13; members 8–17; methodologies 18–22; pure and applied economic theory 21–2, 29; rational mechanics 22, 31–2; research programmes 22–7;

second order dynamics 2, 31–5, 76; welfare economy 104

Pareto, Vilfredo: correspondence with Amoroso 64, 67–8; correspondence with de Pietri Tonelli 13; *Corso* 28, 29–30, 32–4, 35, 37, 101; criticism of utilitarian view 18; dynamic equilibrium 1–2, 23–4, 29–30, 47, 144; dynamic theory 28–47; economic cycle 35–7, 132; economic fluctuations theory 28; *Epistolario* 35; *Le equazioni dell'equilibrio dinamico* 29, 37–41; general economic equilibrium 6, 18–20, 56, 60, 74–5, 109; influence 1, 10, 18–19, 46–7; *Manuale* 9, 22, 23–4, 46, 74, 101; non-competitive markets 18–19; Paretian optimum 101; Pareto school 8; rent theory 11, 20; sociology 46; static analysis 28; time in dynamic theory 46; *Trattato di sociologia generale* 104; welfare economy theorem 100–1, 104; partial equilibrium 7–8, 11–12, 13, 20–1; Marshall's approach 6–8, 11–12, 13

Pietri Tonelli, Alfonso de 50, 86, 94; correspondence with Pareto 13; *Corso di politica economica. Introduzione* 13; criticism of utilitarian school 19; dynamic equilibrium 61–3; empirical research 22; "The Fruitfulness of Pareto Theories" 61; general economic equilibrium 49, 75, 87; generally 12–13, 15; *Lezioni di scienza economica razionale e sperimentale* 9, 13, 32, 68, 102; on development of economic theory 19; Pareto school 1, 8–9, 10, 12–13; rational mechanics 31–2; sociological approach 13

Pigou, Arthur Cecil: *The Economics of Welfare* 25, 101

potential theory 53

probability theory 112

pure and applied economic theory 21–2, 29

Rabbeno, Ugo 5

Ramsay, Frank P. 144; "A Mathematical Theory of Saving" 59–60

rational mechanics 22, 29–34; d'Alembert's principle 30, 32–4, 39, 69; Amoroso 67, 69; dynamic equilibrium 47; economic cycle 140; first order dynamics 29–32; second order dynamics 2, 31–5; statics and dynamics 31; time/space relationship 34, 46

relativity theory 14

rent theory: Pareto 11; Sensini 20

Ricardo, David 19

Ricci, U. 6, 58

*Ricerche Economiche* review 86

Robbins, Lionel: *Essay on the Nature and Significance of Economic Science* 100

Roos, Charles: "A Dynamical Theory of Economics" 56–7; *Dynamic Economics* 57; dynamic equilibrium 2–3, 23, 55–7, 58–9, 72, 125; economic cycle 131, 132, 140, 141; functional calculus 2–3, 47, 50, 55–7, 62, 75, 146; "Mathematical Theory of Competition" 55–6

Rosenstein-Rodan, Paul N. 88; *The Role of Time in Economic Theory* 59

Samuelson, Paul 2, 57–8, 81, 143–4; *Foundations of Economic Analysis* 58, 97; historical equilibrium 58; "The Stability of Equilibrium" 58

Schumpeter, J.A. 8, 23, 130; creative destruction 46; economic dynamics 84; marginalism 28

scientific discipline, development of economics as 6, 22

Scorza, Gaetano 48, 101

Screpanti, Ernesto and Zamagni, Stefano: *An Outline of the History of Economic Thought* 12

Sensini, Guido: *Corso di Economia Pura* 10, 38–40; discussion of rent theory 20; dynamic theory 29, 32, 34, 38–40, 43; general economic equilibrium 19–20, 32, 72; generally 10–12, 123; mathematical analysis 11–12, 21; Pareto school 1, 8, 10–12; synthetic economics 18–19, 21; *La teoria della rendita* 10–12; Shackle, G.L.S. 114, 120, 123; *The Years of High Theory* 22

simultaneous maximums theory: duopolistic market 17; Zaccagnini 17

Smith, Adam 19; invisible hand principle 101

socialist approach 5

sociological approach 5, 22; de Pietri Tonelli 13, 22, 97; dynamic theory 30; Fossati 22; La Volpe 97; Palomba 14–15; Pareto 46

Solow, Robert 81

Spirito, Ugo 25

Sraffa, Piero 69; *The Laws of Returns Under Competitive Conditions* 24

162 *Index*

static analysis 1, 49–53, 65–7, 68–9, 74–8, 87, 145; Cournot solution 55, 67; Lagrange's equation 39, 68, 113; marginalism 23–4, 28; money demand 116; Newtonian physics 111; rational mechanics 31–2; subjective theory of value 28

subjective theory of value 5

synthetic economics 18–19, 21, 49–50

tastes and obstacles: general economic equilibrium 6

*tatonnement* 41–2

temporary equilibrium: Hicks 3, 42, 91, 94–7; La Volpe 3, 60, 87–97

time: dynamic theory 20, 30–9, 41–6, 50–1, 59, 60, 75–6, 144; intertemporal of economic action 3, 101–2; utility function 59, 60; Wieser 109

Tinbergen, Jan 2, 16, 23, 24; "Annual Survey: Suggestions on Quantitative Business Cycle Theory" 125; economic cycle 129–30; economic dynamics 84, 88, 140; function of social welfare 104

trend ratios 51

uncertainty in dynamic theory: Fossati 4, 106–24

utilitarianism: marginal utility and cost of production 6; Paretian criticism 18, 19

value: subjective theory of 28

Vecchio, G. del 115

Vienna Circle: general economic equilibrium 48

Vinci, Felice: dynamic equilibrium 32, 58–9, 126; economic cycle 133–5, 139; *Il significato di alcune teorie moderne della dinamica economica* 40–1; mathematical theory of economic cycle 4; Pareto school 10; "Recent Tendencies of Economic Studies" 135; welfare economics 135

virtual velocities 34

Vito 128

Volterra, Vito 53, 66; functional calculus 2–3; integral equations 2–3, 53, 55, 57, 60, 62; Lotka-Volterra equations 14, 130, 139

Wald, Abraham 121

Walras, Léon 21, 29, 50; dynamic theory 2, 31, 41–3, 47, 56, 61, 70; free competition 8; general economic equilibrium 6, 50, 56, 57, 87, 109; influence generally 1; marginalism 23; *tatonnement* 41–2

Weintraub, E. 53, 96, 140

Weintraub, S. 140

welfare economy theorem: Bordin 16; La Volpe 100–4; Pareto 100–1, 104; Pigou 101; Tinbergen 104; Vinci 135

Wicksell, Knut 126–7

Wieser, Friedrich von 3, 5, 108–10; *Das Gesetz der Macht* 109; *Natural value* 109

Zaccagnini, Emilio: generally 17; *Nuovi Problemi della Polemica Scorza-Pareto* 103; Pareto school 1, 14, 17; theory of simultaneous maximums 17